D0887519

Cologne

INSIGHT *City* GUIDES

Edited by Nina Köster
Photography by Wolfgang Fritz and others
Translated by David Ingram

APA
PUBLICATIONS

NO part of this book may be reproduced, stored in a retrieval system or transmitted in any form or means electronic, mechanical, photocopying, recording or otherwise, without prior written permission of Apa Publications. Brief text quotations with use of photographs are exempted for book review purposes only.

As every effort is made to provide accurate information in this publication, we would appreciate it if readers would call our attention to any errors that may occur by communicating with Höfer Media (Pte) Ltd., Orchard Point Post Office Box 219, Singapore 9123. Information has been obtained from sources believed to be reliable, but its accuracy and completeness, and the opinions based thereon, are not guaranteed.

COLOGNE

First Edition
© 1992 APA PUBLICATIONS (HK) LTD
All Rights Reserved
Printed in Singapore by Höfer Press Pte. Ltd

ABOUT THIS BOOK

Long gone are the days when it was Cologne's stench more than the sweet smell of its toilet waters that established the city's reputation abroad and prompted William Thackeray to comment: "Cologne… is in size considerable, in aspect unpromising and in smell odious". On the threshold of the 21st century, the city is more attractive than ever. The cranes and building sites that dominated the skyline for so long after the devastation of World War II have disappeared. New parks have been created. The museum complex next to the cathedral, initially so controversial, is now accepted as an architectural masterpiece.

The Writers

Apa Publications assigned *Cityguide Cologne* to the sociologist and journalist **Nina Köster**. Having contributed articles to such Insight Guides as *Düsseldorf* and *The Rhine*, her experience stood her in good stead when it came to portraying the unique symbiosis between past and present that Cologne represents. Her fascination for the city's history is reflected in her contribution to the book, describing developments from Cologne's first cultural heyday during the Roman period to its emergence as a modern metropolis after the devastation of World War II.

The history of a city has a great impact on the character of its people. Cologne has its very own rich cultural tradition; confronted by their carnival and cuisine, the locals' piety, pubs and pretty girls, all garnished with copious amounts of the proverbial *joie de vivre*, the visitor will certainly want to know what makes them tick. An answer has

been provided in this book by the great German writer and Nobel laureate **Heinrich Böll** in the article "What is Kölnisch?". Böll was in a good position to know: he was born in the city and lived there until shortly before his death in 1985.

The phenomenon of Heinrich Böll himself is the subject of an article by local literary critic and travel writer **Michael Bengel**, who has also contributed to other Apa guides. Bengel deals with literary figures in his article "City of Poets". Having also taken a look at the attractions of the opposite bank of the Rhine (the right) and discovered some of the monuments that the Romans left behind, he takes a look at what's on offer at the Cologne Trade Fair, before finally satisfying his thirst for the city by sampling its famous beer, known locally as *Kölsch*.

Renate Bach, who has observed the theatre scene in Cologne for more than 15 years, covers the topic in this book, including a feature on the life of Cologne's stage institution Willy Millowitsch. **Dr Wolf Bierbach** of the WDR (Western Germany Broadcasting Corporation) describes the city's importance as a media centre in his article "Cologne Calling".

The delights of the Carnival are revealed by **Engelbert Greis**, the director of a local TV news programme *Kolnische Rundschau*; since the mid-1980s, he has reported for the ARD on the spectacular carnival parade on the Monday before Lent and has often written about this famous Rhenish folk festival.

The art historian **Klaus Hardering** is particularly interested in Gothic architecture. You can't get any more Gothic than Cologne's cathedral, which he has helped to administer since finishing his studies.

Born in nearby Düsseldorf, **Dr Günther**

Köster   *Böll*   *Bengel*   *Bach*

Henneke has lived in Cologne for 30 years. He provided the article on Cologne's Neustadt (New Town). Having worked for a long time as editor of the *Neuer Ruhrzeitung*, he is now press officer of the Rhineland Countryside Commission and writes reviews for the Zurich-based *Neue Zürcher Zeitung*.

Marie Hüllenkremer looks at the art scene in the city. Before she took over as head of the editorial on the *Zeit* magazine in Hamburg, this art connoisseur managed the cultural section of the local *Kölner Stadtanzeiger* and worked as a correspondent for the magazine *Art* in New York. In addition, she is the editor of a highly respected book on art in Cologne.

Petra Pluwatsch writes travel articles, features and reviews for children's books. She studied German and history and now works for the *Kölner Stadtanzeiger*. In this book, she reveals the delights of the local cuisine in a city famed for its gastronomy, and also explores the possibilities of cruising on the Rhine.

Dr Gérard Schmidt went to school in Cologne, but rediscovered the attractions of the city only after landing here again after his world travels. He became a journalist for the *Kölner Stadtanzeiger*, then directed the National Theatre and now has a career as a publisher and author of successful theatre pieces in the local dialect. He provided the chapter on the city centre.

Rainer Sattler grew up in Baden in southwestern Germany, came to study in Cologne some 20 years ago and never left. He works as a journalist and photographer and here presents the attractions of the city's green areas, goes shopping and looks at Cologne's contribution to rock music.

Hannelore Schubert, who has worked as a journalist since 1954, now freelances for the WDR cultural department, specialising in architecture and the protection of ancient monuments. Here she writes about what's on display in the city's museums, takes us to the suburbs on the left bank of the river and out into the countryside to discover attractions within easy reach of the city.

The sports scene in Cologne is dominated by ice-hockey and soccer. The changing fortunes of the city's teams and the sporting aspirations of the city as a whole are outlined by **Bernd Stemmler**, sports editor of a private radio station in Koblenz. **Dr Werner Strodthoff** is one of the city's best known architecture critics and edits the arts pages of the *Kölner Stadtanzeiger*. He takes us on a tour of the wonderful Romanesque churches which have now all been superbly restored after the war damage of the early 1940s. Last but not least among the authors comes **Karin Hackenbroich**, who as journalist and photographer, has followed developments in her home city for 20 years. She compiled the extensive "Travel Tips" section, which was translated into English by **Susan Sting**.

The photographers

Cityguide: Cologne maintains Apa's high standard of photography. Most shots are the work of **Wolfgang Fritz**, who has made a name for himself through his contributions to numerous other Apa guides, and of **Margarethe** and **Günther Ventur**.

The book was translated into English under the direction of **Tony Halliday** and produced in Apa's London editorial office under the supervision of editorial director **Brian Bell**. The proof-reading and indexing were undertaken by **Mary Morton**.

Greis

Hardering

Hackenbroich

Hennecke

History and Culture

Maps

TRAVEL TIPS

For detailed information see page 219

A CITY OF SAINTS AND SALESMEN

"Cologne has lost its 'holy city' image: these days its main significance lies in trade and industry", was the complaint in a guidebook written in the second half of the 19th century. Commerce versus the church? Hardly. From time immemorial, the people of Cologne have known all about secular business, despite the reverence they have for their saints. If the two could be combined, then so much the better. In the Middle Ages, the clergy were just as pleased as the merchant classes to see the pilgrims stream into the city. These devout "tourists" swelled the coffers of Cologne's business-men, and the bishops profited in turn. Indeed, the "Rome of the North" would never have existed had it not been for the generous contributions of its wealthier burghers.

And today? Even in the 20th century, Cologne's appearance is still characterised by a mixture of bourgeois piety and bourgeois prosperity. Its garland of restored Romanesque churches is unsurpassed, its Cathedral unique.

Naturally, industrialisation and the economic upturn after World War II have left their mark on the city's appearance. In the 19th century factory chimneys were built rather than church towers, and in the 20th century huge administrative structures, chic hotels and striking-looking public buildings such as the museum complex next to the Cathedral have all created new architectural accents. But wherever you are in the city, the Cathedral, with its mighty twin towers, is always in view; something doubly fortunate for visitors, in that it provides them with a document of perfect Gothic architecture while at the same time helping them get their bearings.

The people of Cologne forget all about church and business just once in the course of each year – at Carnival time. What the church does for the soul and commerce does for well-being, the Carnival does for the heart. The origins of this "festival of fools" go back to Roman times. Since then, the manner of celebration has altered, but the Cologne Carnival still remains very much a genuine folk festival.

It is seldom that one experiences such unrestrained merriment in the city's inhabitants as in the "fifth season", but that doesn't mean that they don't know how to enjoy life the rest of the time. Cologne's 4,000 restaurants, pubs, bars and discotheques speak for themselves. Indeed, no other city in Germany contains as many restaurants in relation to its population. Cologne's theatre and music scene, too, compares favourably with that of other cities, and as a metropolis of art, it is famed the world over.

Preceding pages: the Wallraf-Richartz Museum bows before the cathedral; reflections of a long history; the swing bridge at the Rhine Harbour; the Hohenzollern Bridge with the cathedral. **Left**, dressed up for Carnival.

Cologne has no less a person to thank for its foundation than Roman emperor and general Julius Caesar. Marching eastwards in 53 BC, he very quickly wiped out the tribe of the Eburones, who lived on the left bank of the Rhine and had dared stand in the way of his urge for conquest. Another Germanic tribe was more intelligent, however: the Ubii. Instead of fighting their conquerors, they formed an alliance with them, and the Roman general Agrippa moved the Ubii from the right bank to the left bank of the Rhine, which had been depopulated after the slaughter of the Eburones. The fortified settlement of the Ubii, founded in 39 BC and known as *oppidum Ubiori*, was the seed from which Cologne sprang.

The site of the new settlement was chosen with great care; it was, after all, to form the capital of a province named Germania extending as far as the Elbe. In an area free from floods, on a plateau situated right next to the river, at the intersection of two important trading routes, and also equipped with its own natural harbour because of an island in the river, the "city of the Ubii" had every chance of becoming an important trading centre. Although the Roman plan of conquering all of Germania never came to fruition, Cologne, even in its capacity as a frontier city and later as the capital city of Lower Germania, still assumed a great deal of importance.

The rights of a Roman city: In AD 50 Emperor Claudius, at the instigation of his niece, Julia Agrippina the Younger, who had been born in Cologne and whom he had recently married, granted Cologne the rights of a Roman city. Thereafter it bore the name "Colonia Claudia Ara Agrippinensium" (CCAA), meaning a city with Roman rights (Colonia) founded in the reign of Emperor Claudius (Claudia), the site of an important altar (Ara), and initiated by none other than Agrippina (Agrippinensium). Now Romans

Left, **the Tomb of Poblicius, now housed in the Roman-Germanic Museum.**

from all kinds of different social classes – retired soldiers, traders, artisans, officials and officers – mingled with the Ubii, and they all left their own individual mark on life in Cologne.

The city was then given its first defensive wall. It enclosed an area of roughly 1 sq. km, and it had nine gates and 19 defensive towers. The city streets were laid out like a chessboard, from east to west and from north to south, and the main traffic arteries were the

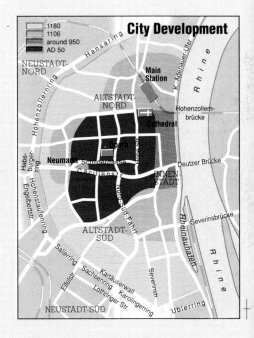

cardo maximus (today's Hohe Strasse), running south, and the *decumanus maximus* (today's Schildergasse), which ran west. The city was provided with fresh spring water via an 80-km (50-mile) long aqueduct from the Eifel Hills; there was an underground sewage and drainage system; and half-timbered and stone houses lined the city's paved streets and generously-proportioned squares.

The interiors of the Roman villas must have been a magnificent sight. Floor mosaics, such as the 70 sq. metre (80 sq. yard) Dionysos Mosaic, which today is the main attraction of the city's Roman-Germanic Museum, were not isolated cases. Even the smallest houses had artistically decorated walls. Excavations have also revealed that some buildings even had heated floors.

No wonder, then, that the Ubii quickly learnt to appreciate the Roman way of life, and in AD 70 they fought on the side of their newfound allies against their Germanic blood-brothers. Germanic tribes rebelled against the Romans on several occasions, and successfully at first. To save their own skin, the Ubii swore an oath of allegiance to these new lords. But when the rebels then ordered them to pull down the city walls and

flourished. In its heyday, Roman Cologne had around 20,000 inhabitants. The city also played an important role politically and economically within the Roman Empire as a whole. Vitellius, the popular general, was being proclaimed emperor in Cologne by the Lower Germanic army as early as AD 69.

Thirty years later, Trajan, the Roman governor of Cologne, ascended the imperial throne, and one and a half centuries after that, the city was the capital of a splinter empire ruled by Postumus of the Rhine, comprising Gaul, Britain and Spain. The remains of the enormous Roman governor's palace, the Praetorium, can still be seen

to murder the Romans, they refused. They argued that the Teutons could not expect them to kill their own fathers, relations and children. There again, the Ubii were quite unscrupulous once the tables had been turned and defeat was looming for the Teutons; any rebels still left in the city were murdered on the spot.

However, it soon transpired that the Ubii had made the right decision. Rome's decision to divide up the occupied territory on the Rhine into two provinces meant that Colonia became the capital of the province of Lower Germania in AD 90. As a result, the city

beneath today's Town Hall.

A trading centre: Cologne, situated at the intersection of several important traffic routes, became a trading centre for goods from many different countries. Brisk trading even took place with the Teutons living on the right bank of the Rhine. Soon the Roman upper classes would only rest their heads on pillows filled with Germanic goose-down, while the women of Rome preferred to wear blond wigs. In return, the Teutons discovered the delights of Italian wine and olive oil, and exchanged natural products such as grain, animal skins, honey and wax for fine glassware, clay bowls, exquisite jewellery and elaborate weaponry. Cologne's artisans were unsurpassed when it came to ceramics and glass-blowing. Production took place outside the city walls to avoid the danger of fire; most houses were made of wood.

The dead were also buried out beyond the city walls, along the highways, as a warning and a reminder to the living. The largest and finest of the tombs were often situated right at the roadside. Many of them were commissioned by their occupants during their lifetimes, and banqueting and battle scenes were popular motifs. Just how magnificent these tombs actually were can be seen from the enormous monument to the legionary Poblicius, on display today in the Roman-Germanic Museum. Poorer citizens were buried behind the ornate tombs of the wealthy, and extensive cemetery areas thus arose, which the first Christians also used for burying their dead.

Tolerance towards people of differing beliefs was a matter of course in Roman Cologne. Roman temples to Jupiter, Mars or Mercury stood peacefully alongside Germanic shrines to goddesses of fertility. The Syrian soldier-god Jupiter Dolichenus was worshipped just as much as the Egyptian goddess of love, Isis, or Mithras, the Persian god of light. Soldiers and merchants from all over the world brought their various deities and beliefs with them to Cologne.

The Christians: A Christian community existed in Cologne probably as early as the 2nd century, and by the 4th century, in the Roman cemeteries outside the city, the first Christian chapels were being built above the tombs of St Ursula the martyr and St Gereon; another chapel was later consecrated to St Severinus. There are still traces of a Christian assembly room not far from the Praetorium. The first reference to the city as a bishopric dates from the year AD 313. It was at that time that Maternus, representing the Christian community of Cologne, took part in the Roman synod.

Meanwhile, the Roman Empire was beginning to show signs of decline. Its frontiers were seething with unrest. At first, however, the Romans successfully managed to defend themselves against the onrush of tribes from the right bank of the Rhine. In AD 310, in order to protect the border, the emperor Constantine the Great founded *Castrum Divitium* (today's Deutz) on the right bank, and had a permanent bridge built across the river to connect it to the city. But in 355 the Frankish general Silvanus, who had been sent to Cologne to protect the Roman borders, sided with his own tribal brothers and had himself proclaimed emperor of Rome. He didn't enjoy his imperial reputation for very long, though: Roman revenge was swift

and Silvanus was put to death. That same year, however, the Franks plundered and devastated the city.

Roman Cologne never really recovered from this shock. Julian did have Cologne rebuilt a year later, but after the Roman legions were recalled from the Rhine border in 401 it was only a question of time before the Franks took over the city completely. They did so in 450. It soon became the residence of kings of the Ripuarian part of the Frankish kingdom, and the Roman era, which had brought the city such prosperity and security, finally came to an end.

Left, the arch of the Roman North Gate. **Right**, brickwork designs on the Roman Tower.

With the arrival of the Franks, Cologne sank into centuries of obscurity. The former cosmopolitan city of tradesmen and artisans became a city of farmers once more. The fact that the Ripuarian Frankish kings had their residence here – as did the Merovingians for a while – did nothing to change things. It was the Christian church that came closest to filling the vacuum left behind by the Romans. Long before the bishops were officially appointed lords of the city they still had it very much under their thumb, and Christian chapels were being built over Roman ruins; one such was St Mary's in the Capitol, built on the foundations of the Roman temple to Jupiter, Juno and Minerva.

A new role: Cologne began to flourish once more under Charlemagne. The Carolingian made the city an archbishopic in 795, and nine years later, after conquering the Saxons, he moved it from the edge to the very centre of the Frankish Empire. His victory not only gave new impetus to the city's economy, it also strengthened Cologne's new role as a religious centre. The influence of the archbishopric of Cologne now extended from the Meuse as far as the Elbe. At the head of the new ecclesiastical empire was Charlemagne's adviser, Hildebold, who first became bishop of Cologne in 787, pontiff at the imperial court four years later, and then Cologne's first ever archbishop in 795. Hildebold started on the construction of a new episcopal church, the forerunner of today's Cathedral, as a symbol of his power.

His successors, too, knew how to preserve and increase Cologne's newly-won influence and wealth. An important role in Cologne's rise to becoming the largest city in Germany was played by archbishop Bruno: he was the youngest brother of the emperor Otto I, and in 953 he became not only archbishop of Cologne but also duke of Lorraine, thus putting combined spiritual and secular power into the hands of one person for the

Left, the magnificent Romanesque Church of the Holy Apostles in the Neumarkt.

very first time. He also laid the foundations of "holy Cologne" when he had two extremely valuable holy relics transported to the city from Rome.

Extending the city: It was during Bruno's rule that Cologne was first extended, something that was to prove of great economic importance for the city. The trading suburbs which had grown up on the old Rhine island after the former Roman harbour, full of silt, had been filled in, were incorporated into the city and fortified during Bruno's rule. This new trading district was then given the monastery church of Great St Martin's as a spiritual focal point. The collegiate church of St Andrew also owes its existence to archbishop Bruno. But Bruno's main interest was the construction of St Pantaleon's, the first monastery church to be added to the garland of collegiate churches outside the city – St Ursula's and St Gereon's to the north, and St Severinus's to the south. Archbishop Bruno was also buried in his favourite church.

In 1020, a third collegiate church was consecrated under archbishop Heribert on the site of the former Roman camp at Deutz. It was here that Heribert was laid to rest one year later. The valuable gold shrine containing his remains can be admired today in New St Heribert's Church. During the rule of his successor, archbishop Pilgrim (who made more of a name for himself as a military leader than as a man of the cloth), the collegiate Church of the Holy Apostles, begun under Heribert, was completed.

Archbishop Anno II, who ruled from 1056 to 1075, went down in the annals of history for a very different reason. It was during his rule, in 1074, that the people of Cologne – whose self-confidence had grown along with the wealth of their city – first rose up against their bishop. Archbishop Anno II had a lucky escape from the enraged burghers, though their uprising was soon quelled by the superior strength of the archiepiscopal army. However, the conflict continued to smoulder, and little by little the burghers of

Cologne succeeded in squeezing more and more rights out of their bishops.

Their first real opportunity as far as this was concerned presented itself at the beginning of the 12th century, when the burghers took the side of the Emperor during the Investiture Controversy and thus went against their archbishop; the Emperor rewarded the people of Cologne by conferring on them military sovereignty. After that, in 1106, the city succeeded in incorporating the suburbs that had sprung up beyond the former Roman walls to the north, west and south within its belt of fortifications.

It was just six years later that the burghers back from defeated Milan to *Sancta Colonia*, thus finally making the city the most important place of pilgrimage in the western world next to Rome and Jerusalem. Nicholas of Verdun, a goldsmith from Lorraine, then created the magnificent Shrine of the Three Magi to house their sacred remains, and apparently on feast days up to 100,000 pilgrims would converge on Cologne, thus providing the city with yet another lucrative source of income alongside its craft and trade: tourism.

By the 12th century, the population of Cologne had risen to over 35,000 and so in 1180 the medieval city had to be extended

banded together to form a "sworn alliance for freedom", in order to protect themselves against interference from the bishops. It was at this stage that the so-called *Richerzeche* was formed, an association of rich burghers for the control of craft and trade; it held its meetings in the "Burghers' House" (Bürgerhaus), the forerunner of the city's Town Hall.

Sancta Colonia: Cologne continued to flourish, despite the friction between its burghers and its bishops. In the summer of 1164 Rainald von Dassel, archbishop of Cologne and a successful military leader, brought the holy relics of the Three Magi for a third time. The city contented itself at first with enclosing the settlements that had sprung up around the large monasteries and churches beyond the fortifications within a large semicircle, made up of a wall and a ditch. Around the year 1200, construction work began on a huge stone wall, which on completion was 5.5 km (3 miles) long on the land side and 2.8 km (1.7 miles) along the Rhine bank, and enclosed an area measuring a full 400 hectares (1,000 acres). Cologne was now the largest city north of the Alps. Twelve gates – just as many as "Holy Jerusalem" – provided land access to the city, while there were more than 30 entrances along the Rhine. Cologne's city boundary was now placed so far out that its wall was to last for another 500 years before finally being forced to give way to the hectic pace of 19th-century development. Sections of medieval fortifications do still exist, though, and the course of the wall can still be followed, from the Severinus wall in the south all the way to the Thürmchen wall in the north.

Building boom: The Cologne of those days must have resembled nothing more than one vast building site. And not only because of the new city wall – church building was flourishing, too. Dominicans, Franciscans, Benedictine monks, Benedictine nuns – all of them were busy building. Within the space of 100 years (from 1150 to 1250) almost all of the large Romanesque churches of the city assumed their present-day appearance. The last to be consecrated was the collegiate church of St Cunibert, in 1247.

One year later the foundation stone was laid for the Gothic Cathedral which was to put all the other churches of the city in the shade. Based on the great French cathedrals, a mighty house of God was created, rearing up into the sky; the choir was consecrated after 74 years of construction work, but the completion of the Cathedral as a whole was to last for centuries.

The only reason all this building activity was possible in the first place was because wealthy burghers were donating large sums in order to finance it. Cologne's merchants and artisans, who assumed that they were assuring themselves of a safe place in heaven, could afford to support church-building with generous contributions. Cologne had long since regained its former role as a trading and manufacturing metropolis. It had begun exporting wine to England quite early on, and – alongside Bordeaux – was gradually developing into Europe's largest centre of the wine trade.

Wine wasn't the only major product: the city's merchants were also doing good business with salt and herring, wool and cloth, swords and jewellery, and basalt and slate.

Left, Archbishop Englebert on his shrine in the cathedral. **Right**, St Severinus's Gate.

Trade was given a further boost in 1255 with the introduction of the so-called "Staple Right", whereby non-local merchants who transported their wares by cart or by boat via Cologne had to pile them up and leave them in the city for at least three days, offering them for sale to the people of Cologne.

No wonder, then, that the burghers, rich and getting even richer in the second half of the 13th century, were also striving ever more energetically for political hegemony. However, by cleverly playing off merchants and artisans against one another, the city's archbishops successfully managed to fend off the burghers' claim to power on several

occasions. However, the showdown arrived on 5 June 1288: the archbishop and the burghers, each with their respective allies, stood facing each other on the battlefield at Worringen. After the largest battle ever fought on Rhenish soil was over, the archbishops had lost their role as the city's rulers once and for all. They were forced to leave Cologne and renounce their claim to power. From then on they resided in Bonn, Brühl or Zons. The only privilege left to them was their right to pronounce death sentences. From that day on, Cologne was *de facto* a Free Imperial City.

After the Battle of Worringen, Cologne's leading families, or *Geschlechter*, assumed control of the city. Most of them were rich and distinguished merchants, and had already been calling the tune in the city's first autonomous bodies such as the *Richerzeche* or the City Council. Essentially, 15 patrician families in Cologne shared power among themselves.

The university: The merchants ran the city self-confidently. In 1359 they had the old "Burghers' House" replaced by the "Hansasaal". In 1388, they founded the university, the first ever institute of higher education on German soil to be opened by someone other than emperors or princes. The Dominican Order had laid the foundation stone for the university a good century previously with the construction of a college for novices, which attracted several famous medieval scholars to the city. The first ever head teacher at the college was the renowned theologian and scholar Albertus Magnus, or Albert the Great, and his most famous pupil was no less a person than the celebrated philosopher Thomas Aquinas.

The merchant families were more than familiar with finance, and in the 14th and 15th centuries Cologne went on to become the richest city in the German Empire. It was a prominent member of the mercantile Hanseatic League, and its merchants probably had the most extensive connections and the most varied trade of all the cities in Germany. The merchants were only one pillar of Cologne's prosperity, though: the other was formed by the city's artisans. "Made in Cologne" stood for quality and guaranteed good sales. Not surprising, then, that Cologne's artisans also wanted to have their own say in the running of the city.

The artisans had begun organising themselves into guilds relatively early on, initially as a result of religious and charitable motives and only later for professional rea-

Left, the Jan von Werth Fountain in front of the late-Gothic town hall tower.

sons. The most important guild was that of the weavers, and related activities such as wool washing, dyeing, spinning, twining, and cloth-cutting. Gunsmiths, too, as well as goldsmiths and silversmiths were also held in high regard. Even today, street-names such as Weberstrasse (Weaver Street) and Streitzeuggasse (Armourers' Lane) still reveal where the various guilds once traded.

The weavers' uprising: Since the wealthy patricians were rather enjoying being in sole control of the city, and were showing no intention of voluntarily giving the guilds any share in their power, the result was inevitable: the guilds were forced to resort to open

artisans took advantage of this in order to overthrow the authorities, who were only concerned with themselves, once and for all. The families that were prepared to relinquish their claim to sole right of representation were allowed to remain; those that were not were hounded out of the city and their property confiscated.

Under the terms of a new municipal constitution, the *Verbundbrief*, a division of power was agreed upon between the artisans and the merchants. Every fully entitled citizen of Cologne – which meant roughly 10 percent of the population – was allowed to vote and be voted for. The following were,

warfare. Leading the uprising were the city's weavers, who constituted what was by far the largest and most important guild. The rebellion in 1370 ended with the dissolution of the *Richerzeche* and the admission of the guilds onto the City Council, where the weavers immediately took control. However, in the autumn of 1371 the merchants took the reins in their own hands once more. After a bloody battle, the weavers were beaten, and banished from the city.

So the patricians were again in charge. But not for long. The city's families kept on arguing among themselves, and in 1396 the

however, excluded from the very start: women, day labourers, beggars, bondsmen, journeymen, clergymen and Jews. The City Parliament was organised into 22 subdivisions known as *Gaffeln* which, depending on their importance, were allowed to choose two or four out of a total of 36 councillors. The City Council voted for another 13 council members from whichever *Gaffeln* they wished. All 49 councillors thus elected then appointed two mayors. The period of office was one year, and re-election was only possible after two years.

Nepotism: Although well meant, this new

arrangement was all too easy to abuse. Very soon it became quite commonplace for just a few councillors to take turns at being mayors. In the intervals between their terms of tenure they took on other lucrative posts. Corruption was rife. In February 1482, the burghers could no longer contain their wrath, and they rose in rebellion. But the storming of the Town Hall ended with the rebel leader being beheaded. Thirty years later, in December 1512, there was more unrest. This time, heads rolled in the city government. In the *Transfixbrief*, an addendum to the *Verbundbrief*, the burghers' rights were extended, and further controls

gogue, the Town Hall chapel was built, containing the famous Altar of the City's Patron Saints painted for it by Stephan Lochner. Today this fine example of late medieval painting of the Cologne school can be admired in the Cathedral.

Persecution of the Jews: Just before the Town Hall chapel was built, the Jews had been driven out of Cologne once and for all. Jews had been living in Cologne as early as Roman times. In the 10th century, many of them settled in the area around today's Town Hall. From that time onwards they were subjected to repeated pogroms. The persecution reached its peak with the pogrom of

were imposed upon the City Council.

In 1407 the guilds had begun work on the construction of the Town Hall Tower, as a symbol of their victory over the city families. The construction work was probably financed with money confiscated from the banished patrician families. A few years later, the Town Hall complex was further extended. On the site of the former Syna-

1349: there was an outbreak of the plague in Cologne that year, and a rumour was circulating that the Jews had poisoned the city's water supply. The Christians' rage was appalling; at the end of what came to be referred to as "Bartholomew's Night", not a single Jew was left alive in Cologne.

A few years later, Jews were re-admitted to the city under the auspices of the archbishop and the emperor, who in so doing were both more than conscious of the income they would generate. But the Jews were no longer needed: the Christians were just as good with money now, and the newcomers

<u>Left</u>, council session in the town hall. <u>Above left</u>, baroque ostentation in the former Jesuit Church. <u>Above right</u>, the Gürzenich, Cologne's oldest banqueting hall.

just meant troublesome competition. In 1424 the Jews were banned from Cologne for good. They were denied right of domicile in Cologne for centuries, and it was only finally restored to them in 1797, after the city had fallen to the French.

But however hard they were on the Jews, the burghers of Cologne were far more progressive when it came to their treatment of women. Even though women were not allowed to vote, they still enjoyed a comparatively large degree of independence in relation to other medieval cities when it came to trade and commerce. Woman merchants and woman artisans contributed a great deal to

even called the tune. In important businesses such as threadmaking and silkmaking, women were left entirely to themselves. Here they were responsible for fixing wages, checking goods, and training employees.

Witch-hunts: This early economic independence did not, however, protect the women of Cologne from being persecuted as witches, just like women everywhere else in the 16th and 17th centuries. Cologne, which liked to portray itself as so liberal, actually played a leading role – on paper at least – in this sorry chapter of German history. The infamous *Malleus Maleficarum*, or "Hammer of the Witches", written in 1487, which

the prosperity of their city. They were allowed to sign contracts, bring debtors before the courts and make statements under oath; other women in other cities could only dream of being accorded such rights.

There was scarcely any business in which women did not do just as well as men. Stina Waveren, for example, controlled nearly 20 percent of the Cologne cloth trade in the 15th century, and Cathringin Broelman occupied a similar leading position in the steel market. Many women in Cologne were also eager and industrious artisans. They had equal rights in many of the guilds, and in some they

provided the ideological basis for witch-hunting as well as being the textbook for torture and executions, was actually the work of two Dominican monks from Cologne: Henricus Institor and Jacob Sprenger.

The city only became really active as far as witch-hunting was concerned in the 1620s. Cologne had not pursued the practice all that eagerly until then. But during the Thirty Years' War, around 30 women were burnt to

Above, Cologne Cathedral took centuries to complete; the state of progress in the 15th century. **Right**, bronze bust of Nikolaus Gülich.

NIKOLAUS GÜLICH

Favouritism, intrigue and gossip exist all over the world, but the nepotism known as *Klüngel* is a typical Cologne phenomenon. Nepotism in Cologne is nothing to be ashamed of; it's as much a part of the city as the Carnival or the Catholic church. Little tricks to gain personal advantage are the spice of life as far as the citizens of Cologne are concerned; that's what makes life really worth living. Everybody "pulls strings" as best they can, tricking others and getting tricked themselves. And nepotism in Cologne isn't limited to an elite, either; it's practised all over the place.

Civic anger at excessive nepotism has been a recurring phenomenon throughout Cologne's history, but no event has remained more firmly fixed in the memory of the population than the uprising led by Nikolaus Gülich roughly 300 years ago. Gülich, a ribbon merchant, became one of Cologne's historic figures when he rebelled against the nepotism that was rife in the city. At the end of the 17th century, mismanagement, and the preferential treatment of a handful of ruling families who were lining each other up for influential posts in the civic administration, and generally abusing the constitution, had reached such proportions that it took very little for the burghers' dissatisfaction to break out into public fury.

The rebels found their spokesman in Nikolaus Gülich, who had himself been a victim of the authorities' nepotistic practices, but was unwilling to accept that fact without protest. Gülich voiced what many people had been thinking but none dared publicly admit: that the machinations of the ruling clique had to be stopped, and the constitution made relevant once again. Unwavering in the face of repression, Gülich managed in 1680 to have an independent commission of enquiry appointed, and the first conclusion it reached was that certain persons in high office should be immediately dismissed from their posts and brought to trial.

If the City Council had been hoping to take the wind out of the opposition's sails by making this concession, then it was very soon disappointed. The verbal attacks by Gülich and his supporters on the corrupt civic authorities only became more intense after this initial success. The Council finally resorted to arresting Gülich, but it had misjudged things yet again: Gülich's popularity had grown so much by then that the Council soon saw itself compelled to release him.

With more support among the population now than ever before, Gülich continued his fight against the civic authorities. The burghers' resistance became more organised, and in the summer of 1683 they succeeded in putting an abrupt end to the entire City Council.

But the promised reforms still hadn't arrived. The city had new rulers, true enough – but their method of ruling had not changed a great deal. Gülich had settled in comfortably in a new and influential post, and seemed more concerned with having the new civic authorities sanctioned after the event by the emperor than with fulfilling the population's hopes for justice and equality for all.

The emperor, however, far away in Vienna, who had been following all the unrest in Cologne with disfavour now for quite some time, had no intention of giving his official approval to the new authorities. Quite the reverse, in fact: in August 1685, Gülich and two of his leading comrades-in-arms, Abraham Sax and Anton Meshow, were put under the ban of the Empire. In the same month, they were arrested: Gülich and Sax were sentenced to death by the sword, while Meshow was given a whipping and sent into exile.

On 23 February 1686 in Mülheim, the executioner did his duty. Afterwards, Gülich's head was placed on an iron spike up on the Bayenturm, his house was demolished and a pillar of shame, with a bronze effigy of his head on the top, was erected on the site.

In November 1685, by imperial decree, the former City Council and all the other members of the former authorities had already been restored to office. Nepotism was back in the saddle and, as for the constitution, it remained what it had always been from the very start: a paper tiger, its stipulations having very little in common with reality.

death. Even members of the city's leading families fell victim to the madness: Katharina Henoth, for example, the daughter of the city postmaster, was burned alive as a witch in 1627 at Melaten Cemetery. Usually all that was necessary was a simple accusation to set the gruesome machinery of torture, self-incrimination, trials and executions into motion. It could be a coincidence, but it is still remarkable that witch-hunting reached its peak at a time when the city's economy was suffering a rapid decline, and women were no longer playing an important role.

When Cologne was officially raised to the status of a Free Imperial City by the emperor Luther's theses had dealt the sale of indulgences a sharp blow. Thus, the Cathedral's only provisionally completed choir and the unfinished southern tower with its huge wooden construction crane were to determine the city's appearance for the next 300 years or so.

But Cologne hadn't yet lost all of its grandeur. In 1561, the Staple House beside the Rhine was completed, in 1573 the Town Hall received a magnificent Renaissance Loggia, and the city's Arsenal (Zeughaus) was finished around 1600. Cologne had already been given its most important municipal building, next to the Town Hall, in 1444: the

Frederick III in 1475, it had reached the zenith of its development in every respect. Trade and craft were flourishing, and the emperor held the city in great esteem. But less than a century later, Cologne had already begun to show unmistakeable symptoms of decline.

Economic decline: In 1560, construction work on the Cathedral was suspended, for what had once been a steady flow of donations and contributions had now degenerated to a mere trickle. This was partly due to the Reformation, however. True, Protestantism had failed to find a foothold in Cologne, but magnificent Gothic banqueting and festival hall known as the Gürzenich. Emperors and princes were frequent visitors to this "grand and marvellous dancing hall", as one contemporary described it. Emperor Frederick III enjoyed holding banquets here just as much as his son Maximilian, or the emperor Charles V. Splendid gatherings, often with more than a thousand guests, were quite a common occurrence in the Gürzenich.

The only church worthy of note to have been built at that time was the Church of the Assumption (St Maria Himmelfahrt), begun in 1618 and consecrated in 1678, one of the most important Jesuit buildings in Germany and the largest Baroque church in Cologne. With this magnificent construction, the Jesuits – who had become a spearhead of the Counter Reformation in Cologne – succeeded in giving physical expression to their religious credo: its Gothic and Romanesque elements bear witness to the traditions of earlier epochs.

The Thirty Years' War: Displaying their characteristic inclination to avoid major confrontations if at all possible, the burghers of Cologne succeeded in keeping their city out of the turmoil of the Thirty Years' War (1618–48). While half of Europe was being

in the face of new products and new production methods. So, instead, they clung stubbornly to outmoded customs and habits, dodged anything involving any kind of risk, and steered clear of all innovations.

In the 17th century, as the city's trade and craft became less and less important, corruption and the proverbial Cologne brand of nepotism known as *Klüngel* increased as never before. Under the leadership of ribbon merchant Nikolaus Gülich, the City Parliament succeeded in having an impartial commission of inquiry set up, which went on to drive the mayors, councillors and several administrative officials out of office before

reduced to ashes, Cologne did good wartime business: it provided the troops with weapons, provisions and clothing. But even this could not stave off the city's decline.

Cologne, spoilt by success, was unable to find any recipe for dealing with the continual shifts in the world's economy; its merchants were helpless as long-distance trade shifted to ocean-going traffic after the discovery of America, and its artisans were helpless too,

Left, the "Cologne Farmer" at the Eigelstein Gate. **Above**, the old arsenal (Zeughaus) now houses the municipal museum.

placing itself in charge of the city. Gülich's attempts at reform did not meet with the approval of the emperor, however. Gülich and his colleagues were declared violators of the peace, arrested, and then publicly beheaded in February 1686.

A full century was to pass before this "rebel against nepotism" was done proper justice, albeit rather too late: Gülich was posthumously honoured as a freedom fighter by the French when they entered the city in October 1794, after the Revolution. The arrival of the French, however, also marked the end of Cologne's era as a Free Imperial City.

COLOGNE GOES INDUSTRIAL

On 6 October 1794, the day the French entered the city, everything changed. The event marked not only the demise of Cologne's long period of civic autonomy, but also the end of the Middle Ages. Liberty, equality and fraternity were the watchwords of the French Revolution. The Tree of Liberty became the symbol of the new era. Just three days after the French marched in, the first Tree of Liberty had already been set up during a ceremony in the city's Neumarkt. Bit by bit, the old order disintegrated.

In place of the special courts customary until then, a standard system of justice, Napoleon's *Code Civil*, was introduced. The city's economy was also given a boost with the dissolution of the guilds. Moreover, the right to practise their religion without hindrance turned Jews and Protestants, after centuries of persecution and discrimination, into fully-fledged Cologne citizens, and this also found its expression in the economic life of the city, where Jews and Protestants were soon occupying leading positions thanks to their readiness to innovate and to take risks.

Secularisation: Most far-reaching of all, however, was secularisation, which shook the Catholic church – until then it had occupied an all-powerful position – to its very foundations. Convents and monasteries were expropriated, their treasures sold or destroyed, their buildings torn down or turned into warehouses, factories or hospitals. A few parish churches remained unscathed by secularisation, which is the reason why some collegiate and monastic churches hastily passed themselves off as parish ones, thus escaping destruction. The reason most people in Cologne don't like to talk about those 20 years of French rule is probably largely because of the rough treatment the Catholic Church received.

Nevertheless, while the French era had begun promisingly enough, the same cannot

<u>Right</u>, the equestrian statue of King Frederick William IV at the east end of the Hohenzollern Bridge.

be said of the start of the Prussian era. The decision taken at the Congress of Vienna in 1815 to award the left bank of the Rhine, and thus Cologne as well, to Prussia was not well received in the city. The mentalities were too different: the Rhinelanders, such lovers of life, on the one hand, and the duty-conscious Prussians on the other. The fact that not Cologne but Koblenz had been made the centre of the Prussian province on the Rhine in 1822, and that Cologne's university, closed by the French, had not been re-opened since, only served to fuel Cologne's resentment. Nevertheless, the Prussians had big plans for Cologne. Within just a few years it

trip from Cologne to Müngersdorf. By mid-century there were already several dozen steam engines in operation in Cologne. The modern era had arrived.

Visible signs of the new age, apart from the tall factory chimneys everywhere, were the railway station, which was built right next to the Cathedral, and the first permanent Rhine bridge ever to be constructed since Roman times, completed in 1859. At the request of King Frederick William IV the road and rail bridge – the forerunner of today's Hohenzollern Bridge – was aligned precisely with the choir of the Cathedral.

From 1842 onwards, the Cathedral was a

had been turned into the most important fortified city on the Rhine. Forts and other defensive installations sprang up around the medieval city wall, and large barracks were built in the Neumarkt and in Deutz.

Full steam ahead: However, a crucial role as far as the development of the city over the next decades was concerned was played by something else entirely: the invention of the steam-engine. In June 1816 a steamer moored in Cologne for the very first time; in 1828 the first industrial steam-engine began operations in a Cologne corn mill; and in August 1839 a steam train made its first-ever

building site once more. As he laid the foundation stone for the extension work, the King said that the main body of the great Cathedral was to be completed as a symbol of "German unity and strength". In 1880, the work was finished. But what should have been a triumph for the Catholic church instead fell victim to the general quarrel between church and state that Bismarck had provoked: the great celebration in the Cathedral took place in the absence of the city's archbishop – he was living in exile.

But not only the Cathedral was surrounded by construction cranes in the mid-19th century; new tenement blocks and new factories were springing up all over the place. Many of the city's artisans saw their chance, and switched over to mass production. New technology quickly gained a foothold, above all in the textile industry, the breweries, sugar refineries, mills and metalworks, and it brought several Cologne citizens wealth and respectability.

Nikolaus August Otto became world-famous when he developed the world's first four-stroke internal-combustion engine at his factory in Deutz. The internationally famous firm of Klöckner-Humboldt-Deutz developed from this factory, which was

paid for dearly, however, by mass misery. Up to 16 hours' work a day, preposterously low wages, women and children being forced out to work, dark and damp tenements – this was the harsh reality facing most of the working people of Cologne in the 19th century. Considering these conditions, it is astounding that no blood was shed in the city during the revolutionary year of 1848.

Perhaps the strong presence of the Prussian military nipped any inclination to start an armed uprising in the bud. Even Karl Marx – co-editor of the *Neue Rheinische Zeitung* with Friedrich Engels in Cologne at that time – who called upon the populace in

founded in 1864. Another firm of international importance, the cablemaking firm of Felten & Guilleaume, was founded by master ropemaker Theodor Felten and his son-in-law Carl Guilleaume in 1826. Franz Stollwerck, a confectioner, made his fortune with the industrial manufacture of cough sweets and cakes. Sugar refineries made Carl Joest the richest man in Cologne.

Mass misery: This economic upswing was

Left, the French left their mark on the city – street names were written in both languages. **Above**, the erection of the tree of liberty in the Neumarkt.

the Gürzenich to begin the class struggle was unable to bring the revolution to Cologne.

After the failure of the 1848 revolution the city experienced an unparalleled surge of growth. It was not long before the last remaining open spaces within the medieval city walls had been built up. New housing estates and factory areas thus began to appear beyond the fortifications, out in front of the city gates. Cologne's first suburbs developed along the major arterial roads to the north and south: Nippes and Bayenthal. Ehrenfeld grew up in the west and, on the right bank of the Rhine, Kalk and Mülheim.

The New Town: The old city wall, nearly 600 years old by then, was proving more and more of a hindrance. In 1881, after lengthy negotiations, the city finally managed to acquire the area beyond the walls, fortified by the Prussians, for 12 million gold marks. In June of the same year, work began on dismantling the wall. Only St Severinus's Gate in the south, the Cockerel Gate in the west and the Eigelstein Gate in the north were allowed to remain, along with a few other smaller structures.

It then took less than 20 years for the New Town (Neustadt) to be built according to plans drawn up by city architect Joseph

parishes of Müngersdorf, Longerich, Bocklemünd, Mengenich, Volkhoven and Weidenpesch. On the right bank of the Rhine, Deutz and Poll were also included.

The city's surface area had thus increased tenfold to more than 11,000 hectares (27,000 acres), making Cologne, in terms of the land it occupied, the largest city in Germany – just as in medieval times. The number of inhabitants increased by around 80,000 to more than 260,000.

The fact that the population of Cologne actually doubled before 1910 makes it clear just how rapidly the city grew during the years that followed. No wonder the city

Stübben; it was based on the Ring Roads of Vienna, and extended around the Old City in a semicircle. Cologne was now roughly 236 hectares (600 acres) larger in size.

Only a few years later, the city expanded yet again. On 1 April 1888 the communities surrounding Cologne were incorporated into the city itself. The new city limits on the left bank of the Rhine now extended along the Militärringstrasse, and, in addition to encompassing the Old City and New Town, they also included the new suburbs of Ehrenfeld, Nippes, Bayenthal, Lindenthal, Sülz and Zollstock, as well as the older rural

authorities were already considering incorporating even more suburbs. In 1910 Cologne swallowed up the towns of Kalk and Vingst, and in 1914 Mülheim and Merheim. For the first time ever in the city's history, the areas to the right and left of the Rhine were now roughly the same size. At the outbreak of World War I, Cologne covered an area of 20,000 hectares (80 sq. miles), and had a population of over 630,000.

Left, complete but still a building site: inspecting damage to the cathedral. **Right**, a French corporal numbering house No. 4711 in the Glockengasse.

EAU DE COLOGNE

Johann Wolfgang von Goethe thought very highly of it, Wilhelm Raabe attributed life-saving powers to it, and Napoleon Bonaparte's officers gave it its name: Eau de Cologne. No other Cologne product is so inextricably linked to the city as this subtle mixture of ethyl alcohol, orange, lavender and other essential oils matured in wooden casks, and its precise recipe has been a rigorously well-kept secret for generations.

The city may contain more important firms – the automobile manufacturing company of Ford, for example, Cologne's largest employer, or the mechanical engineering firm of Klöckner-Humboldt-Deutz, responsible for the historic development of the Otto engine – but you'll find that the famous perfume is still always the only name to be mentioned all over the world in the same breath as the Cathedral.

Strangely enough, the mixture was originally created as a medicine – good, it was claimed, for curing heart trouble, gout, coughs, the plague and all sorts of other nasty diseases. The reason it didn't remain one is thanks to Napoleon: in 1810 he issued an imperial decree ordering the recipes for all medical remedies to be handed over.

This created a thorny commercial dilemma. Faced with the choice of either having to reveal their secret or to sell their product as a perfume in future, the makers of *Kölnisch Wasser* – and there were several of them at the time – decided to switch to the camp of toiletry article manufacturers and have their product struck off the medical list altogether. This was how the Eau de Cologne so familiar to us today was born, and it soon became incredibly popular with Napoleon's officers. Its aromatic perfume was just the kind of amorous souvenir to suit French tastes.

Today, roughly 20 different firms in Cologne produce the famous perfume. Only two of them, however, were there from the very start: the firm of "Johann Maria Farina opposite the Jülichs Platz GmbH", founded in 1709, who were the first to put the *Eau Admirable* on the market, and the firm of "Ferd. Mülhens Eau de Cologne and Perfume-factory No. 4711 Glockengasse opposite the mail-coach station in Cologne on the Rhine", founded in 1792 and known as 4711 for short.

As for the origins of the perfume, nobody is all that sure. Farina is supposed to have obtained his recipe from an Italian compatriot named Giovanni Paolo Feminis, and at No. 4711 the story goes that the banker's son Wilhelm Mülhens was given the precious formula as a wedding present by a Carthusian monk. Since that time the newer firm has successfully drained off a lot of "Eau" from the older one, and the French had their share of responsibility here, too.

For it was a French corporal who wrote the house-number 4711 on the Mühlens' home in the city's elegant Glockengasse while the French were numbering the city's buildings, thereby giving Wilhelm Mülhens the brilliant idea of labelling his flasks with precisely this number and providing his perfume with an unmistakeable brand-name. No wonder that the descendants of the banker's son are still retaining the legendary 4711 number, even though a whole range of new products – among them "Tosca" and "SIR" – are also making the cash-registers ring these days and have already achieved the status of classics.

Anyone who wants to contact the most famous firm in Cologne by phone only needs to dial 4711, and for anyone interested in the firm's history, No. 4711 Glockengasse is definitely the right address. Here, the Mülhens family has painstakingly reconstructed its original headquarters, destroyed in World War II, according to the historic plans.

Even though production has now been shifted to the Cologne suburb of Ehrenfeld, the neo-Gothic building in the Glockengasse has remained the outward and visible symbol of the firm. Here, visitors can savour the swell smell of success by trying out the Mülhens' very latest perfume creations, lose themselves in appreciation of the remarkable art and architecture, or just observe that memorable French corporal as he rides into the Glockengasse to the tune of the Marseillaise – all electronically controlled, on a carillon built into the facade of the 4711 building.

The outbreak of World War I was greeted in Cologne with much enthusiasm. However, as the hunger and the cold resulting from the British naval blockade became more and more unbearable, as the initial news of success at the Front gradually turned into news of defeat, and when even a few bombs were dropped on the city at Whitsun in 1918, people changed their minds. The discontent made itself felt shortly before the end of the war. Spurred on by the German naval mutiny in Kiel, the people of Cologne, too, rose in revolt. On 8 November 1918, a Workers' and Soldiers' Council took control of the city. The revolution only remained a brief episode, however – when the British occupation forces marched in that same year it quickly came to an end.

The mayor of the city at that time, Konrad Adenauer, was a lot more successful in realising his ideas. In 1917 Adenauer, who until then had been deputy mayor, assumed his predecessor's official duties and despite the British occupation, which lasted until early 1926, succeeded in putting his own individual stamp on Cologne's post-war development. In June 1919, the university was reopened at his instigation. Today, with over 50,000 students, it is one of the largest institutes of higher education in Germany. And in 1921 Adenauer ordered the construction of the Müngersdorf Stadium, which at that time was the largest in Europe.

In 1922, helped by the Provincial Parliament, he succeeded in having the municipality of Worringen made part of Cologne. The incorporation of what until then had been a primarily agricultural municipality made it possible for a huge industrial harbour to be constructed between Niehl and Merkenich, and for accommodation for those employed there to be built in neighbouring Worringen. In the same year, construction work was begun on the trade fair complex in Deutz, where the historic Millenium Exhibition of

Left, the girders of the destroyed Cologne-Deutz bridge were raised in 1974.

1925 was held, as well as the international Press Exhibition (PRESSA) in 1928, with its 5 million visitors.

From 1924 onwards, Adenauer took advantage of the removal of the Prussian fortifications stipulated by the Treaty of Versailles to lay out, under the supervision of Fritz Schumacher, the 7-km (4-mile) long Inner Green Belt and the 30-km (19-mile) long Outer Green Belt, with their children's playgrounds, sports facilities, meadows and ponds, thus creating a local recreation area that is the envy of many other large cities even today. The National Socialists put an end to Konrad Adenauer's work in 1933. True, they were the strongest party in the local elections held on 12 March that year, gaining nearly 40 percent of the vote, but they still remained without a majority in the City Council. This did not stop them, however, from grabbing power for themselves and from bringing the administration and the whole of public life "into line" with their policy of *Gleichschaltung*.

The cells in the basement of the former Gestapo headquarters in the El-De-Haus bear witness to the horrors inflicted under the Nazi regime: the walls still bear inscriptions scratched there by suffering prisoners. Today, an exhibition in the building documents the history of Cologne during the Third Reich. The city's synagogues were burnt down on 9 November 1939, shops and houses belonging to Jews were looted and destroyed, and the Jews themselves tortured and murdered.

The National Socialists had shown their true face in 1936 when they had their soldiers march across the Hohenzollern Bridge to the left bank of the Rhine, thus breaking the terms of the Treaty of Versailles. Eighteen years after the end of World War I and the demilitarisation of the Rhineland it had helped to bring about, the barracks in Cologne were being filled once more, and preparations for war were in full swing.

World War II began on 1 September 1939, when Hitler attacked Poland. On the night of

31 May 1942 Cologne suffered its first massive aerial bombardment at the hands of the Allies. Many more were to follow. When the German Army High Command took its leave of the city on 6 March 1945 with the phrase "The wreckage of Cologne has been left to the enemy", there were still roughly 40,000 people living in Cologne, compared to a figure of 768,000 at the beginning of the war. 20,000 of the city's population had been killed, buried beneath the rubble.

More than 90 percent of its housing had been destroyed or damaged beyond repair, and most of the churches and almost every civic building lay in ashes. All the Rhine bridges had been destroyed.

But new life soon began to stir among the debris. By the end of 1945 over 400,000 citizens of Cologne had already returned to their native city. Reconstruction began on a provisional basis at first. People settled in, removed the rubble and repaired anything that could still be repaired. Then, after the currency reform in 1948, plans for the city's reconstruction were drawn up. Bit by bit, historic buildings were either restored, such as the city's garland of Romanesque churches (1985), or completely rebuilt, like the Gürzenich (1955). Modern structures such as the "Vier-Scheiben-Haus" housing the WDR radio station, or the Severinus Bridge, supported by its single pylon, gave the city a new look.

The reconstruction phase has now come to an end. The last extension of Cologne took place in 1975, when it gained another 18,000 hectares (44,000 acres), thereby increasing its surface area to more than 400 sq. km (150 square miles), and its population to nearly 1 million.

Taken together with its surrounding communities, today's Cologne is an industrial centre with over 2½ million inhabitants, making it the third largest industrial area in Germany. In 1987 the working population of 420,000 in Cologne alone managed to achieve a gross net product amounting to more than DM 42 billion. The city's industry, exhibitions, banks and insurance companies, traders and artisans all contributed to the economic upswing.

Leader in car manufacturing: The service sector has gained an enormous amount in importance in Cologne over the past few years, but this has had little if any effect on the city's industry. In 1989, industrial turnover totalled DM 33 billion, with nearly one in four members of the population employed in industry. Leading the field is the car manufacturing industry, responsible for one quarter of the city's industrial turnover.

American car manufacture pioneer Henry Ford had recognised Cologne's advantages as a production centre as long ago as 1930. Nowhere else, in Ford's opinion, were the transport connections so ideal as in Cologne. This is even truer today than it was then.

Over 1,000 trains a day thunder over the Hohenzollern Bridge. Ten autobahns connect with the autobahn ring around Cologne, and 12 major federal highways in every direction complement the transport network. There are eight bridges across the Rhine, and the Rhine itself is an important transport route, too: nearly 14 million tons of goods are traded in the city's harbours annually. And Cologne is also connected to all the world's major industrial centres by air via the Cologne-Bonn airport – the second largest air-freight centre in Germany.

The Ford company workforce, which

originally numbered around 600, has grown today to over 25,000. Ford is by far the largest industrial employer in Cologne. 1,200 new cars a day roll off the production line at the Ford plant in Niehle. Meanwhile, other firms such as Citroën, Mazda, Renault and Toyota have also taken advantage of Cologne's ideal location. The city also produces tractors and farming machinery.

The chemical ring: The chemical and petrochemical industries are of immense importance to the region. Dozens of refineries and chemical works extend in a kind of ring around Cologne. They have almost 70,000 employees, and their combined turnover

the firm of Stollwerck was much appreciated by previous generations. And there are also far more breweries in Cologne and its environs than anywhere else in Germany: a total of 24, to be precise. The famous Cologne beer known as *Kölsch* belongs as much to the city as marzipan to Lübeck or *Weisswurst* to Munich. But of course it was another product that made Cologne famous throughout the globe: Eau de Cologne.

"Learn a trade and you'll never starve" goes the saying, and Cologne's 6,500 craft businesses are proof of it. Alongside trade, it is the city's most traditional branch of industry, employing a total of 65,000 people. Most

totals more than DM 20 billion every year. Further pillars of industry are the machine-tool and electrical industries. The traditional firm of Klöckner-Humboldt-Deutz is the world's largest producer of air-cooled diesel engines. Also well-represented in Cologne is the food, beverages and tobacco industry. Cologne sugar, too, has been famous since the last century, and chocolate produced by

Left, a memorial to two world wars: Barlach's "Angel of Death" in the Antonite Church. **Above**, symbol of the new beginning: Cologne's trade fair centre.

of the inhabitants of Cologne earn their living in the service sector, however. In 1987 the figure was 230,000 and two years later it had already risen to 240,000.

As the headquarters of 60 insurance companies, Cologne ranks as one of the most important European insurance centres, and it is certainly one of the oldest. Even the ancient Romans made payments during their lifetime in order to be given a decent burial, and in the Middle Ages merchants also insured themselves against losing their ships or cargo. Banking in the city also has its roots in the Middle Ages. After all, businesses needed to be financed back then, too. Today, there are 29 credit institutions in Cologne, including several large private banks. Alongside banks and insurance companies, quite a few associations, too, have chosen Cologne as their base of operations – 350 in all. They include the Federal Association of German Industries, the German Congress of Municipal Authorities, the National Housing Association and the Central Association of the German Retail Trade.

A media centre: The West German Radio Company ("Westdeutscher Rundfunk", known as WDR for short), the largest of Germany's broadcasting companies, is

ceives over a million visitors every year, nearly half of them from abroad. New luxury hotels are bringing in an increasing amount of money to the city.

The boom in visitors has also been highly profitable for the city's restaurants. No other city in Germany has as many pubs and restaurants in relation to its population as Cologne. One clever person once estimated that if all the counters from all the bars in Cologne were placed end to end, they would extend for 10 km (6 miles). Not only Cologne's restaurant owners, but its retailers too have been very happy about the soaring increase in tourism. As early as 1985 their

based in Cologne. The "Deutsche Welle" (the German equivalent of the World Service), the "Deutschlandfunk" and the satellite TV station "RTL-Plus" all broadcast from here too. Cologne's reputation as a media centre is further enhanced by a full 80 film and TV production companies, plus over 130 publishing companies and more than 200 printing firms. The "Media Park" is sure to strengthen the city's reputation even further; it is presently under construction, on the site of the former Gereon freight depot.

Cologne has enjoyed steady popularity for years as a tourist destination. The city re-

cash registers were taking in 30 percent more money per customer than the national average – and the trend is continuing.

The people of Cologne would be even happier, though, if their guests stayed a little longer; most of them pack their suitcases and leave after only one or two nights. The reason for these "flying visits" to Cologne could very well be the city's Trade Fair Complex in Deutz: by the beginning of the 1990s, it had more than a million visitors.

<u>Above</u>, Cologne in ruins. <u>Right</u>, Konrad Adenauer was once lord mayor of the city.

KONRAD ADENAUER: A COLOGNE LEGEND

"To be successful in politics you have to be able to remain seated for longer than anyone else." Had this phrase not been uttered by Konrad Adenauer himself one might have been inclined to consider it an evil insinuation on behalf of some of his rivals. But Adenauer, mayor of Cologne for many years before later becoming the Federal Republic's first ever Chancellor, was never too fastidious in his choice of methods, and openly admitted that the end justified the means.

He thought nothing of using his own vote to elect himself Chancellor in 1949, and even during his term as mayor in Cologne he was never afraid of achieving his objectives, even if the manner in which he did so was often rather unusual, to put it mildly.

The story of the Rhine Bridge at Mülheim is an outstanding example of Adenauer's political style. Adenauer was in favour of a suspension bridge, but a specially formed committee of experts, and also the City Parliament, decided in favour of an arch bridge. Anyone else would have accepted this decision. Not so Adenauer. In order to achieve his original aim he adopted a strategy that was effective, if somewhat time-consuming: in a series of private meetings, he took each of the city councillors to task individually.

He had so much success among the communists that one of their representatives, named Knab, had himself brought into the decisive meeting on a stretcher just so that he could vote in favour of Adenauer's suspension bridge (Adenauer had convinced the communists with an enthusiastic portrayal of the beauty of Leningrad and its suspension bridges). At the end of the meeting, the representatives decided on a suspension bridge after all.

A few years before this, when he was nurturing his dream of surrounding Cologne with a "Green Belt", Adenauer hadn't even bothered to ask the City Parliament at all. Its representatives only learned of Adenauer's plan after their mayor had already convinced the British and the Prussians, single-handedly, of his ideas, and had had an expropriation law from the National Assembly in Berlin tailored to his needs.

His methods might not always have been democratic, but his success usually proved him right in the end. Adenauer left more of a mark on his native city than anyone else before him. He restored glory and greatness to weary Cologne.

He had not been destined for a political career by any means, though. Adenauer was born on 5 January 1876 in Cologne's Balduinstrasse, the third son of a minor civil servant. His childhood and youth were marked by piety and thrift. Financial problems almost resulted in his being unable to study. But then events moved quickly.

In 1894 he began studying law at Freiburg University, in 1897 he took his law examinations in Bonn and in 1901 his assessor examinations in Berlin; in 1906 he was working as a lawyer in Cologne, in 1909 he was deputy mayor of the city, and in 1917 he became lord mayor of Cologne, the youngest in all Germany. He remained in his post until 1933. Years of persecution at the hands of the Nazis then followed, before he was eventually reinstated as mayor by the Americans in 1945.

And Adenauer might even have ended his career as mayor of Cologne had it not been for the British; they removed him from office in October 1945. Adenauer's reaction to this was typical: he added a new file to the one in his archive that read "removed from office by the Nazis" – the new one read "removed from office by the Liberators". Then he turned his attention to fresh tasks. He was 70 years old when he started to build up the German Christian Democratic Union (CDU), and 74 when he was elected Chancellor in 1949. He retired at the age of 88, having left an imprint on the Federal Republic as lasting as the one he had previously left on his native city of Cologne.

The integration of the Federal Republic into the West was his achievement, and the decades-long separation of the two Germanies was the price paid. On 25 April 1967 Konrad Adenauer was buried at the cemetery in Rhöndorf. He had become a legend in his own lifetime.

WHAT DOES "KÖLNISCH" REALLY MEAN?

Heinrich Böll assesses the spirit of Cologne.

The non-*Kölner* probably tends to associate the word *kölnisch* with something dark, devout and bourgeois; something consisting – in varying degrees – of the Cathedral, the Carnival, the Rhine, Wine and Women. As far as the people from the surrounding areas who stream into the city on Saturdays and Sundays are concerned, Cologne's attractions are varied and full of contrasts. Cologne is still a pilgrimage city; for many people its places of pilgrimage are of a discreet and often only apparently conflicting nature. Will anyone ever manage to put things together in such a way that piety, common sense and human nature can co-exist without colliding with one another?

Some paintings by Max Ernst show a human ear in the foreground; the mouth that goes with it is off hovering in a distant corner of the picture. Max Ernst, born in the Cologne area, fell under the city's spell; its holy mysteries were a kind of magic for him. In the cool of the Cathedral, the father confessor performing his duties; an ear that hears and yet doesn't; a mouth far removed from that ear, able to absolve what not every priest can absolve. The Cologne saying *"Der muß im Dom beichten gehen"* ("He'd better go and confess in the Cathedral") conveys a mixture of reverence and terror similar to that experienced in prison by small-time confidence tricksters, thieves and opportunists in the presence of genuine gangsters.

I often used to watch my father's helpers poring over the plans for confessionals, trimming the wood and assembling the whole thing with its individual sections; in the remarks they made about communists and atheists they were as outspoken and as critical as only former Catholics can be, but there was still a kind of invisible limit that no-one would have dreamt of crossing in the presence of a child; even in the Carnival, at the point where it feeds off the very depths of vulgarity, this limit is never violated either; in fact the only time it does is when something as untypical of Cologne as *Fasching* gets confused with the Carnival; the Carnival is vulgar, with all the majesty and horror that vulgarity entails, but it is never frivolous; *Fasching* is a Bohemian invention, while the Carnival has its roots in the people; it is classless, and like an infectious disease it knows no class barriers. *Fasching* isn't a noticeable part of city life; it can be ignored; but it would be useless to try to ignore the Carnival in Cologne; all one can safely do is remove oneself from the zone of infection.

The Carnival is unthinkable without that ever-present ear, that Max Ernstian ear, hovering above it; if I ever had to come up with a suggestion for a new coat-of-arms for the city, the ear would be an integral part of a rather complex piece of heraldry providing information about the character of Cologne; the mouth to go with it would certainly be visible, too, up in another corner.

The Cathedral wouldn't be in my coat-of-arms, though; the fact that it was so obviously spared by the bombs – something the magnificent Romanesque churches were considered unworthy of – belongs among the sentimental errors as to what Cologne really represents; the Cathedral is a lot less characteristic of Cologne than its other churches; indeed, it's never really suited the city at all, even as an episcopal church.

Cologne argued with its bishops for centuries; battles were fought, tricks were devised, papal bans were proclaimed in Rome, and the city was deprived of priests and sacraments; and all largely because of money, property and privilege. After all, most of Cologne's bishops were more secular princes than bishops, and most of the princes in those days were princes with debts to pay. The city only began to tolerate its bishops when the latter renounced their princely role; this tolerance is only just 150 years old, and not without a certain irony;

Preceding pages: escaping the guests. **Left**, enjoying a cruise on the Rhine. **Following pages**: *Brightening up her day.*

everyone knows only too well that the bone of contention has now been removed, for there was no bone more worth fighting over than the good old Cologne *thaler*. The bishop has been back in the city for just 150 years, and since then all the pastoral letters and sermons have had a reconciliatory, almost canvassing tone to them, and this in a city where almost 20 percent of Catholics fulfil their church duties; the bishop still has not lived long enough in the centre of the city, and his church, the Cathedral, is unfavourably located, on a slight rise, surrounded by huge hotels, next to the station, in the windiest part of the city which must have

printed in so many brochures, the Madonna among the Ruins and her sister in Lochner's painting still have a freshness about them that is utterly typical. And they keep turning up, too, in all ranks of society, rich and poor: in the tram; at the wheel of a sports-car; selling lipstick at Woolworths; listening to lectures on existentialism. There aren't too many of them but they're somehow always around: those faces that are so *kölnisch*; the serious ones have a slight hint of mockery to them, and yet – the perfect Madonna. The others are gentler, friendlier and yet – the perfect Madonna as well.

Ear, mouth, St Gereon's, the bishop's

been cursed for its draughtiness by Romans on sentry duty all those years ago.

No, the Cathedral wouldn't suit my imaginary coat-of-arms. St Gereon's, on the other hand, would do the job nicely: a church of martyrs, a church of mutineers. It was named after a Theban who rebelled against Rome, and its chief architectural point of interest has such a cosy-sounding name to it, too: "decagon". A small ear, a tiny mouth, and St Gereon's in my imaginary coat-of-arms; half a bishop's crook, and then to wind up the clerical and religious emblems, a picture of the Madonna. Seen on so many posters,

crook and a Madonna; that's probably enough religious emblems to be getting on with. Then we'd need some secular ones: an insurance building, perhaps, or a bank. And beside them we'd certainly have to have two hands, one of them washing the other; the rest of the world can keep its compromises and gentlemen's agreements, its corruption and bribery – *Der Klüngel*, Cologne's particular brand of nepotism, is something else entirely; it's the Cologne version of "being Nice". If someone asks you Nicely for a loaf of bread, and you can't give it to him, you do have the power as well as the right to say no

– but if you give him three slices of bread and he throws them at your feet, and insists on the entire loaf, then he's just not being Nice, or typically Cologne, about things.

If the ancient wisdom of this city is anything to go by, he'd probably be surprised and overwhelmed at being given those three slices at all in the first place. And hovering above the two hands washing each other we'd need to have the *Grielächer*, the person whose back gets scratched and who sometimes scratches other people's; the *Grielächer* takes nothing seriously, not even those things that need to be; everything's like one big Carnival to him; male voice choirs,

women's rights, education reform and deportation; it's all just another chance for him to tell jokes and insist on everyone being Nice to each other; if we had him between the two hands we could give him a vulgar-looking face, and dress him like a patrician, with Schäl's winking eye and with the nose of someone with circulation problems, like Tünnes; delicate hands and plump feet, or vice versa; he has a horror of things intellectual which can sometimes even make him forget his basic characteristic, his sense of

Left and **right**, two pleasant faces of the city.

humour; when a *Grielächer* starts getting serious, it's not a pleasant feeling; he's sensed the presence of his arch-enemy, the intellect, and he gets filled with apprehension as he realises that something Not Nice is going to be unavoidable – and if it's not Nice, then Cologne ain't Cologne any more, and what's a feller to do then? *Grielächer* is a word that's impossible to translate.

And those certainly aren't all the ingredients, by any means, that make *Kölnisch* into a true adjective that can lay claim to being a word in its own right. Although every city has a prison – and some even have suburbs, Roman walls and the Rhine – the city prison at the Klingelpütz would still have to be mentioned as being typical; it's a horrible-looking building, everyone is familiar with it, it's permanently overcrowded, it hasn't been brought "up to date" for years, and yet the plans presently under way for a new building are filling both its former and its potential inmates with a certain sadness; what the experts refer to as crime is so widespread in Cologne, for reasons as yet unexplained, that it's only really comparable to the crime level in harbour cities.

The expression "*Er sitzt im Pütz*" ("He's doing time in the Klingelpütz") usually refers more to a case of bad luck than real misfortune, and the number of people in Cologne who've experienced the *Pütz* from the inside is so high that one can safely speak of a certain familiarity. I wonder whether as many people know the Cathedral as well from the inside as they do the Klingelpütz? However, I shall attempt to remain Nice. One thing's certain, though: the prison chaplain has the largest congregation in all of Cologne. There they sit now, those who knew not how to practise nepotism, that complicated instrument, those whose Not-Niceness had to be put on the record.

Come to think of it, a little wrought-iron grille, evoking plenty of associations – park gates, prison bars – might rather suit my imaginary coat-of-arms.

From: Essayistische Schriften und Reden, Volume I by Heinrich Böll, Cologne 1979. Reprinted by permission of the Cologne publishing house of Kiepenheuer & Witsch.

A City Of Writers

"My ambition is," said Thomas Mann in 1926, "to prove that Lübeck... can be found in all my writings, from the beginning to the end, and that the city both decisively determines and controls them." Cologne is often associated in a similar manner with Heinrich Böll, but in fact Böll never cherished any such ambition: "If the Nazis hadn't arrived, and if the war hadn't happened, and I'd become a writer, I expect I'd be living in Berlin today."

"The apple never falls far from the bough" – a metaphor adopted by Thomas Mann, and it is certainly true of Böll. He was born in Cologne. The city's other famous writers only chose to move to Cologne from elsewhere: Paul Schallück (1922–76) was Westphalian, Hans Bender (born in 1919) came from Kraichgau, and Dieter Wellershoff (born in 1925) came from the Lower Rhine. True, Jürgen Becker was born in Cologne in 1932, but he grew up far from his native land: all of them apples minus the bough?

Thomas Mann's apt metaphor has the same problem as all comparisons: it doesn't stand up to scrutiny. Authors can't be compared to fruit, they don't have a bough, and they strike their own roots.

And Cologne is a particularly suitable place to do just that: the city has around 160 bookshops and several more publishing companies, a whole handful of radio stations, editorial offices and educational institutions: all in all, a countless number of places for literary life to meet. Too many perhaps, for Cologne still hasn't been provided with a proper centre for it all, a kind of "house of literature".

Writing tends to be only very seldom pursued as a main profession. Authors are often more inclined to congregate in the media as critics, lecturers and literary advisers – Werner Koch, for example, or Jürgen Becker, who works at the *Deutschlandfunk*

Preceding pages: a night at the opera. **Left,** Cologne's most famous poet: Nobel laureate Heinrich Böll.

but also happens to be a well-known lyric poet; or Dieter Wellershoff, who read manuscripts for many years in Heinrich Böll's publishing house of Kiepenheuer & Witsch before going on to write his own stuff exclusively. The novelist Hans Werner Kettenbach, born in 1928, is today deputy editor-in-chief of Cologne's largest daily newspaper.

It's when they have the safe background of a paid job that many authors are often at their most effective, the best example perhaps being Dieter Wellershoff, who became the mentor of his own "Cologne School" of new realism, with its famous names: Rolf Dieter Brinkmann (1940–75), who also lived in Cologne, and Nicolas Born (1937–79) are the two most notable.

Historically, close affiliation between authors and professions has been quite common in Cologne: Albertus Magnus, or Albert the Great (1200?–80), taught here as a "Doctor universalis", his pupil Thomas Aquinas (1225–92) became a "Doctor angelicus" and also taught in Cologne as well as elsewhere; Master Eckhart (1260?–1327) had a professorship in the city from 1320 onwards; Johannes Duns Scotus (1256?–1308) earned himself the title of "Doctor subtilis" for his perspicacity; and Friedrich von Spee (1590–1635), famed as a poet and as an opponent of witch-hunting, taught at the city's Dreikönigs Gymnasium.

They all had their roots firmly fixed in scholastic life – and not one of them was born in Cologne. Only one other scholar actually was: the famous necromancer Agrippa of Nettesheim (1486–1535). He, however, used to practise his art in Bonn – his creditors and opponents of his cabalistic teachings having forced him to flee there.

Karl Marx from Trier, who edited the *Neue Rheinische Zeitung* in Cologne from 1848 onwards, might have become a citizen of Cologne had the Prussians not expelled him as a stateless person in 1849. But anyone who wants to claim Marx for Cologne and accord the city a progressive tradition should also mention Robert Blum, who was born at the fish market near the church of Great St Martin's in 1807, and shot dead as a revolutionary in Vienna in 1848. One should also mention Heinz Steguweit (1897–1964) and Ernst Bertram (1884–1957); both were born in Cologne, both died there, and both were lyric poets infected by nationalism.

Cologne writers have hardly ever treated their native city as the "intellectual lifeform" that Thomas Mann famously considered Lübeck to be. And the anecdote handed down to us by Hans Bender, about Jürgen Becker accusing him of "living in Cologne like a tourist!" certainly reflects the feelings of many. There again, Cologne occasionally

Alongside dialect literature, the songs of Willi Ostermann (1876–1936), or the poems of Albert Vogt (better known under his pseudonym of "B. Gravlott"), only one more present-day Cologne speciality needs to be mentioned: the so-called *Köln-Krimis* ("Cologne Crime Stories") by Christoph Gottwald (born in Cologne in 1954), who has provided his city with a whole genre. The first book of the series, *Tödlicher Klüngel* ("Deadly Nepotism"), however, was shifted to Cologne only when it was certain that it would be published there. "I can write books anywhere, but the only place I ever want to live is Cologne," said Gottwald.

turns up as a theme in their work: Dieter Wellershoff has recently written a book on his native city (*Pan und die Engel*) and Jürgen Becker has been on the trail of his old and new home since writing *Felder* (1964).

Publicists Carola Stern (born in 1925) and Vilma Sturm (born in 1928), as well as Günter Wallraff (born in 1942) are natives of Cologne, though the city is not that important to them as authors. And Cologne often forms the background of books: Graham Greene (*Stamboul Train*), Gerhard Zwerenz (*Casanova*) and in the novels of Bernd Sülzer (*Bensberger Zwischenspiel*).

Whether Heinrich Böll would ever have become a "Berliner" now that the post-war era is over is more than questionable. But Werner Kettenbach is quite clear on this point at least: "Even if Cologne had a literary scene similar to the one Berlin used to have, and I had the time as well as the inclination to get involved in it, the fact that I live here in Cologne and that I want to stay here would be based on quite different reasons."

Two writers of the post-Böll generation: (above left) Jürgen Becker and Dieter Wellershoff (above right). <u>Right</u>, the grave of Heinrich Böll.

Heinrich Böll: Author Without a Native City

Heinrich Böll (1917–85) was born in Cologne. The city would happily have provided him with his last resting-place, too, at the Melaten Cemetery. But he lies buried in Merten instead, in a pretty little graveyard high on the slopes of the *Vorgebirge* (foothills to the west of the city). From here, on a clear day, one can make out the towers of St Severinus's in his native city. For Merten isn't all that far from Cologne; but – and this is the crucial point – it's also just far enough away *not* to be Cologne.

This small distance, though, somehow symbolises Böll's relationship with his native city. It was one characterised by love, certainly, and by a certain amount of oversensitivity too; and certainly never one of unqualified harmony. In 1982 there was a huge fuss made in Cologne when Böll moved house for the last time – almost as if he was trying to stir up trouble yet again just by changing his address – but in fact all he was doing was returning to his family, at his son René's house.

Böll has been criticised often enough: he has been branded a "nest fouler" and a "defeatist", and if not as "a man without a native land", at least as someone without a native city. One only has to read a few of his many essays, though, to realise just how idiotic such accusations are, and to discover just how closely and inextricably involved Böll actually was with "his" native city. At the age of 50 he said: "I believe that in general, that is to say beyond any subjective point of view, that the city in which a person has lived until he is 21 will always have a determining and a decisive effect on him."

Böll was born at No. 26, Teutoburger Strasse, in the New Town area of the city. He himself spent three times longer than his own figure of 21 years in Cologne. His is the story of someone who gradually fell out of love with his native city.

"When we saw Cologne again, we wept", he wrote describing his return home in 1945. His loss of his *Heimat* had of course begun far earlier, with the sight of the brown-shirted ranks marching through the city, "desecrating the streets", as he put it. His way to school, through the area of the city surrounding St Severinus's, took him past the newsstand with its Nazi newspapers. It was at this point that he began to spend his afternoons writing, at No. 32, Maternus Strasse. Years later he was to say: "I do not believe that one can write, paint, compose, or be an artist at all without resistance…"

But even if Böll's motivation to write was based on his experience of life – and thus his experience here in Cologne – his work is far from biographical. He would seek the settings for his books elsewhere, or simply invent them; Cologne is hardly ever the scene of the action.

Böll did erect a literary monument to the nation's capital of Bonn, though, but it was one that didn't exactly meet with approval: *Ansichten eines Clowns* ("The Clown").

His favourite theme was the history of the middle classes – the kind you find everywhere, but particularly in the New Town area of Cologne, where he and his family had lived. His last apartment before World War II began was also in the New Town, at No. 17, Karolinger Ring. It was destroyed by the bombs, and Böll thus became homeless in his own home city.

Years later, when he moved back to the New Town (to No. 7, Hülchrather Strasse, which is where he also received the news of his Nobel Prize in 1972), it was really only a half-hearted attempt at trying to feel at home. He could never come to terms with what he called "traffic Cologne". The "war and the north-south interchange" were two things Böll tended to mention in the same breath from then on.

Nevertheless, Cologne was still his *Heimat*, and there were many aspects of it he loved. At the age of 60, in 1977, he was proud to remember what he had experienced as a 16-year-old: even during the March elections in 1933 (that is, after the seizure of power), the Nazis had still not managed to win a majority in Cologne.

In 1983, just two years before his death, at a ceremony held in the Town Hall, Cologne made Heinrich Böll an honorary citizen.

THE THEATRE SCENE

Visitors to Cologne probably can't help noticing that the city exudes a discreet, and to some extent quite pleasant, whiff of provincialism; this has occasionally been known to cause problems for the city's actors, for provincial attitudes tend to abound wherever you go.

In 1930, Konrad Adenauer, who was mayor of Cologne at the time, censored the first performance of Brecht's *Dreigroschenoper* ("Threepenny Opera") in the city. Certain "political and moral" aspects of it were watered down as a result. Hansgünther Heyme, director of Cologne's Schauspielhaus from 1968 to 1979, got into trouble for taking a collection to pay for terrorist Gudrun Ensslin's dental bill, as well as for his accurate portrayal of a paranoid Martin Luther (*Luther & Thomas Münzer*).

His successor, Jürgen Flimm, placed himself between all political stools with his play *Absa(h)nierung* (a pun on the German word for "redevelopment" and the verb meaning "to rake it in") about the decline of the Stollwerck section of the city. "Crises come and crises go" is the name of another play from the Flimm era.

Before 1900, Cologne had never been an exciting city for theatre. Historic theatre buildings are conspicuously absent. The oldest theatre, in fact, is the one belonging to Willy Millowitsch on the Aachener Strasse, where plays have been staged since 1936.

Even as early as the serious days of the High Middle Ages, people here preferred to concentrate their energies on the Carnival, which at that time provided more than enough visual effect for a city which today has several museums and around one hundred art galleries. Cologne has never been a seat of royalty; princes have never shown off their wealth here, and so stage performances as such never had a chance.

As late as 1592, "English acting troupes" were being driven out of the city. In the 17th

Left, the Schauspielhaus and Opera House on Offenbachplatz.

and 18th centuries, travelling theatre groups from Holland, Belgium, France, Italy and Poland were only reluctantly admitted into the city, and only under certain strict conditions. The city didn't care for what they did, and made as much plain to them. *"Hängt die Wäsche weg, die Gaukler sind in der Stadt"* ("Get yer washing off the line, those jokers are back in town again"), as the saying went.

Theatre in Cologne developed only very sporadically. In 1783, the people of Cologne were able to proudly announce the presence of the first proper theatre in the city, in the Schmierstrasse (today's Komödienstrasse), right next to the Cathedral. The site has been occupied by a bank building for many years, for the theatre soon went out of business, despite the fact that Albert Lortzing and Jacques Offenbach kept it going for a while.

Then in 1872, finally, there it was: the first respectable "Civic Theatre". It opened its doors in the Glockengasse, right opposite the place where the Opera House stands today. But it was destroyed in World War II. The site of the former Civic Theatre today has a neo-Gothic structure built on it, displaying the city's most famous perfume, Eau de Cologne.

After the war, plays were put on in the assembly hall of the University, in pubs and in community halls. Herbert Maisch, the director in those days, writes in his memoirs: "And so we drove through the villages in a furniture van to show people that plays were being put on once again in Cologne". On 8 October 1962, a new theatre designed by Wilhelm Riphahn opened with a performance of Schiller's *Die Räuber* ("Robbers"). The play was directed by Oscar Fritz Schuh.

Since the beginning of the 1990s – after a five-year-long lapse under helpless director/ dramatic advisor Klaus Pierwoss – exciting, committed theatre has been staged here once again, and has made a name for itself outside the region. With Günther Krämer as director, the theatre on the Offenbachplatz has someone who has successfully dissected the weirder sides of human existence with an

Theatre 65

aggressively sharp disrespect, yet at the same time very aesthetically; someone who has brought momentum, colour and an earthy sensuality to all the plays he has tackled, whether by Brecht or Heiner Müller, Goethe or George Tabori, whether in the Schauspielhaus, the Kammerspiele or the Schlosserei. The director crisis, the asbestos crisis, and also the long closure of the theatre have all been forgotten now. What were the magic words in the days of Flimm? – "Crises come and crises go."

Cologne has developed a lot more of a feel for the avant-garde over the last few years. "Squat", "Living Theatre" or Robert Wilson

though perhaps somewhat more alternative. The speciality here is highly colourful children's theatre.

Another firm favourite with children and adults alike is the "Hänneschen Theater" in the Eisenmarkt. Founded by Christoph Winters in 1802, it is the oldest local puppet theatre in all the German-speaking countries, and today it is run by the city. Typical aspects of Cologne are parodied here, much in the style of the Italian *commedia dell'arte* – and all of it, of course, in Cologne dialect.

The "Keller Theater" in Kleingedankstrasse stages drama relating to contemporary problems, and has also put on several

have been welcome guests in the city. Cologne now has its very own, and very active free theatre scene, with around 20 alternative theatre groups.

Alongside the "Theater am Dom" in the "Schweizer Ladenstadt" (near the Opera House) and Millowitsch's "Volkstheater" on the Aachener Strasse, the "Senftöpchen" is another highly regarded place of entertainment, where cabaret, musicals, nostalgia and even travesty shows enjoy great popularity. Cabaret and music are the most popular of all. The "Comedia Colonia" in Löwengasse (near the main police station) is similar,

neglected plays from the 1950s. In "Bauturm", opposite Millowitsch's theatre, the plays are modern and often home-made, but they also do Horvath and Büchner. One oddity is the "Freie Werkstatt Theater" in Zugweg, in the Südstadt. Here, they're really up-to-date in true 1968 fashion, with plays featuring old people, foreigners and the unemployed, and dealing with topics such as cancer or anorexia nervosa.

Left, a performance of Brecht in the Schauspielhaus. Right, cheers! Now over 80 years old, Willy Millowitsch still performs on stage.

THE MILLOWITSCH FAMILY

It's quite possible that we have Liebig's invention of artificial fertiliser to thank for Willy Millowitsch's famous Volkstheater in Cologne. One day Franz Andreas Millowitsch, born around 1790, a *Spezereikrämer* (grocer) by trade, and forefather of Cologne's favourite actor, was unable to sell his fertiliser from Gerberlohe to the local cabbage farmers, because the latter preferred Liebig's artificial equivalent. So instead, Franz Andreas began travelling around as a street-singer and puppeteer – and became quite a character in his own right.

His descendant Willy is continuing the long tradition; wherever he turns up, the crowds go wild. He captivates his audience time and time again with his special Cologne mixture of character comedy and one-liners, and in his role as a *Jrielächer*, which is roughly the equivalent of a rogue.

If it's traditional, it must be good, and over 80 years old now, he remains loyal both to himself and the dynasty as the lovable lad from the "Veedeln" (Cologne's old districts) in *Nacht jackenviertel*, a play written by his grandfather Wilhelm Joseph, or as the worthy citizen thirsty for adventure in the comedies of mistaken identity written by Arnold and Bach, in which morality and family life always win out in the end, despite the odd touch of irresponsibility in between.

In the playhouse on the Aachener Strasse, where the Millowitsch family have been entertaining their audiences since 1936 with their popular brand of theatre, continuity is seen as all-important. *Tante Jutta aus Kalkutta* ("Auntie Jutta from Calcutta") remains a perennial favourite with audiences. And *Fussig Julchen* provided – and still does provide – a great opportunity for all the female members of the family to shine, from Willy Millowitsch's grandmother Emma all the way to his daughter Mariele. Son Peter helps to stage his father's productions.

The most powerful moving force in the history of this old German family of popular actors seems to have been grandfather Wilhelm Joseph, ex-puppeteer and author of around 30 works for the stage. In 1894 he flung his puppets aside and announced: *"Ich will es Euch bekunden, die Puppen sind verschwunden, es war mir zu gewöhnlich, wir spielen jetzt persönlich."* ("There's something that I have to say, the puppets all have had their day, I found them rather boring, in person's more rewarding.")

He then put all his energy into plays starring real flesh-and-blood characters, also bringing those two famous Cologne character-types Tünnes and Schäl, who had originally been featured in the puppet theatre, onto the stage, thereby making them famous far beyond Cologne.

Willy Millowitsch, such a quiet person in private, and such an explosively charismatic individual the moment he's up on stage, had to suffer for many long years from the arrogance of highbrow criticism, which successfully denied him any entry into professional associations as well as a place in works of reference.

But today, that's no longer a problem: he is an honorary citizen of Cologne, he has been awarded the Federal Service Cross as well as the Telestar Prize, and Hollywood, television and "serious" acting have now beckoned. He has played Molière's *Bourgeois gentilhomme* as well as the philosophical gravedigger in Noelte's *Hamlet*.

His daughter Katarina says that he's remained a modest person. She is a teacher, with two children and a doctorate in German studies, and has made what amounts to quite a prolific contribution to the free theatre scene in Cologne. She often talks admiringly of how calm a person he is, of his inner dynamism, of his "positive conservatism", and even of a "certain childlike side" to him.

Cologne's most famous actor is being plagued by ever-increasing sprightliness in his old age. Television and guest appearances in public go on piling up, and on top of all that Willy spends more than 90 days of the year on his own stage. Even when he's on holiday on the island of Elba, the telephone isn't left alone for a second, and he writes hundreds of letters and postcards to his fellow-actors and friends.

Cologne has a long tradition as a musical city, and offers an astounding range of both old and new music. Very few other cities contain so many active musicians and composers, and concerts, performances and live shows take place almost daily. The city has almost 300 choirs, and 100 serious rock and pop groups. Concerts are staged regularly in the Philharmonie and in the Music Academy, and on top of all that there are also the hundreds of performances that regularly take place in the city's numerous churches.

The opening of the Cologne Philharmonie in 1986 provided the city's two biggest symphony orchestras, the municipal "Gürzenich Orchestra" and the "Cologne Radio Symphony Orchestra", as well as the "WDR Big Band", with a new home. The Philharmonie, designed in the shape of an amphitheatre by Cologne architects Busmann and Haberer, could only be built with the support of the WDR, which contributed a third of the costs.

Inside the Philharmonie, the audience and the musicians sit in a circle, with the conductor or soloist standing in the middle. This means an uninterrupted view from each of the two thousand seats in the auditorium. The acoustics are also excellent; in order to insulate the hall from the sounds of steamers chugging past up the Rhine, and noisy railway trains, the entire auditorium was embedded inside a twin-walled concrete cradle which actually floats on the water-table, and is anchored firmly to the ground. The 11-metre (37-ft) high glass cupola above the podium ensures excellent sound quality and makes the auditorium a great deal larger.

For many years the musical centre of the city used to be the ancient banqueting-hall known as the Gürzenich. In 1821 it was Cologne's turn to organise the Lower Rhine Music Festival, and it decided – at first only on a provisional basis – to do up the rooms in the Gürzenich. Since 1832, the room most often used by musicians is the casino hall,

where Franz Liszt and Clara Schumann, among others, once performed.

Günter Wand did a great deal to promote the "Gürzenich Orchestra"; he conducted it from 1947 to 1974, and made a lasting personal contribution to the musical life of the city. During the course of the orchestra's 100-year history, numerous famous composers and conductors have stood before the musicians and the members of the choir as their guests: Felix Mendelssohn and Brahms, Richard Wagner and Tchaikovsky, and, after the turn of the century, Gustav Mahler, Weingartner and Pfitzner.

For the Cologne Radio Symphony Orchestra of the WDR, too, with its wide range of music both old and new, the new location in the Philharmonie has many advantages. Indeed, the WDR is of immense importance to the city as a whole: as well as being a radio station, it also commissions new works of music on a regular basis – from the Music Academy, for example. The radio station was one of the pioneer centres of electronic music, especially the works of Karlheinz Stockhausen, who still lives in the city. The WDR also acts as a nationwide mouthpiece for composers and musicians, and naturally for music lovers as well. The radio stations "Deutsche Welle" and "Deutschlandfunk" play a leading role in this respect too, one example being the various concert series they put on in their own concert halls.

The city's Opera House, built between 1957 and 1962, with a seating capacity of 1,400 has long earned itself a reputation both nationally and internationally. Guest performances, and co-productions with other opera houses in Paris and London have been extremely successful. The programme features works from Slavonic countries, Italy, France and of course Germany, too. Today's Opera House on the Offenbachplatz was built during the 1950s; the old one, on the Ring, was destroyed towards the end of World War II.

The vocal music scene lends extra strength to Cologne's already excellent musical repu-

Left, the acoustics are excellent in Cologne's Philharmonie.

tation. The Cathedral Choir, the Bach Choir, the Philharmonic Choir and the Gürzenich Choir are just four of the three hundred choirs based in the city that have won various awards in national and international competitions. The ensembles for old and new music are just as important and varied, too. Keep an eye out for performances by *Musica Antiqua Köln*, who perform Baroque music on period instruments.

Closely associated with a city's musical life are, of course, its music schools. Cologne's Music Academy and its Rhenish School of Music provide a wide range of different training programmes, as well as

salon"; concerts featuring Dixieland, Swing and trad Jazz take place there daily – and admission is free. The band at the "Biersalon" plays music from the 1920s, and the pianists, who play in a lot of different styles, change every day. There's a cabaret, too. Jazz performances also take place regularly in the subway, in the "Klimperkasten" and in the Municipal Gardens (Stadtgarten).

The choice of rock and pop music on offer is just as vast. Depending on their fame, the groups play in the Cologne Sports Hall (Sporthalle), in the "alter Wartesaal", in the Stadthalle at Mülheim or in the Life-Musik-Hall (sic!) in Ehrenfeld. The club scene in-

various opportunities to perform. And the Music Academy was the first in all of Germany to introduce a "jazz studies" course – no wonder, when one considers the active jazz scene in the city, with famous line-ups such as Saxofon-Mafia, Härte 10 and Nana. And the *Jazzhaus* initiative, with its 50 musicians, has done much to promote jazz via its annual festival, which has been going for 10 years now.

Particularly popular on the Cologne jazz scene are the performances at bar owner/pianist Papa Joe's establishments, known as "Em Strechstrump" and "Papa Joe's Bier-

cludes the "Luxor" (rock and pop), the "Cauri-Club" (Afro and Latin-American), the "Rose Club" (Punk and Heavy Metal), the "Popocatepetl" (Blues), and the "Underground" (experimental rock).

Anyone interested in hearing Cologne's most famous rock bands, however, may not get the chance to do so: "BAP" and the "Bläck Fööss", who were very successful in the 1980s, only very rarely perform their *Kölsch-Rock* in their native city these days.

Above, female rock. Right, BAP, Cologne's most famous band.

ROCK 'N' ROLL COLOGNE-STYLE

Times have changed. Cologne's dialect only used to really come into its own during Carnival time. No longer: the city's musicians, who wear their "heart on their tongue" (*et Hätz op de Zung*) rather than their sleeve, have used it to lend new charm to their songs, making them famous far beyond the city's borders.

Ever since the group known as the Bläck Fööss (literally: "bare feet") sang *Linda Lou*, the first ever rock song in "Kölsch", the local dialect, at the 1973 Carnival session, the sound of the language has become an accepted part of the rock and pop scene. The Bläck Fööss are now very popular right across Germany, Carnival time or no Carnival time.

What makes them so special is their combination of cleverly-written lyrics, based on everyday situations, and their quite often excellent musical arrangements.

It's actually astonishing that no one thought of it sooner. The fact that the Cologne dialect, Kölsch, flows off the tongue just as smoothly as the beer of the same name was proven by such poets as Willi Ostermann years ago. Kölsch has a vividness and precision that is unparalleled. A common verb in post-war Cologne was *fringsen*, which meant to pinch (as in money); no one is sure to this day whether the archbishop of that time, Cardinal Frings, quite approved.

But the Bläck Fööss were by no means the only group to realise that the adaptable, soft sound of "Kölsch" was far more suited to rock music than the more common and universally accepted "high German". This was more than proven by the overnight success of Wolfgang Niedecken's group "BAP": their winning formula of committed lyrics combined with catchy mainstream rock have since turned songwriter and singer Niedecken, guitarist and arranger Klaus Heuser (alias Major Healy) and a handful of local heroes from southern Cologne into an internationally famous band.

And it was the group "BAP" who were the first to use the term "Kölschrock" on one of their posters in 1978. The breakthrough as far as other linguistic areas of Germany were concerned came in 1981 with their third album, *für usszeschnigge!* ("cut-out"). Since that time they have made eight more successful albums, and all the group have become millionaires. BAP proved that they were not only successful with audiences at home but also abroad when they toured China (where they played eight concerts to a total audience of 120,000) and the Soviet Union.

Jürgen Zeltinger, known as "de Plaat" ("baldy") because of his lack of hair, is another famous name. In his songs, this "underdog" of the scene touches on controversial topics such as homosexuality in the track *Tuntensong* ("Fairy Song"). His song *Müngersdorfer Stadium* has become the national anthem of Cologne.

The German group that goes by the English name of "The Piano has been Drinking" set Tom Waits' music to texts in Cologne dialect, and are considered relative newcomers on the "Kölschrock" scene. This band, too, has had considerable success on radio as well as on smaller stages.

Holger Czukay, a member of the group "Can", which enjoyed international success in the early 1970s, especially in Great Britain, is still a well-known musician today. He is particularly famous for his "radio collage" activities.

Purple Schulz, a singer from Cologne with texts in High German, who also has a penchant for melancholy ("*Ich will raus*" = "I want out"), has sung his way into the ranks of Cologne's rock musicians, as have Wolf Maahn and his "Deserters" as well as Arno Steffen, who used to be Zeltinger's songwriter/producer.

By far the best way of getting to know the estimated 150 groups who took part in the Rock Contest sponsored by the city is to hear them perform live in Cologne's numerous music venues, such as Luxor, Underground, Life Musik Hall, Basement and Wartesaal. The fact that several major stars have recently chosen to live in Cologne makes it clear just how attractive the city has become as a centre of music: artists such as Tina Turner, Herbert Grönemeyer and Ina Deter have all settled here.

Munich considers itself a "media city" as a matter of course, as does Hamburg; and Berlin would love to be one again too. Cologne, though, has been a media city for decades, indeed it may even be *the* media city of Germany. But it's only recently that it has begun emphasising the fact.

Cologne, with its three daily papers, compares very favourably with Germany's other large cities. The biggest paper is a tabloid, *Express,* which, including subeditions, was selling 440,000 copies a day at the start of the 1990s. *Express* has thus long since elbowed the local Cologne edition of the *Bild-Zeitung* into second place. The same publishing house, DuMont Schauberg, also produces the more traditional *Kölner Stadt-Anzeiger.* This liberal paper (circulation 290,000) is one of Germany's most highly regarded regional newspapers.

The *Kölnische Rundschau* (circulation 160,000), from the Heinrich-Heinen publishing house, is generally regarded as the city's "number two" newspaper, and politically is somewhat more conservatively inclined. The "Rundschau" is actually very much in the tradition of the city's former *Kölnische Volkszeitung,* but without the latter's clerical line.

But it is the radio and television stations in Cologne that really make it a media city. The city did lose the "BFBS" (the British Forces Broadcasting Station) to Herford in Westphalia a few years ago, true, but with its five radio stations and numerous commercial production companies, Cologne has now become a centre of the electronic media. The largest radio station by far is the *Westdeutsche Rundfunk* (WDR) which has more than 4,500 employees. Its productions mostly take place in the city centre, at the studios in the radio building on the Wallrafplatz, next to the Cathedral terrace. The WDR transmits more than 135 hours of

music and information daily on its four different stations – and a fifth one is at the planning stage. On top of that, there are roughly 20 hours of television daily, broadcast in the First Programme of the ARD as well as in the Third Programme, *West 3.*

The two federal broadcasting corporations, the *Deutsche Welle* and the *Deutschlandfunk,* are both located in the southern part of the city on the "Raderberggürtel". The "Deutsche Welle" broadcasts 90 hours of programmes daily on short-wave, in 34 different languages (including German!), worldwide. It thus provides an important link for Germans living overseas as well as keeping other countries up-to-date on events inside Germany and internationally. The "Welle" has a staff of 1,450.

Right next door, the 740-strong staff of the "Deutschlandfunk" provide a 24-hour information and music service in German. Another 12 hours of programmes are transmitted in 11 different European languages.

RTL-Plus, one of Germany's two large commercial television stations, has its production centre west of the city, on the Aachener Strasse. RTL has around 700 employees and transmits a good 20 hours of television each day.

Finally, mention should also be made of *Kanal 4*, owned by the Holtzbrink publishing group from Stuttgart. "Kanal 4" produces television programmes with the emphasis on culture – much like its English equivalent, Channel 4. Still in its infancy is *Radio Köln*, the local commercial radio station, financed and run by newspaper publishers DuMont Schauberg and Heinen.

Two factors are sure to turn the city into a "media mecca": the College for Media Studies (Medienhochschule), which started taking on students in autumn 1991, and the Media Park. The aim of the college is to prepare its students for careers in film, radio and television, while the Media Park is a huge studio production complex, on the site of the former Gereon freight depot, housing numerous firms with up to 3,000 employees.

Left, filming of the popular WDR TV series *Lindenstrasse*, Germany's answer to *Coronation Street*.

Cologne without the Carnival is unthinkable. The Carnival isn't just a huge folk festival, it's an explosive "happening", an enormous popular movement; the Carnival is Cologne's "fifth season" of the year. On "the 11th of the 11th" – that is, on 11 November each year – the starting pistol is fired at 11 minutes past 11 o'clock, marking the beginning of the Carnival Season. And the "fifth season" comes to an end on Ash Wednesday, at the beginning of Lent.

Hundreds of thousands of people spend weeks celebrating *Fastelovend*, as the Carnival is called in Cologne dialect. Over a million *Jecken*, or "Carnival Fools", gather in the streets for the climax: the *Rosenmontag* Carnival Parade; the parade on the Monday before Lent. Millions more watch the entire crazy event on television.

This "festival of fools" originated as early as Roman times; it has its beginnings in the Roman cult of Bacchus, the god of drunkenness and ecstasy, and the Saturnalia. The customs and rituals of the Carnival have changed continually over the centuries – often quite radically so. The *Fastelovend* assumed its present-day appearance in 1823, when the "Festival Organisers' Committee" was formed. As is clear from the name, the festivities certainly did need to be organised; there had been occasions in the past when the Carnival had threatened to go out of control because of rowdiness and promiscuity – and in "Holy Cologne" of all places, too.

The gentlemen on the committee thus made it their noble task to reform the festivities and also to organise the whole thing properly. Today they would be the equivalent of the "festival management", though in those days, altering the actual content of the Carnival played a major role.

The trade-mark of the new, improved, transformed and thus socially acceptable Carnival was the first ever *Rosenmontag*

Parade in 1823. Until that time there had been a variety of sporadic, very easygoing processions throughout the entire city, many of which had had anything but happy endings. The Parade, on the other hand, gave the city a new direction, it united the whole festival in one huge and colourful finale.

And things have remained like that to the present day. The smaller processions in the "Veedeln" (districts) and other suburbs have been retained, however; though less im-

moral than they used to be, they also tend to be far more basic, and potentially explosive, than the "official" Carnival itself.

After World War II, a second Carnival procession through the city centre was introduced: the so-called *Schull- and Veedelszög* (the schools' and districts' procession) on Carnival Sunday. This is the more popular and traditional procession, while the *Rosenmontag* Parade, despite its satirical elements, tends to be a lot more pompous and perfectionist.

The Rose Monday Parade: On the Monday before Lent, all the various guards, corps,

Preceding pages: Carnival partners. Left, "Funkenmariechen". Right, one of the floats in the parade on the Monday before Lent.

traditional associations and clubs that have connections with today's festival committee assemble together – there are over 50 of them altogether. The Parade is one of the most unique and impressive spectacles ever: it's around 6 km long, and takes no less than three hours to pass by.

Around 7,000 *Karnevalisten* wearing colourful costumes and fine uniforms march, ride or otherwise travel along with it. Dozens of oversized carnival floats – which have taken several months to build – satirising contemporary issues with their political effigies, roll through the city.

Several tons of *Kamelle* (sweets), choco-

January they are officially inaugurated at Cologne's historic venue for costume balls, the Gürzenich.

The forerunner of the Prince was "Hero Carnival", who was originally the only one to rule with the fools. The Peasant and the Maiden joined him later. The sturdy Peasant represents the historical fighting spirit and loyalty of Cologne. The Maiden symbolises "the untainted and independent city, free from subjection to any foreign tyranny."

When the Maiden is a man: The Maiden in the "big three" has traditionally always been played by a man. Indeed, the Carnival is, and always has been, very much a male affair.

lates and *Strüßger* (posies) are thrown from the floats. The whole spectacle costs several million marks, and is financed by the festival committee, the societies, those participating in the parade as well as by a subsidy from the city (which, naturally, the *Karnevalisten* think is far too low).

The highlight of the *Rosenmontag* Parade is the so-called *Dreigestirn* (literally, "triple star" – the "big three" who hold sway in Carnival time). The roles of Prince, Maiden and Peasant are traditionally performed by well-to-do Cologne men, and at the beginning of the Carnival *Sitzung* ("session") in

There have only been two occasions in Cologne's history when the Maiden was actually played by a young girl, and both were during the Nazi regime.

Male predominance at the Carnival is obvious wherever you look. Even in the dancing groups of the Corps, men have been dressing as woman dancers for decades. It was only in 1936 that a woman first danced as *Funkemariechen* with the *Rote Funken* ("Red Sparks" – men dressed in 18th-century military outfits). Although emancipation and equal rights are certainly on the increase in today's *Fastelovend*, women have been an accepted part of the *Rosenmontag* Parade and the "sessions" for many years now.

The societies form the basis of the organised Carnival, and no one is really sure how many of them there are. The "Red Sparks", like all the other Carnival societies, are a colourful parody of militarism, which has never been too popular in Cologne. The Prussians and their regimented existence had little in common with the people of Cologne: in 1823 they were in the city during the first ever *Rosenmontag* Parade, and were sent up by the "Red Sparks".

But the original "Sparks" they are based

are the *Bütenredner*, or "wash-tub speakers", who make their comic speeches, in accordance with tradition, from a wooden wash-tub. Unlike the *Fastnacht* in Mainz, the speeches are not at all intellectual or didactic. The sheer sense of fun for fun's sake, and an earthy sense of humour that verges on stupidity – but in a positive sense – are the chief characteristics of the Cologne *Fastelovend*.

A folk festival: Hundreds of thousands of people attend the "sessions" and the costume balls, which of course also make the Carnival important from an economic point of view. One single session brings in over DM

on were anything but brave soldiers. In the 17th and 18th centuries, the *Funken* were actually the Cologne city guard. They were certainly no brave elite troop. Quite the reverse in fact: they used to earn a bit extra on the side, on top of their soldier's pay, by knitting and babysitting, and war-cries were quite alien to them. The *Funken* then rapidly "funked" the moment the French besieged the city in 1794.

The juiciest part of the Carnival sessions

Left and **above**, dressing up is all part of the fun, for bystanders and participants alike.

900 million. The Cologne Carnival is a folk festival in the truest sense – a festival for young and old, and rich and poor; it is valued because it does not divide, it unites. It functions as a melting-pot, and symbolises the tolerant side of Cologne, which can best be summed up in the saying *Jeder Jeck ist anders* – best rendered as "We're all crazy in our different ways."

The battle cry of the Carnival is "*Kölle alaaf*" – anyone interested in knowing what that means really has to visit the city during the *drei tolle Tage* ("three crazy days") at the peak of Carnival time.

There are several reasons for Cologne's excellent sporting reputation, and one of them lies over to the west of the city: the only Sports Academy in Germany. It's a research institute just as much as an educational one, with room for 6,000 students, and it has produced many world record-holders and Olympic athletes.

Only 500 metres away from the Academy is the edifice that has made every Cologne sports fan's heart beat faster for the past 40 years: Müngersdorf Stadium, home ground of the first division team "1. FC Cologne". The stadium, constructed on the western edge of the city between 1921 and 1923 at the behest of Konrad Adenauer, who was mayor of Cologne at that time, was the largest sports complex in Europe when it was completed, and even today, with enough covered seating for 60,000 people in the main part of the stadium, it still compares highly favourably with many newer structures. "Hännes" the billy-goat, the stadium's mascot, has already made the internationally famous club German champions on three occasions, and Cup-winners on a further four.

The other main club in the city, "SC Fortuna Cologne", is just about managing to stay in the second division, with varying degrees of success.

The city's hockey-players are exceptionally successful, though: Cologne's red-and-white, blue-and-white and black-and-white hockey stars regularly make the headlines in field and indoor hockey.

The focal point of the city's ice-hockey is the Ice-Hockey Oval on Lentstrasse; the whole place always goes wild when the *Haie* ("Sharks") from the Cologne Ice Hockey Club, known as "KEC" for short, race after the puck in important league games.

The pace is also just as hectic at the Gallop Racing Track ("Galopp-Rennbahn") in Weidenpesch. The track is only part of what is one of the largest horse-racing courses in Germany, and more than a dozen exciting meetings take place here between March and October each year, including the trials for the German Derby as well as the "Preis von Europa", a flat race with Germany's highest prize: DM 400,000.

The annual highlight of athletics in Cologne, the International Sport Festival, is also attended by the world's best. Several world records have been set during the Grand Prix event (in late summer).

Another centre of exciting sporting activity is the Sports Hall at the Trade Fair Grounds (*Messegelände*) in Cologne-Deutz. Here one can find boxing, handball and motocross events as well as the famous "Six-Day Cologne Cycle Race".

No other city in Germany has so many teams in the various top national leagues as Cologne. A total of 29 different clubs represent the city, and they specialise in 19 different kinds of sport, ranging from baseball to underwater rugby.

As far as the disciplines of judo, hockey, athletics and swimming are concerned, top athletes are trained in Cologne for participation in international championships.

Alongside its leading role internationally from the point of view of competitive sports, Cologne also has extensive sports facilities for the general public. Every sixth person in the city belongs to a sports club, and Cologne has 700 of them, featuring around 50 different kinds of sports, ranging from riding and rowing to tennis, golf and flying.

Anyone in Cologne who doesn't feel like indulging in competitive sports can still find what he's looking for: 19 indoor swimming-pools, 10 outdoor ones, three spas and one thermal bath all provide recreation and relaxation. And the city's numerous fitness clubs and bodybuilding centres, with their weights and home-trainers, are also a good way of keeping fit.

Information is available from either the Cologne Municipal Sports Association (Stadtsportbund), Tel. 2401214, or the "Sport-und Bäderamt", Tel. 4983222.

Left, torchlight vigil at a home game of the Cologne ice-hockey team "The Sharks".

Traces of Cologne's 2,000 years of history can be found everywhere in the city. Roman tombs and Romanesque churches, the old Town Hall and the famous Cathedral, a unique collection of museums and the much-vaunted *Altstadt* (Old City): there are things to see wherever you go. But don't try to see everything at once – it can't be done. The Cathedral of course is a "must", but everything else should depend on the time you have to spare, and on your personal preferences.

Don't let the city's fascinating past let you forget the delights of the present: take time off to relax from your journey through past centuries and knock back a *Kölsch* beer in one of the city's highly *gemütlich* taverns, or spoil yourself with a relaxing trip on one of the Rhine steamers. Or why not take a refreshing breather in one of the city's many fine parks? And a piece of advice: Cologne is a very good place to eat out, however bizarre your culinary tastes may be.

Of course, it's not just its buildings and treasures that give life to a city, "it's the people that make the place". It can take a while to get to know them, however, so in the meantime remember that the magic ingredient in Cologne is "leisure". Just take short breaks wherever you happen to be: in one of the museums, in the Old City or in the Cathedral square. It's always easy to find somewhere to sit down and relax.

An even better idea, though, is to leave the beaten tourist track altogether and get a real feel of the city in its traditional districts, known as "Veedeln". You won't need to go far either, for some of the most original and lively of the "Veedeln" can still be found within the city's Rings, in the Eigelstein and Südstadt sections of the city. Anyone with time to spare should also take a quick trip to the sections of the city over on the right bank of the Rhine, or out beyond the Rings.

Modern art enthusiasts can fill an entire holiday just touring around Cologne's galleries. Most of the city's art dealers can be found in the streets around the Neumarkt. One good idea is to combine a stroll through the galleries with a walk through Cologne's shopping streets: the most famous of these are the Hohe Strasse and the Schildergasse. Locals and tourists stroll up and down here today just as the ancient Romans once used to: indeed, the street pattern hasn't changed significantly since those times.

Preceding pages: the choir stalls in Cologne Cathedral; a minister lights the candles. **Left,** the Corpus Christi procession outside the main portal.

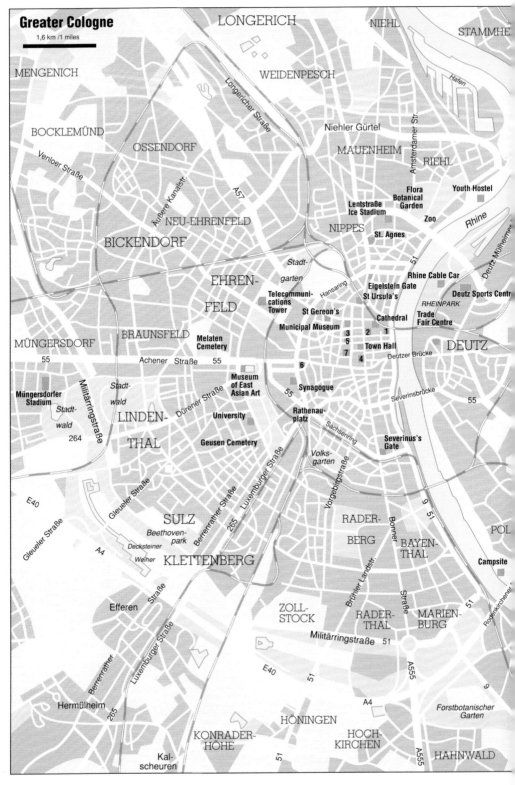

Greater Cologne

1,6 km /1 miles

LONGERICH

NIEHL

STAMMHE

MENGENICH

WEIDENPESCH

Longericher Straße

Hafen

BOCKLEMÜND

OSSENDORF

Niehler Gürtel

MAUENHEIM

RIEHL

Venloer Straße

Amsterdamer Str.

Außere Kanalstr.

A57

Flora
Botanical
Garden

Youth Hostel

NEU-EHRENFELD

Lentstraße
Ice Stadium

Zoo

Rhine

BICKENDORF

NIPPES

St. Agnes

Stadt-
garten

EHREN-

FELD

Hansaring

51

Rhine Cable Car

Telecommuni-
cations
Tower

Eigelstein Gate
St Ursula's

Deutz Sports Centr

Deutz Müllheim

RHEINPARK

BRAUNSFELD

St Gereon's

Cathedral

Trade
Fair Centre

Municipal Museum

3

2

1

MÜNGERSDORF

Melaten
Cemetery

5

7

DEUTZ

55

Achener Straße 55

Town Hall

4

Deutzer Brücke

Stadt-
wald

6

Museum
of East
Asian Art

Müngersdorfer
Stadium

Dürener Straße

55

Synagogue

Severinsbrücke

55

Stadt-
wald

264

LINDEN-

University

Rathenau-
platz

THAL

Geusen Cemetery

Sachsenring

Severinus's
Gate

Militärringstraße

Volks-
garten

E40

Gleueler Straße

Berrenrather Straße

Luxemburger Straße

Vorgebirgstraße

9

51

POL

SULZ

Beethoven-
park

RADER-

Bonner

A4

Decksteiner

265

BERG

BAYEN-
THAL

Weiher

KLETTENBERG

Campsite

Gleueler Straße

Efferen

Straße

ZOLL-
STOCK

Brühler Landstr.

RADER-
THAL

Straße

MARIEN-
BURG

51

Rodenkirchener

Luxemburger Straße

Militärringstraße 51

A555

Berrenrather

E40

51

9

Hermülheim

265

A4

Forstbotanischer
Garten

HÖNINGEN

KONRADER-
HÖHE

HOCH-
KIRCHEN

A555

HAHNWALD

Kal-
scheuren

51

1 Wallraf-Richartz-Museum/
  Museum Ludwig /Philharmonie
2 Roman - Germanic Museum
3 Museum of Applied Art
4 Gürzenich/Old St Alban's
5 Opera House/Theatre
6 Hahnen Gate
7 St Cecilia's/Schnütgen Museum

DELLBRÜCK

Gronau

HOLWEIDE

Bergisch Gladbacher Straße

Berliner Straße

E35

51

506

MÜLHM.

A3

506

Frankfurter

Dellbrücker

Bensberger

Marktweg

Refrath

Strunderbach

MIELENFORST

BUCHHEIM

Bruchbach

Mauspfad

BUCHFORST

55

MERHEIM

Flehbach

55

Lustheide

HÖHENBERG

Straße

BRÜCK

Brück
Game Enclosure

Brücker Mauspfad

Flehbach

Rather Weg

55

55

KALK

VINGST

E35

A3

8

NEUBRÜCK

STAATSFORST

KÖNIGSFORST

UMBOLDT

Rösrather

OSTHEIM

Frankfurter Straße

Straße

Rather Mauspfad

RATH

GREMBERG

E40

A4

A4

Kölner

8

A559

HEUMAR

A3

E35

Heumarer Mauspfad

FORST

WESTHOVEN

Straße

GREMBERG-
HOVEN

8

straße

A59

Leidenhausen
Estate

WAHNER

ENSEN

Hauptstr.

Stein-

Berger

Straße

Frankfurter Straße

EIL

HEIDE

Grengeler Mauspfad

Campsite

RODEN-
KIRCHEN

Campsite

Weißer Straße

ner Straße

Hauptstr.

PORZ

Airport
✈

WEISS

ADELEN-
HÜTTE

8

URBACH

GRENGEL

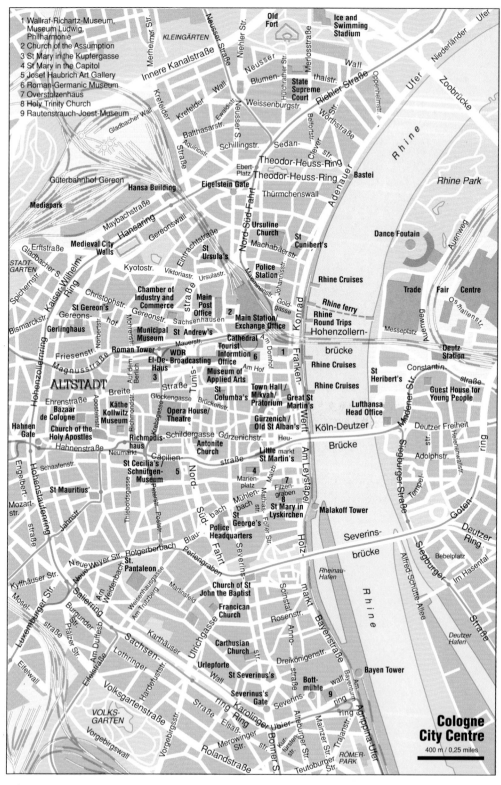

1 Wallraf-Richartz-Museum,
  Museum Ludwig,
  Philharmonie
2 Church of the Assumption
3 St Mary in the Kupfergasse
4 St Mary in the Capitol
5 Josef Haubrich Art Gallery
6 Roman-Germanic Museum
7 Overstolzenhaus
8 Holy Trinity Church
9 Rautenstrauch-Joest-Museum

**Cologne
City Centre**

400 m / 0,25 miles

THE CITY'S MAJOR LANDMARK

"The Cathedral Church of St Peter in Cologne is both mother and mistress of every church in Germany"
– Matthew of Paris, early 13th century

The number of titles and names that **Cologne Cathedral** has been given through the centuries could easily be extended, too. In its time it has been called a "papal basilica", and art historians have referred to it as "the youngest and prettiest sister of the great French cathedrals" or quite simply as "the absolute cathedral". "God's battle cruiser" is another name that made the headlines, as did the fondly ambiguous "Rome's dearest daughter". Cologne, despite its unique series of Romanesque churches and its wonderfully varied museums, has really always remained first and foremost a cathedral city.

An early Christian church site: The area around the Cathedral was densely populated as early as Roman times. An early Christian episcopal church with a west choir, atrium and a separate baptistry came into existence after 313 during the rule of Maternus, Cologne's first documented bishop. The edifice was based on Old St Peter's in Rome. In 817, after Charlemagne had appointed his friend and advisor Hildebold bishop of Cologne, and had raised the city to the status of an archbishopric, work began on the new Carolingian structure.

The "Old Cathedral", as it is called, a triple-aisle pillared basilica with two choirs, two transepts, and towers flanking the choir on the westwork is known to us not only from the results of excavations but also from a drawing on the dedicatory picture in the Hillinus Codex (*circa* 1025).

It was when the holy relics of the Three Magi were brought from Milan to Cologne in 1164 by archbishop Rainald von Dassel – a coup that transformed Cologne into one of the most important

places of pilgrimage in the West – that plans were drawn up for the construction of an entirely new cathedral. In 1248, archbishop Konrad von Hochstaden laid the foundation stone for the new Gothic Cathedral, which was to be modelled on the great French cathedrals (and on the one in Amiens in particular). On 27 September 1322, the choir was consecrated; it was closed off towards the west by a huge temporary wall.

The wooden construction crane on the provisional roof of the south tower, completed in 1410, was a distinctive feature of the city for centuries. In 1560, construction work on the Cathedral was abandoned. At this stage, roughly 90 percent of the planned total area of the Cathedral could be used for services; a provisional wooden roof above the arcades closed off the inner area.

Late completion: It was not until the 19th century that the Cathedral was finally completed as a "German national shrine". The foundation stone for further construction work was laid on the southern side of the Cathedral in 1842, in the presence of King Frederick William IV of Prussia. Thanks to various advances in technology, the Cathedral was then completed in only 38 years by church architects Zwirner and Voigtel. On 15 October 1880, 632 years after the medieval foundation stone had first been laid, the final phase of construction – the placing of the finial on the south tower – was complete.

The largest medieval section of the building consists of the high choir and the garland of choir chapels, or chevet, with its filigree support system. The facade of the southern transept, designed by Zwirner, is considered a masterpiece of neo-Gothic architecture. The sculptured figures on the portals are the work of Christian Mohr. The bronze doors were built by Ewald Mataré, with the help of his pupil Joseph Beuys, between 1948 and 1954.

The Cathedral is at its most imposing-looking when seen from the west. The two towers rear up above the 7,000-sq.

metre (8,300-sq. yard) facade, the largest in Christendom; its design was largely based on the original medieval plans for the west front. The five axes of the facade find their reflection in the division of the interior into five aisles. Of the three doors, only **St Peter's Door** (to the south) dates from the Middle Ages. A new section built into the northern buttress, consisting of 30,000 bricks, is a reminder of the heavy damage the Cathedral suffered during World War II. At 157.38 metres (516.52 ft), the northern tower is exactly 7 cm higher than its southern counterpart.

Imposing-looking nave aisle: If you enter the Cathedral by the central doorway of the west front, the view stretches right down the complete length of the narrow, towering nave aisle (119 metres/390 ft long). The best place to begin a walk around the Cathedral is in the northern side-aisle. Here, the magnificent stained-glass windows dating from the beginning of the 16th century strike one immediately; the sketches they are based on were executed by noteworthy representatives of the Cologne school of painters. Just before one reaches the northern transept, the **Clares Altar** comes into view; it was created around 1360, and was transferred to the Cathedral from the former convent of Poor Clares in 1821. Twelve Franciscan saints are depicted on the outer sides of the altar wings – the oldest preserved painted wooden panels in the world.

Passing beneath the organ loft, we reach the ambulatory. The mosaic flooring, which covers the full length of the ambulatory, was designed by August von Essenwein between 1885 and 1897, and executed by the firm of Villeroy & Boch, Mettlach. The first large portrait as one enters the ambulatory is of archbishop Hildebold with the model of the "Old Cathedral". On the east wall of the Chapel of the Cross (*Kreuzkapelle*) hangs the **Gero Cross**, commissioned by archbishop Gero (969–76), and showing Christ on the cross at the moment of his death, with

Ordination in the cathedral.

his eyes closed and head bowed. This over-life-size Ottonian sculpture is thought to be the oldest monumental crucifix in the western world. The Gero Cross was incorporated into the Baroque altar in 1683.

Virtues and vices: Separated off by a stone parclose and Baroque choir screen, the **high choir** (which can be entered only on conducted visits) has retained its medieval appearance almost completely: the magnificently carved **choir stalls**, with their depictions of human virtues and vices, were built between 1308 and 1311, and with 104 seats are the largest in Germany. Special stalls were kept reserved for the Pope and the Emperor, members of the Cologne cathedral chapter from the early Middle Ages.

The paintings on the 14th-century choir-screens show scenes from the lives of various saints specific to Cologne. On the choir pillars, the life-size statues of Christ, the Virgin and the 12 Apostles, standing on piers, are among the masterpieces of Cologne sculpture between 1280 and 1290. Angels playing music can be seen above their ornate baldachins. The medieval windows of the clerestory show 48 kings (the 24 kings of Judah and the 24 elders of the Apocalypse), with and without beards respectively, and an Adoration of the Magi in the axis window.

The mighty **high altar**, covered by a single slab of black marble, is decorated with arcades of figures carved from white Carrara marble, representing various scenes, prophets, apostles and saints. It was only after the end of World War II that the **Shrine of the Three Magi** was shifted to its present location in a glass case behind the high altar. Begun around 1190 by Nicholas of Verdun, the shrine, which houses the relics of the Three Magi that were brought from Milan to Cologne in 1164 by Rainald von Dassel, is considered the most outstanding example of medieval goldsmith's work from the Rhine-Meuse area.

The famous Shrine of the Three Magi in the high choir.

Further noteworthy works of art can be found in the seven choir chapels. The second chapel in the ambulatory, **St Maternus's Chapel**, contains the tomb of archbishop Philipp von Heinsberg, with a sepulchral monument that is quite unique: the recumbent stone figure of the archbishop is surrounded by a fortified city wall, complete with towers and gates, reminding us that even though Philipp had his ups and downs with the burghers of Cologne, he finally decided in favour of the construction of the Hohenstaufen wall around the city.

Next door, in **St John's Chapel**, is the tomb of archbishop Konrad von Hochstaden. The recumbent figure of the archbishop, modelled after similar French statues, is considered the most important 13th-century bronze figure in Germany. Moreover, this chapel also contains the so-called *Fassadenriß F*, a detailed architectural plan made in about the year 1300, on a piece of parchment over 4 metres (13 ft) long, of the projected facade with its two towers.

The **Three Kings' Chapel**, the axis chapel of the ambulatory, contains the oldest stained-glass window in the Cathedral. This "Old Bible" window, as it is called, contrasts 10 scenes from the Old and New Testaments respectively. The window was installed around 1260, and is still Romanesque in style. Opposite the axis chapel and behind the choir screen is the tomb of archbishop Dietrich von Moers. Instead of the usual form of tomb, church architect and sculptor Konrad Kuene here chose a group of figures instead, showing the adoring Magi and the kneeling archbishop beside the Virgin on her throne.

The last of the chapels in the ambulatory contains the tomb of archbishop Gero, and also the so-called "New Bible" window, similar to the older one in design but already showing Gothic influence. It was transferred from the former Dominican church to the Cathedral in 1892.

Altar of the city's patron saints: The three eastern arches of the southern nave together form the **Lady Chapel**. The famous **Altar of the City's Patron Saints** by Stephan Lochner has been here since 1856. This masterpiece of the Cologne School of Painters, painted between 1440 and 1445, was originally created for the Town Hall chapel. It portrays several saints closely associated with the city: on the wings we see St Ursula with her companions, and St Gereon with the soldiers of the Theban Legion, who all died as martyrs in Cologne, and on the central panel, the Adoration of the Magi.

The Lady Chapel also contains three more magnificent works of art: just to the left of Lochner's altar is the ornate tomb of archbishop Friedrich von Saarwerden, with a recumbent statue in bronze surrounded by figures inside Late Gothic arcades; to the west, on the outer wall of the chapel, the tomb of archbishop Rainald von Dassel, and in the direction of the ambulatory, the tomb of Count Gottfried von Arnsberg, with a metal grille placed over the recumbent figure – ostensibly with the aim of protecting it from the Count's disappointed heirs.

On the eastern side of the southern transept, the **Altar of St Agilulph** can be seen: it is 5.5 metres (18 ft) high, and was created in Antwerp in 1521. The central shrine depicts the Life of Christ and the Passion.

The most magnificent works of art in the southern side-aisle are the five **"Bavarian Windows"**, commissioned from the royal stained-glass works in Munich and presented to the Cathedral by King Ludwig I of Bavaria in 1842.

No visit to the Cathedral would be complete without a visit to the **Treasury**, which contains a collection of reliquaries, chalices, monstrances and other liturgical objects from medieval times to the present day. The so-called Staff of St Peter (10th–11th centuries), the Byzantine Reliquary (11th–12th centuries) and the baroque shrine of canonised Cologne archbishop Engelbert (1632) are especially noteworthy.

The cathedral seen from a different perspective.

THE ROMANESQUE CHURCHES

Contrary to the popular lay perception, churches aren't like simple interchangeable, standardised containers that can just be set down anywhere at random. Churches "grow" rings of stone over the years like the rings in tree-trunks – it's often impossible to work out exactly how old many of them really are. The same applies to Cologne's "garland of great Romanesque churches", all of which, without exception, have now been rebuilt after their destruction in World War II.

The churches – formerly lay canonical foundations and religious institutions for ladies of rank – attracted small clusters of buildings around themselves, made up of collegiate institutions, cloisters and parish churches, right up to the beginning of the 19th century. They celebrated their heyday in the 12th century, however, in the so-called "Hohenstaufen period".

A plethora of churches: The period between 1150 and 1250 has been described as "the greatest century in Cologne architectural history". And justly so, for where else at that time, not to speak of later – and not only in German-speaking countries – could one find such a wealth of massively constructed collegiate and abbey churches within the bounds of a single city? Around the year 1200, the broad, semicircular Hohenstaufen city fortifications were complete.

Before this, for almost a millenium, Colonia had not dared venture beyond its original Roman rectilinear grid. **St Severinus's Church** (St Severin) to the south and **St Cunibert's** (St Kunibert) to the north of medieval Cologne marked the boundaries of the city's historic Rhine panorama, as indeed they still do today.

More churches then appeared in the High Middle Ages: **St Gereon's** (St Gereon), to the north-west, the **Church of the Holy Apostles** (St Aposteln), to the west on the Neumarkt, **St Mary's in the Capitol** (St Maria im Kapitol) on the Heumarkt, **Great St Martin's** (Gross St Martin) east of the Old Market (*Alter Markt*) inside the Old City, **St Pantaleon's** (St Pantaleon) to the south-west, **St Andrew's** (St Andreas) immediately west of the Cathedral, **St Ursula's** (St Ursula) to the north of the old Roman city gate, **St George's** (St Georg) opposite police headquarters, **St Cecilia's** (St Cäcilien) which has housed the Schnütgen Museum of medieval art for decades, and last but not least, the church of **St Mary's in Lyskirchen** (St Maria in Lyskirchen) – incredibly, the 13th-century frescoes on its vaulting survived World War II, the only fresco cycle in Cologne to have done so.

At the turn of the 18th century, the Old City of Cologne contained – believe it or not – 149 churches, with all of 171 towers. Most of these structures, as well as various cloisters and monastery

Preceding pages: the Church of St Martin. Left, relics taken to extremes in the Golden Chamber of St Ursula's. Right, a detail of the portal of St Mary's in the Capitol.

walls were torn down both during and after the wave of secularisation at the beginning of the 19th century.

The large collegiate churches and abbey churches, however (and St Mary's in Lyskirchen was the only church not be counted as one), were spared and were turned into parish churches. Until their destruction in the bombardments of World War II they were restored several times, usually in accordance with the taste of the time – i.e. with plenty of colour, and a great deal of mosaic work.

The spirit of the 1950s: Hardly any of these 19th-century embellishments can now be found in the proud "corner-stones" of Cologne's architectural history, which have been open again to the public since 1985 (Great St Martin's, St Mary's in the Capitol and St Gereon's were all building sites up till then, and St Cunibert's westwork still is).

The incredibly complex reconstruction of this former garland of Romanesque churches was done in the purist spirit of the architects of the 1950s: they loved the simple stonework, and removed what was left of the 19th-century mosaics. In the Church of the Holy Apostles, for example, the open stonework of Speyer Cathedral served as a model, and the Cologne architects of the 1950s still remembered "cryptical" interior concepts such as those practised by Clemens Holzmeister in St George's church during the 1920s.

Alterations: The present trend in Cologne seems to be towards giving one or other of these venerable, and yet also rather "neo-Romanesque" churches more ornate interiors, and the results have been highly controversial. Thus the former Benedictine abbey church of Great St Martin, restored highly sensitively and with graphic bareness by the architect Joachim Schürmann after the war, has now been provided with new and highly colourful windows (very much in contrast to the architect's cautious mode of operation).

At present, Hermann Gottfried is in

The Hohenstaufen westwork of St George's Church.

the process of painting the trilobate choir of the Church of the Holy Apostles in lively neo-Expressionist style; and even the simple coffered ceiling above the Ottonian nave of St Pantaleon's won't be visible for much longer because it is due to be replaced by a new and more colourful one of richer design.

Visitors to St Gereon's, too, should not assume that the relatively topsy-turvy interior of the architecturally magnificent Decagon, which dates from the Roman and Hohenstaufen periods, is the last word in wisdom of design: the window cycles by Georg Meistermann and Georg Buschulte will of course be staying, and yet the Decagon and high choir, taken together, convey a very strong sense of disunity. In itself very beautiful, the Baroque altar that was taken from the destroyed Gothic church of St Columba doesn't fit in very well between the Decagon and the high choir: its style and dimensions seem all wrong. And the blood-red of

the cupola clashes with the blue-green walls of the choir.

And yet: whether one is in Great St Martin's, the Church of the Holy Apostles, St Gereon's or even St Mary's in the Capitol (where the magnificently restored Renaissance rood screen has been jammed far too much between the nave and the choir section), the sense of space that is so characteristic of all the Romanesque churches in Cologne overpowers one time and time again.

Most of the churches were first built above Roman and early Christian tombs, St Severinus's and St George's being two examples. St Gereon's was built as early as the 4th century AD, as a Roman imperial building and martyrs' church (for soldiers in the Theban Legion, according to legend). Others, such as St Mary's in the Capitol, for example, with its 11th-century trilobate choir and ambulatory – quite unique in the entire history of western architecture – were constructed above the foundations of former Roman temples.

The splendid dome of St Gereon's.

In the case of St Mary's, the church was probably built over a temple dedicated to the Capitoline triad situated above an arm of the Rhine, which in Roman times used to flow directly beneath it.

Traces of "paganism": St Mary's in the Capitol dates back to the 7th century. Plectrude, wife of Pepin of Herstal, the ruler of the Franks, founded a religious house for noble ladies here which managed to raise enough money to pay for the later magnificent trilobate choir. The choir and crypt were consecrated in 1065. Despite the church's destruction and its "purified" reconstructed version, in the stonework one can still make out the Roman remains of the "pagan" temple dating from the 1st century AD.

The nave, before it was destroyed (the crypt, west tower and nave vault collapsed on 2 March 1945), used to be covered by a Gothic ribbed vault. Today the central aisle, rounded off at its western end by a fine imperial gallery, is covered by a wooden "emergency ceiling" dating from 1957. Despite its destruction and simplified reconstruction – the eastern conch has no dwarf gallery – this church still retains much of its former beauty. The pillared trilobate choir is indisputably one of the greatest architectural experiences one can have in Cologne.

The immediate vicinity of this beautifully rounded church, founded in the depths of Roman times, has only very recently been adapted to suit the style of the building (as have the areas surrounding the Church of the Holy Apostles, Great St Martin's, St Cunibert's and St Gereon's).

The trilobate choir in St Mary's in the Capitol provided the inspiration for similar architectural achievements in the Church of the Holy Apostles (choir section with dwarf gallery, built around 1200) and in Great St Martin's (choir consecrated in 1172).

Both of them – the Church of the Holy Apostles with its mighty, fortress-like west end, and Great St Martin's with its eye-catching square tower and its four corner turrets, are among the finest of Cologne's Romanesque churches. All in all, there really was quite a varied collection of buildings in the city just before work began on the Gothic Cathedral in 1248. But now we will take a closer individual look at some more of the more interesting churches.

St Andrew's Church: St Andrew's, that marvellous mixture of Romanesque and High Gothic elements (porch at the west end, nave basilica and high choir), was first consecrated in 974. In the mid-13th century it was restored in High Romanesque style, and in 1420 was given a shrine-like glass filigree high choir, modelled on the choir of the Coronation Chapel in Aachen. The high, Gothic roof had to give way to a simple flat sloping emergency one after the serious destruction wrought during World War II.

Stylistically, the tower with its four turrets draws heavily on the tower of the Minster in Bonn; the crypt was recon-

Left, exquisite stained-glass in St Cunibert's. Right, the nave of St Severinus's.

structed after 1950 by Karl Band. St Andrew's – still the home of members of the Dominican order – with its magnificently structured interior, is one of the most atmospheric churches to be found anywhere.

Church of the Holy Apostles: This church is situated to the west of the Neumarkt, directly behind the site of the former Roman west gate. The Neumarkt is the only large square in Cologne not to have been built over since Roman times, and is thus of great archaeological interest. The church, with its magnificent trilobate choir, made up of three conches, a cupola and a small lantern, and its remarkable rectangular hall at the west end with its open tower, assumed its present shape and size between 1150 and 1230.

Like the eastern choir of Great St Martin's and its tower, the trilobate choir of the Church of the Holy Apostles, too, was also created expressly to be seen – the former for people looking across at the city from the Rhine, the latter giving the Neumarkt its distinctive appearance. The three-aisled nave is impressive for its solid structure (arched nave arcade on tetragonal, cruciform pilasters). Inside the church, bare stone predominates, though the choir section and the cupola are being given a great deal more colour at present by the painter Hermann Gottfried.

St George's: Founded as a lay canonical foundation above the remains of a Roman temple in 1059 by archbishop Anno II, the church was consecrated in 1067, and its nave and choir were vaulted around 1150. The westwork was added as early as 1188, but left unfinished. Constructed as a three-aisled pillared basilica (enriched during the Hohenstaufen period by two central supports), this church is fascinating for its compact plasticity, particularly evident in the Hohenstaufen westwork – a masterpiece of its type.

The walls of the westwork are nearly 5 metres (16 ft) thick, and were apparently planned as the external base for a tower. The restoration work on the church, which suffered heavy damage during World War II, was finally completed in 1964.

St Gereon's: This church is a grandiose decagonal structure on an elliptical ground-plan, built above 4th-century Roman foundations. A canons' choir with two towers was added by archbishop Anno II and consecrated between 1067 and 1069, and renewed extension work took place in the mid-12th century with the addition of an apse. The decagonal Roman central structure was remodelled between 1219 and 1227 to form the present Decagon, with its unique three-dimensional effect; architecturally, it is without a doubt one of the most impressive testimonies to the Hohenstaufen period.

St Severinus's: St Severinus's was built above a Roman cemetery, as a cemetery chapel consecrated to St Severinus. There were several stages of development in its construction, just as with the other churches. Its various sec-

Left, "Death" by Zurich graffiti artist Harald Nägeli, on the walled-up west portal of St Cecilia's. Right, St Ursula's Romanesque west tower is crowned by a baroque cupola.

tions date from the 10th, 11th, 13th, 14th and early 15th century, and elements from the late Hohenstaufen period in the eastern part of the church combine with Late Gothic elements in the westwork to create an overall effect of austere, luminous beauty.

St Pantaleon's: Formerly a Benedictine abbey, the church was founded around the year 957 by archbishop Bruno, on the site of an extensive Roman villa. Bruno is buried here, as is the Empress Theophano (Emperor Otto II's Greek wife), who added the mighty westwork.

Also badly damaged during the war, and subsequently restored, this church still gives one a strong sense of the imposing, imperial nature of Ottonian architecture. Traces of Baroque alterations and additions can still be found in the choir section (high altar and chancel), and the rood screen dates from the early 16th century.

The massive and imposing westwork is most impressive. The long building with its striking west end is surrounded on three sides by a fine lawn – a reminder of the former monastery's area of sanctuary – creating a restful oasis in the centre of the city.

St Cunibert's: Finally, St Cunibert's, the sepulchral church of canonised bishop Cunibert of Cologne, who is said to have been laid to rest here in 663. After several previous structures, the present building, with its double tier of windows and dwarf gallery in the choir, was only finally erected in the late Hohenstaufen period.

Its foundation stone was probably laid in 1215, and most of the choir completed by 1222–24; the church was then finally consecrated in 1247, one year before work began on the city's new Gothic Cathedral. Although it suffered heavy bombardment in World War II, the church was opened again as early as 1956, with the exception of its west end, which is soon to be restored without its original high spire.

Under cover of darkness: Of all the churches in Cologne dating from the Hohenstaufen period, St Cunibert's is considered to be the most uniform in style. Its interior is surprisingly bright and cheerful. The magnificent windows at the east end date from the time it was built (1220–30). During the war, an unofficial rescue operation took place under cover of darkness, and the windows were shifted to the Siebengebirge (hills on the eastern bank of the Rhine). The Gothic baptistery, installed in the south wing of the eastern transept and decorated between 1260 and 1270, also escaped destruction.

In 1247, construction work had been completed on St Cunibert's, and the mighty Gothic choir of the city's new Cathedral had not yet been built: it was at this point, with the completion of St Cunibert's, that the Romanesque, late Hohenstaufen period drew to a magnificent close, its roots still firmly in the old style, yet presaging Gothic brightness and clarity of contour.

The churches of Cologne are referred to as "Romanesque", but in fact they passed through nearly all the important construction periods from the early Middle Ages onwards, and parts of them even date from late Graeco-Roman times.

The High and the Late Middle Ages as well as the Early and High Gothic periods also left their traces, later followed by the odd Baroque insertion. In the 19th century they were cleaned up and renovated, and received several historicist additions; then they were destroyed during the bombardments of World War II, before being rebuilt in a largely "purist" manner.

Now their doors are open once more to visitors, worshippers and all those interested in art and architecture: a garland of churches with no counterpart anywhere north of the Alps, and quite unique in having been constructed within such a small area; an ancient heritage that Cologne has painstakingly restored over the past 40 years, and has now finally regained.

St George slays the dragon.

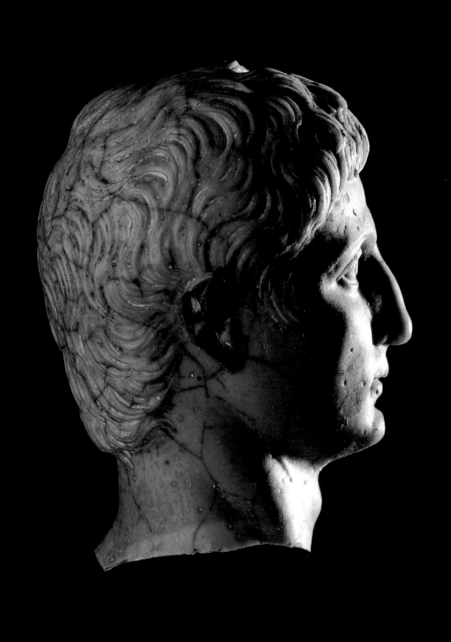

ON THE TRAIL OF THE ROMANS

"Taking the lift back to Roman times"; seldom has a book-title been so apt as that of the popular work by Rudolf Pörtner. The lift does actually exist: the shaft leads from the new Town Hall down into the Roman Praetorium beneath it. But it's the metaphor in the title that is most significant: the heart of the city is rather like a palimpsest, an old piece of parchment from which the writing has been removed to make room for new writing, thus allowing traces of old texts to be discovered beneath newer ones.

Soil steeped in history: Anyone who descends to these levels – whether he takes the lift or just uses a spade – very soon comes into contact with the city's Roman past. To give a recent example: in the summer of 1990, the medieval quarter of St Alban was discovered between Martinstrasse, Quatermarkt and Gülichplatz, to the north of the famous Gürzenich. Here, traces were found revealing that the area had been densely populated as early as Roman times, and further down, a stone decorated with a floral relief was discovered: it had apparently fallen from a great height, and had once perhaps even formed part of the **Temple of Mars**, which many people think once stood here.

At the other end of the Roman city, the **Roman Tower** (Römerturm) of the city's former fortifications has been visible for almost two thousand years. Street names such as "Griechenpforte" (Greek Gate), "Hohe Pforte" (High Gate) or the "Alte Mauer am Bach" (Old Wall by the Stream) are reliable clues to where the old Roman walls used to run, and the greatest temple of any Roman city, the **Capitol**, built to honour the triad of Jupiter, Juno and Minerva, is both apparent and non-apparent in the name as well as the foundations of St Mary's in the Capitol, one of the city's most important churches.

Around the middle of the 1st century AD, Cologne began its history as *Oppidum Ubiorum*. Caesar had annihilated the Germanic tribe of the Eburones on the left bank of the Rhine roughly 100 years before, and had then established relations with the Ubii. Under Augustus, the Ubii rose to become part of the Roman federation, and were settled on the left bank to fill the vacuum left by the Eburones. Even this first Ubii settlement had its own fortifications.

The so-called **Ubii Monument** still stands; it was probably the corner bastion of the former entrance to the harbour. It was only in 1965, during construction of an apartment building on the corner of "Mühlenbach" and "An der Malzmühle" that the mighty squared-stone masonry – the oldest stone monument in the city – was first discovered and exposed.

In AD 50, the Emperor Claudius, at the request of his wife Julia Agrippina, raised the city to the status of CCAA: Colonia Claudia Ara Agrippiensium. Soon afterwards, construction work began on renewing the city walls, and the mighty **Roman stone wall**, with its 19 towers and nine gates, was completed as early as AD 70. The limestone arch of the **northern gate**, which once lay on the road to Neuss, has been reconstructed in the Roman-Germanic museum. On the side facing away from the city one can still clearly see the proud abbreviation "CCAA".

The wall enclosed an area which some sources say measured as much as one kilometre square. The two main thoroughfares, the **"cardo maximus"** which ran north-south, and the **"decumanus maximus"** which ran from east to west, are still the two main streets in the heart of the city today: the Hohe Strasse and the Schildergasse.

Anyone who doesn't just want to sense ancient Rome in Cologne's streets, but to see it and actually experience it at first hand should take a walk along the section of original Roman wall situated to the north of the city; it

Preceding pages: evening light falls on the Wallraf-Richartz Museum. Left, Roman head of Augustus in the Roman-Germanic Museum.

runs from the Cathedral – where a good section of it can be seen near the entrance to the Cathedral underground car park – along the street called "An der Burgmauer" in a westerly direction, past various remnants and ruins, all the way to the Roman Tower (Römerturm) one kilometre away.

The slope between "An der Burgmauer" on the one hand, and Komödienstrasse and Zeughausstrasse on the other is a present-day reminder of the former difference in elevation between the walls surrounding the city and the broad ditch that lay beyond the fortifications. The **Roman Fountain** in front of the Arsenal (Zeughaus) with its Municipal Museum dates from 1915 (it was renovated in 1955) and is thus somewhat newer than the **Roman Tower**, which is just as richly decorated as it was 1,900 years ago. The mosaic pictures in its stonework can still be easily detected.

The only non-genuine feature of the tower is its crenellation. One theory goes that the tower was twice as high in Roman times. During the Middle Ages it served as a lavatory for the Franciscan nuns from the convent of Poor Clares; in the 19th century an extra storey was added to provide living quarters; and finally it was purchased by the city and restored.

Truth and legend: During the Middle Ages, people could often make no sense at all of the Roman ruins; instead of the truth, they were far more prone to believe in legends, such as that of Master Gerhard, the architect of Cologne Cathedral, who made a pact with the devil that he would complete the Cathedral before the devil could bring water to the site all the way from Trier, in the Eifel. The devil, it is said, won the wager by making use of the Roman aqueduct, whereupon Gerhard flung himself to his death from the Cathedral's scaffolding.

But the Roman aqueduct actually extended no further than the "Marsilstein", or Marsil Stone, which at that time was outside the city limits. Only

A Roman lion.

very little is known of the water system within the city walls, and what some people take to be a section of Roman aqueduct in Theo-Burauen-Platz (named after the popular mayor and honorary citizen of Cologne from 1956 to 1973) is actually part of the **drainage system** which extends underground here along the length of the Budengasse (the former entrance to the Praetorium).

Inside the city itself, traces of the Roman **drinking water canal** exist only in the form of exhibits: in the park at the Museum of Applied Art, for example; in front of the Stadtsparkasse's "City-Treff" on the Habsburger Ring; in front of the main entrance to the *Fachhochschule* (Polytechnic) in Cologne-Deutz, or at the Geological Institute on Zülpicher Strasse. Many of these sections of stone come from far outside Cologne – just like its drinking water 2,000 years ago.

The local water wasn't good enough for the fastidious Romans, anyway. Very soon after Colonia was founded,

an aqueduct was built to carry water from the nearby foothills into the city, and it was then followed in the 2nd century AD by a technological masterstroke: the Roman aqueduct leading from the Eifel Hills at Nettersheim, an area that even today still contains best water for miles around.

The aqueduct, which was built underground because of the harsh climate, begins at a height of 420 metres (1,370 ft) above sea-level and then, descending very gradually, covers a distance of 9 km (55 miles) – though only around 50 km (30 miles) as the crow flies – before it reaches the Cologne area, which lies 50 metres (160 ft) above sea-level. It's possible to visit the original source, and inspect a reconstructed section of the aqueduct in the Eifel even today, and various parts of the canal have now been exposed; in 1988 the Eifel Association ("Eifelverein") opened its "Roman Canal Footpath" for those interested in studying it more closely.

But at the end of Graeco-Roman

Remnants of antiquity in the Roman-Germanic Museum.

times, when Roman domination of the Rhine area came to an end, the Roman aqueduct, too, sank into obscurity. During the Middle Ages, stone from it was used as building material, and fine pillars for churches were cut from it. Anyone accidentally chancing upon the aqueduct, while ploughing or land-clearing, for example, who didn't immediately believe it was the entrance to hell, was even less inclined to believe that people had once gone to all that trouble just to get hold of drinking water.

The aqueduct gets a mention in the 11th-century *Anno Lied* as a *Steinin Rinnen* (stone gutter). And according to another theory the Romans used this long aqueduct to transport their wine from Trier, in the Moselle region, to Cologne. So much for the expertise of the Middle Ages.

The fact that the Romans buried their dead along the highways outside the city limits, firstly in urns and then later in graves, means that another of Cologne's Roman attractions can be found outside the bounds of the former city, even though it has been incorporated into it today: the **Roman burial chamber in Cologne-Weiden** (1328 Aachener Strasse).

It was originally discovered quite by chance in 1843, during some construction work. The burial chamber was refurbished, and now the urns and niches, busts of the deceased, a marble sarcophagus with fine carvings and, above all, the stone furnishings all combine to give one a good impression of the cult of death in those times, at least as far as the wealthy were concerned.

The imposing remains of the **Praetorium**, in Kleine Budengasse, which were briefly mentioned by Cologne chronicler and councillor Hermann von Weinsberg during construction work on the Town Hall Loggia in 1570, have also been made accessible to the public. The impressive walls of what once used to be the palace belonging to the governor of Lower Germania can now be inspected deep below the Town Hall, which was destroyed in World War II; a scale model gives one a good idea of just how mighty this structure alongside the Rhine harbour wall used to be.

The Roman-Germanic Museum: The best place for anyone interested in Roman history is right next door to the Cathedral: the **Roman-Germanic Museum**. Since it was opened in 1974 this unassuming building has had over 10 million visitors.

One could easily spend days on end here studying what Cologne used to be like; the place has everything, from different kinds of everyday implements right up to some of the most magnificent treasures of antiquity. The sheer amount of exhibits is all part of the original idea behind the museum: "a supermarket of early history" is how the collection's founder, Hugo Borger, referred to it.

One of the most important exhibits here is definitely the **Dionysos Mosaic**, discovered in its present position during the construction of a bunker; it adorned the floor of a room in a Roman peristyle house that stood exactly where the museum stands today.

The **Tomb of Poblicius**, above the famous mosaic, was discovered by two young men excavating a cellar in 1965, and the mysterious *diatreta* glass cups, with their delicate network design, were also discovered accidentally during some construction work – as has so often happened in Cologne.

So the more cautious one is when digging away at the ground in Cologne, the better. It will be a long time before the palimpsest is thoroughly deciphered. In 1987 there was a plan to build an underground car park below the Neumarkt, the new heart of the city, once a densely-populated area in Roman times. The car park would have destroyed a great deal. So, despite a lot of protest, the plans have been shelved for the time being, thus giving future archaeologists the chance to stay on the trail of the Romans.

An enduring monument.

THE MUSEUMS AND THEIR PATRONS

While most of Germany's museums have their origins in royal collections, the major museums of Cologne were founded by the burghers of the city themselves. The priest **Ferdinand Franz Wallraf**, who lived from 1748 to 1824, is responsible for many of the collections in Cologne.

Wallraf, like many other of his contemporaries, collected anything that contributed to the cause of furthering science and knowledge, and managed to gather together a vast assortment of books, drawings, etchings, stone monuments, coins and paintings. After Napoleon's occupation of the Rhineland and the resulting secularisation of the monasteries and churches, he became strongly interested in medieval panel paintings, and did his best to save them from destruction.

On his death he bequeathed his collection to the city of Cologne on condition that it be suitably exhibited. To gain some idea of just how passionate a collector this man was, it must be remembered that he alone donated 1,616 paintings, 3,875 drawings, and 42,419 etchings. Parts of his collection were later included in other ones. The various exhibits can be seen today in the Roman-Germanic Museum, the Museum of Applied Art and the Schnütgen Museum. The Municipal Museum also inherited some of his treasures. The main part of his collection, though, is on show in the Wallraf-Richartz Museum, which – as the name makes clear – has another magnanimous patron to thank for its existence.

The merchant **Johann Heinrich Richartz** (1795–1861) donated the sum of 100,000 thalers to the city in order to house the collection. It took a while before the former Minorite convent was deemed to be a suitable site, and it also took yet another donation from Richartz before the museum – built according to plans by Felten and Raschdorf – could finally be opened in 1861.

During World War II the building was completely destroyed, and yet another citizen of Cologne came to the rescue with a generous donation, giving the museum a new lease of life: **Josef Haubrich**. He was a lawyer, and had saved many Expressionist and Modernist paintings from destruction during the Nazi era. His generous donation in 1946 meant that the first new German museum of the post-war era could be constructed. On the original site, the austere, understated design by Rudolf Schwarz and Josef Bernard became a reality, and was opened in 1957. At that time the building was known as the "Wallraf-Richartz Museum and the Haubrich Collection".

The fact that it didn't remain so is thanks to the entrepreneurial married couple **Peter and Irene Ludwig** from Aachen. In 1976, they bequeathed 300 exhibits from their collection of modern art (with the main emphasis on Ameri-

Left, art appreciation in the Ludwig Museum. **Right**, a detail of Stephan Lochner's *Madonna in the Rose-Garden*.

can pop-art and "new realism") to the city on condition that it would be housed in a new museum. The city of Cologne thus decided to erect a large double museum next to the Cathedral: the Wallraf-Richartz Museum and Ludwig Museum.

In 1986 the original and by no means uncontroversial new building, designed by architects Peter Busmann and Godfried Haberer, was formally opened. Then in 1989, the Museum of Applied Art moved into the "old building" at the Minorite convent. So today, monuments to the honourable benefactors Wallraf and Richartz can be seen standing in front of an edifice with little if anything at all in common with their original intentions.

The patron **Josef Haubrich** has had the **Art Exhibition Hall** (Kunsthalle) named after him: it was opened in the Neumarkt in 1967. It acts as a "shopwindow" for other museums, and features alternating national exhibitions.

Before one sets foot in the **Wallraf-Richartz Museum and Ludwig Museum** with the **Agfa-Foto-Historama**, it's best to work out in advance whether one is more attracted by older or more modern art, and then divide up one's visit on that basis. Asking for a plan of the building at the information-desk, which outlines the interior and shows the various possible routes, makes it relatively easy to find one's way about. It is advisable, though, to take a break between the two collections, in the generously laid-out museum cafeteria, for example, or in one of the many restaurants in the Old City (Altstadt) close by.

The highlight of any trip to Cologne's museums is the collection of medieval panel paintings by the Cologne school of painters. The great altars can all be found in one room, standing there at eye-level, some distance away from the walls. The work of Cologne's most famous painter, Stephan Lochner, must not of course be missed (the museum owns a *Last Judgement* by him as well as his magnificent *Madonna in the*

A 17th-century Japanese priest figure.

Rose-Garden), but several other works, such as those by the Master of St Veronica, are worth attention. The two large triptychs by the Master of St Bartholomew are also excellent.

As is always the case with museums founded on donations, not every culture and epoch is dealt with in a balanced manner. The transition to the Renaissance is represented by only a few, though exquisite, works of art: Barthel Bruyn's double portrait of the Salsburgs, husband and wife; Dürer's *Piper and Drummer*; and Cranach's *Judgement of Paris*.

Focal points: 17th-century Dutch art, however, is very well represented in Cologne because the city succeeded in obtaining the Carstanjen Collection in the early 1920s. As early as the stairwell one can already see Rubens' altarpiece The *Stigmatisation of St Francis*. Other highlights include works by Hals, Honthorst and von Heemskerck, and of course there is also the fine *Self-Portrait in Old Age* by Rembrandt.

Another focal point is 19th-century painting. Here we find works by Joseph Anton Koch and Schnorr von Carolsfeld, as well as Caspar David Friedrich and Adolph von Menzel. There is also an important collection of works by the realist Wilhelm Leibl, and Corinth and Liebermann form the transition to the French Impressionists, where Renoir's *Portrait of the Sisleys* is a real highlight.

20th-century art: Munch forms the transition to the Ludwig Collection, and 20th-century art. Going down a few steps at the end of the "Museumsstrasse" one finds post-1960 German art: to the right, in the main hall, Penck, Kiefer and Immendorf, and in the Rhine Halls ("Rheinsäle"), works by Klapheck and Richter.

If one then goes up to the second floor, one passes through a small exhibition room containing works by German avant-gardist Joseph Beuys before reaching a large hall devoted to the work of the German Expressionists, including Kirchner and other members of

A scene from the Ludwig Museum.

the "Brücke" group. A monumental sculpture by Otto Freundlich is particularly eye-catching here, and right beside it is a superb ensemble by Beckmann. Then, via Constructivism and the Russian avant-garde, one reaches Picasso, well represented with works taken from all his periods.

As far as Dada and Surrealism are concerned, the Rhineland has its very own contributor: Max Ernst. He was born in the nearby town of Brühl, and is of course very well represented, above all by his scandalous *Madonna thrashing the Baby Jesus.*

One then comes to abstract art of the post-war era – Wilhelm Nay, who adopted Cologne as his home, has a whole exhibition room devoted to his work (Peill donation). Further on, one reaches "Nouveau Réalisme".

Then it's the turn of the Americans, with work by Jasper Jones, Andy Warhol, Rauschenberg and Lichtenstein. In the stairwell, one is suddenly faced by a very colourful *Nana*. At this point, the two sculpture sections up on the roof deserve a visit; they afford a fine view of the Old City, and from the western one there is a magnificent view of the choir section of the Cathedral, which almost seems to be within reaching distance.

Both museums contain small exhibition rooms devoted to old prints, which, though separately run, can be found in the same area of the building. The reading room, where one can be shown individual pages, is situated on the first floor, close to the entrance to the medieval collections.

A real treat for photography enthusiasts is the **Agfa-Foto-Historama**, on permanent loan to Cologne from Agfa, Leverkusen. One can reach this exhibition – which documents the history of photography from the first ever daguerreotypes to the present day – by crossing over to the other side of the cafeteria, or by going down the stairs at the end of the "Museumsstrasse".

The **Schnütgen Museum**, with its collection of church art from the early Middle Ages to the 19th century, also has a patron to thank for its existence: **Alexander Schnütgen** (1843–1918), a member of the Cathedral chapter, who, 100 years after Wallraf before him, devoted himself to saving valuable works of church art.

He was generally considered a rather odd collector, one who resorted to all kinds of ruses in order to acquire endangered works of art. In 1906 he bequeathed his collection to the city, which initially housed it in a new annexe to the Museum of Applied Art. In 1932, the exhibition was transferred across the river to the former Abbey of St Heribert in Cologne-Deutz. The medieval panel paintings from Schnütgen's collection were then moved to the Wallraf-Richartz Museum.

"**Germany's finest museum**": The abbey was destroyed during the air raids of World War II, but luckily its contents had been moved out in time. They were given a new home after the war in the

An exhibit from the Schnütgen Museum.

Romanesque convent church of St Cecilia. At the museum's opening ceremony in 1956, Federal President Theodor Heuss spoke of it as being "Germany's finest", and the great attraction of this museum even today is still the marvellous combination of the Romanesque church with the medieval masterpieces. One enters the building from the west, and before starting on a tour of the collection one really should allow a little time for the full effect of the interior and the arranged exhibits to sink in.

The exhibition is laid out chronologically, beginning with Romanesque sculpture and ending with the Baroque Heisterbach Grille. There are some real treasures to be found in the choir area, where the crucifix from St George's dominates the crossing, and the alabaster figures from the *Three Kings Gateway* and also the magnificent altar veil from St Ursula's are on view.

The busts of St Ursula, with their endearing expressions, and ostensibly containing the relics of the saint and her 11,000 virgin companions, are a real Cologne speciality.

One magnificent piece of work is the polychromed console bust of a woman carved by one of the Parler family. The western choir contains the mysterious *Siegburg Madonna* which was only discovered in the 1920s. The crypt, finely restored in 1977, and now re-opened, contains valuable liturgical utensils.

The Museum of Applied Art ("Kunstgewerbemuseum"), originally known as the Museum of Arts and Crafts, also has **Ferdinand Franz Wallraf**, whose collections make up the major part of it, to thank for its existence. Again, it was due to the generosity of another patron that the collection was provided with a suitable location. **Otto Gustav Andreae** bequeathed 400,000 marks to the city, and in 1900 an expensive, neo-Renaissance structure was opened on the Hansaring. Several extensions were later added to the building in order to house the

The Rautenstrauch-Joest Museum is devoted to the ethnology of non-European cultures.

Schnütgen Museum and the Museum of East Asian Art. Thanks to generous contributions from the people of Cologne and the acquisition of the collection belonging to Rhenish scholar Wilhelm Clemens, the building soon became one of the most important museums of arts and crafts in all Germany.

After World War II it sank into almost total obscurity, only managing to draw attention to itself via several minor exhibitions in the Romanesque Overstolzenhaus. Until 1989 it was very much a museum of storage boxes and packing-cases. But then, under the careful supervision of architect Von Lom, the now classic structure by Schwarz and Bernard – the original Wallraf-Richartz Museum – was restored to its original form and adapted for the use of the Museum of Arts and Crafts, which is today known as the "**Museum of Applied Art**".

The collection is laid out chronologically and based around particular themes, but these days it no longer relies

on self-contained ensembles; rather, an effort has been made to allow each exhibit to retain its individual aura, while conveying a sense of how it connects with the others. Some of the finest exhibits in the museum are its articles of furniture, ranging from the Middle Ages to the time of the "Vienna Workshops" at the beginning of this century. Some parts of the museum feature collections of jewellery and majolica, and there are also a few pieces of fine porcelain on display.

The entrance to the modern collection is situated on the ground floor beyond the main hall. The museum was founded on condition that it also display a collection of contemporary art. The "Textiles and Fashions" section, housed in a small, darkened exhibition room on the upper floor, is attractively laid out.

There is one other museum which no one visiting Cologne should miss, even though it is not right in the centre of the city: the **Museum of East Asian Art**. It, too, has patrons to thank for its existence: **Adolf and Frieda Fischer** presented the city of Cologne with their collection in 1909 on condition that a museum devoted solely to Asian culture be founded. The collection was thus spared the fate of becoming just another ethnological museum.

In 1913, the museum was opened in an extension building to the Museum of Arts and Crafts, and Fischer then stocked it with all the treasures he had specifically acquired for his collection on two lengthy trips he had taken through Asia in 1909 and 1912.

In 1944, the museum was destroyed during air raids, and it was only in 1977 that it was reopened in a new, harmoniously simple-looking building designed by Japanese architect Kunio Mayekawa, next to the Aachener Weiher (pond). The Japanese garden in the inner courtyard and the terrace facing the Aachener Weiher give the building a calm, Far Eastern atmosphere that is very conducive to meditation. The restaurant here is very popular too, especially during the summer months.

The museum contains works exclusively from Japan, China and Korea. Since many of the exhibits are very sensitive to light, they often get changed. Sometimes, during important exhibitions, whole sections are moved.

Impressive: The Chinese and Japanese bronzes are magnificent, and one particularly impressive exhibit is the wooden figure of *Buddha Amitabha* from Japan. The glass display cases contain porcelain and ceramics from Korea, Japan and China, and of course there are also many fine examples of the lacquerwork for which East Asia is so famous. There are always a few particularly fine examples of the museum's large collection of folding screens on display, and one can always be sure of seeing several of the enchanting scroll wall paintings, with their landscapes and scenes from everyday life.

The **Rautenstrauch-Joest Museum** of ethnology also reveals the names of its patrons. The two Cologne families not only formed the basis of the museum with their collections, they also donated money for the building itself, which was constructed in neo-Baroque style by Edwin Crones and opened in 1906 as the first ever museum devoted entirely to ethnology. Even today it is still the only ethnological museum in all of North Rhine-Westphalia.

The building was badly damaged during the war, and the Museum has been somewhat hampered in its effect by the municipal Little Theatre ("Kammerspiele"), housed in the same building. Plans by Gottfried Böhm for a new building on the Heumarkt are now being discussed, but it is unlikely to be moved into before the end of the 1990s.

At the moment, the following sections are open: Indian cultures – the South Seas – pre-Columbian cultures of America – Khmer and Thai. There has also been a recent addition: a toy collection called "Spielzeugwelten" (Worlds of Toys).

The Schnütgen Museum in St Cecilia's contains a unique collection of church art.

ART AND COMMERCE

Cologne has its art dealers' ingenuity to thank for its leading role as the European metropolis of modern art: in 1967, several of them, including Hein Stünke and Rudolf Zwirner, founded an "Art Market". Back then, the newly-created "Association of Progressive German Art Dealers", made up of 18 representatives from the trade from all over the Federal Republic, put on an exhibition in the Gürzenich of non-establishment, contemporary art. And although the odd connoisseur may have been put off by the light-hearted combination of art and commerce, the exhibition was a great success, with 15,000 visitors in five days.

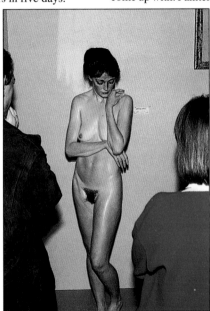

"Art Cologne", as the exhibition has been referred to since 1974, has gone from strength to strength since then, and was shifted long ago to Cologne's Trade Fair Centre. And this despite fierce competition, for the idea of an art market has now gained acceptance and similar fairs are taking place the world over, from Los Angeles to Basle and Paris to Chicago. But only Basle – because Americans prefer Switzerland to Germany – has been providing any really serious competition.

Cologne has reacted to this with fresh ideas: museums and their collections have formed part of the fair since 1978, and there's also room for new talent thanks to a subsidy programme for young artists.

But the main driving force in Cologne's artistic life is less the politicians responsible for its culture than its art galleries themselves. In a city with such magnificent museums, art dealers have been able to set out a selection unparalleled anywhere else in Europe. Anyone interested in art – whether classic modern, constructive, art from the 1950s (when Paris was the artistic metropolis of the Western world), pop or pop art – will find all his heart's desires in Cologne, up to and including the most recent trends.

To make the range on offer even more attractive, the gallery owners have been continually innovative. One example is the "Gallery Weekend" which they stage twice annually, and which brings collectors, artists and museum representatives from all over the world to the Rhine.

But what use are galleries without the artists to go with them? Cologne attracts a lot of artists, and the number is increasing steadily. It's not only the commercial prospects that beckon, either: there's also the basic atmosphere of tolerance here. "*Jeder Jeck ist anders*" ("We're all crazy in our different ways"), as they say in Cologne, reflecting an easy-going attitude towards one's fellow-men, whether or not they happen to come up to accepted norms. On top of this there is also a healthy love of art which the Rhinelanders have retained ever since Roman times.

This unique artistic climate has resulted in a genre that only a place like Cologne could have come up with. Painters, sculptors and video artists do not work separately from one another here; instead, the disciplines tend to blur. Depending on what their subject requires, they can reach for paintbrushes, palette knives or video cameras. This kind of openness and determined lack of narrow-mindedness has resulted in experiments that are making creative art forge ahead. The city plays a leading role in the video arts.

Cologne is not sinking into any kind of regional complacency, though; that is prevented not only by the artists here with international reputations – such as Gerhard Richter, Sigmar Polke, Bernhard Johannes, Ann Blume, Jürgen Klauke, C.O. Paeffgen, Astrid Klein, Walter Dahn and Martin Kippenberger – but also very much by the dealers themselves.

Three gallery-owners in particular had a decisive influence for many years: Paul Maenz, who began by exhibiting Arte Povera and Minimalist art, and was one of the first promoters of "rediscovered painting" (*Transavantguardia* in Italy, and the group "Mülheimer Freiheit" in Germany), took official leave of the business in 1990. Michael Werner, with his consistent exhibition strategy and his mixture of decisiveness and personal commitment, gained international success with his team of artists (Georg Baselitz, Markus Lüpertz, Georg Immendorf, A.R. Penck, Per Kirkeby) and he continues to play an important role. Rudolf Zwirner, really more a dealer than a gallery-owner, still remains one of the great names in the business, not only because of the exhibitions in which he used to mix established names with new ones, but also because of his cultural-political commitment which he continues to display with as much verve as ever, often unsettlingly so. His *Köln Sammelt* ("Collectors of Cologne") exhibition was one of the best in recent years.

Meanwhile, a new generation of gallery-owners is taking the place of the old established names of former years. The dominant figure here is Max Hetzler. Cool and clever, he has built up a gallery in which he co-operates with colleagues in New York. A branch on the West Coast of the USA also means that new talent and new buyers can readily be found. Hetzler represents Günther Förg, Werner Büttner, Georg Herold, Martin Kippenberger, Albert and Markus Oehlen as well as Reinhard Mucha and Hubert Kiecol. He runs his worldwide business from his gallery-house on Venloer Strasse, which was built by renowned Cologne architect Oswald Mathias Ungers.

Roughly 60 different galleries are officially listed in Cologne, but there are actually a lot more, with new ones being founded almost daily. Some of the most important addresses offering a broad range of work in general include: Karsten Greve, with such great names as Jannis Kounellis, Nicola de Maria, Paco Knöller and Lucio Fontana; Monika Sprüth, whose programme also takes in Rosemarie Trockel, Cindy Sherman, Jenny Holzer, Barbara Kruger and Fischli/Weiss; Gerhard Reinz, who with his "Galerie Orangerie" and its works by Picasso, Miro, Fautrier, Ackermann, Nay and Poliakoff, tends to focus on classic moderns and on postwar art in general.

Two major figures among the prime movers are Rolf Ricke, who was the first to introduce the work of American artists Richard Serra and Keith Sonnier to Europe, and Winifried Reckermann with Yves Klein, Arman, Uecker and Calder, as well as several successful young artists such as Thomas Virnich, Dorothee von Windheim and Bodo Baumgarten. Heinz Holtmann has Beuys, Buthe, Banana and Blume on offer, and the Jöllenbeck Gallery looks after Runde Mields, Michael Witlatschil, Rainer Barzen and Frank Dornseif. Several dealers also offer art from the 1920s and 1930s for sale, including the Stolz and Teufel Gallery. And Kicken-Pauseback as well as Johnen & Schöttle both specialise in photography.

Something of a loner on the Cologne artistic scene is the Gmurzynska Gallery. Founded in 1964 by Antonina Gmurzynska, who was born in Warsaw, its clearly-defined, high-quality programme made it one of the top addresses for pioneers of modern art and for the European and Russian avant-garde. Thanks to her excellent contacts, Antonina Gmurzynska succeeded in unearthing key works of the Bauhaus, de Stijl, Suprematist, Cubist and Surrealist movements. Her gallery became a meeting-place from the mid-70s onwards for heads of museums and collectors such as Thissen-Bornemisza and Peter Ludwig. When Antonina died in 1986 and her daughter took over the gallery, many felt that the end was nigh. But Krystyna soon proved she could follow in her mother's footsteps, and the gallery, housed in a new museum-like building, is now in a better position than ever.

Even though no other German city will seriously be able to endanger Cologne's reputation as a metropolis of art over the coming decades, the city will still have to rise to several challenges in the near future. The change in the political landscape means that it will have to re-define its role, and maintain its status as a bridgehead between Paris and Berlin and – thanks to its excellent collection of Pop Art, unrivalled even in the USA itself for size and quality – as a counterpart to New York.

Art and art dealing is thus still very much alive and well in Cologne. And considering Cologne's special mixture of Rhenish cheerfulness, realism, creativity and hard business sense, there really need be no cause for alarm. In the words of Hiltrud Kier, a native of Graz and head of one of Cologne's museums: "The people of Cologne have never been all that concerned with what happens elsewhere, they've always rested safe and secure in the knowledge of their two-thousand-year history." And anyone touring Cologne's museums and art galleries always gets a sense of this relaxed, self-confident feel the city has, along with its cheerful "live and let live" attitude to life.

SHOPPING IN COLOGNE

As far as shopping in Cologne is concerned, a very pleasant transformation has taken place over the past few years with regard to quality and variety, and its been lent extra strength architecturally and aesthetically, too, with the reorganisation of the Ring roads between Zülpicher Platz and Christophstrasse, and the construction of well-designed shopping arcades in the city centre.

Whatever you're looking for – fashions, furniture, porcelain, glass, leather goods, cosmetics or jewellery – you'll find it all in the city centre, between the Rings (from Ebertplatz up to the Südstadt) and the Rhine.

The first shopping district most visitors to Cologne get to know is the one around the Cathedral and the Old City. It's certainly worth taking a stroll between the Wallrafplatz and the Alter Markt – top-quality fashions, crockery, jewellery and carpets are all on sale here. Musikhaus Tönger, with its records, CDs and sheet music, is a favourite haunt for classical music enthusiasts. For pop and jazz the best place to go is the highly popular "Saturn" on the Hansaring.

Incidentally, this brick complex on the Hansastrasse was Europe's tallest skyscraper just after it was built in 1925 – something that seems ludicrous today. Another good place for pop music is WOM (World Of Music) on the ground floor of "Hertie" in the Neumarkt.

In the summer, it's very pleasant to sit outside the "Früh am Dom" beer-hall, or the various other restaurants and cafés bordering the Cathedral square, and enjoy a view of the Roncalliplatz, the "Domhotel", the Roman-Germanic Museum and the western facade of the Cathedral. Anyone who still finds the pace of life too hectic here should head down the Stollwerck-Passage for the distinguished "Gartencafé Reichard",

with its select assortment of cakes and confectionery.

Much of Cologne was destroyed in World War II. The **Hohe Strasse** wasn't spared either, and was rebuilt rather unimaginatively. However, it's still one of the city's most popular and lively shopping streets. Boutiques, jeans shops, fur shops and shoe shops predominate, alongside sex shops and fast-food outlets. At the end of the long, narrow street one arrives at what used to be the Tietz department store, now "Kaufhof"; it has made quite a name for itself with gourmets ever since its new food department opened. Crab, lobster, poultry and game from France, exotic fruit and vegetables from all over the world are permanently available here; at the various "snack-stands" one can sample pasta dishes, vegetarian dishes, fish and meat specialities, and salmon or oysters for a quick meal *en passant*. The range available here should give one more than enough energy to cope with a walk through the next major pedestrian street on the route.

Street performers: The **Schildergasse** got its name from the medieval shield-painters whose guild house once used to stand here, along with some of their workshops. Today the street is lined with clothes shops, large and small; one can buy leather goods, underwear, jewellery and cosmetics, and also find several pleasant places to pass the time of day – in the street café next to the Antonite Church, for example. From spring until autumn this street is a favourite haunt of pavement artists and buskers, as well as mime acts.

The **Neumarkt** was a horse and cattle market as early as the 11th century. Today, depending on the season, this rather unimaginatively designed square is the venue for the "Büchersommer" summer book fair, the antiques market, the wine market and the Christmas market. But market or not, the Neumarkt is still a desirable address.

A further and very recent attraction as far as shopping arcades are concerned is

Preceding pages: faces at a flea market. **Left**, shop-window reflections.

Richmod's. The tower of the former Richmodis building, with its two horses' heads looking out of the window, is being integrated into the new architecture. Meanwhile, the **Neumarkt-Passage** has already been completed, and it now stretches as far as Richmodisstrasse before connecting three major shopping arcades, including Richmod's as well as the exquisite **Olivandenhof** (named after a medieval building that once stood on the site called the "Haus zum Olivunden" – meaning "elephant").

One of the three very well-equipped bookshops in the Neumarkt area can be found right at the entrance to the arcade, next to the "Kreissparkasse" bank. The interior of the shopping arcade is luxuriously laid-out, with a wholemeal bistro and a gourmet restaurant, and a glass lift travels up to the glass cupola of the Käthe Kollwitz Museum, with its permanent exhibition of graphics, posters and sculptures.

Fashion enthusiasts should definitely check out the expensive and lavish articles of clothing, including leatherware, in the **Mittelstrasse** and **Pfeilstrasse** districts. Here, right next to the **Bazaar de Cologne** (near the northwest corner of the Neumarkt), there is a glass-covered shopping arcade with a whole series of shops, pubs and restaurants, chic fashion firms and several elegant boutiques.

The latest and weirdest fashions: Very different fashions – those preferred by the city's young alternatives – can be found in **Ehrenstrasse**, at the end of which one rejoins Pfeilstrasse. Boutiques, some of which contain extremely weird clothing, alternate with flashy shoe-shops, esoteric bookshops, and leather shops to suit all tastes. Here we find alternative cafés and cinemas, an Asian shop, an excellent poultry and game shop, and also Walther König's artistic bookshop which has a superb selection.

Those keen on seeing something a little more elegant and sophisticated after this should turn off Ehrenstrasse into **St Apernstrasse**. Within this area, surrounding the arcade known as the **Kreishausgalerie**, it's worth taking a look inside the various antique shops and art galleries. And from here it's just a short walk to **Breite Strasse**, in the pedestrian precinct, and to the oldest shopping arcade in Cologne, the **Ladenstadt**. Posters, wine, carpets as well as kitchenware can be found here. There's also the celebrated 4711 building in the nearby **Glockengasse**.

A good old-fashioned stroll: Ever since the tram link between Zülpicher Platz and Ebertplatz was moved underground, Cologne's **Rings** have once again become attractive; it has gone to great pains to restore these streets, once so popular with shoppers and strollers. From 1881 onwards, after most of the medieval city walls had been taken down, the Rings were laid out according to plans drawn up by Stübben, Cologne's municipal architect. The streets of the projected "New Town" (Neu-

Hohe Strasse, Cologne's busiest shopping mile.

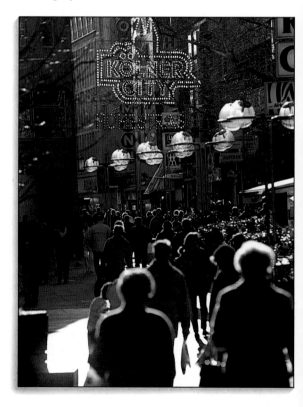

stadt) varied in width as well as magnificence according to the kinds of inhabitants planned for them.

Some of this has been borne in mind during the present restoration work, the quality of which is already evident in the magnificent shop and office buildings on the **Hohenstaufenring**, near the Zülpicher Platz. Here one can find expensive furniture, fashions and computers, fine fabrics and a bookshop with a comprehensive selection of travel books and hiking maps (Gleumes). And just around the corner, at No. 3, **Beethovenstrasse**, a fishmonger's, plus snack bar, with what is probably the most comprehensive selection of Mediterranean fish in the whole of Cologne, the "Neptun Fischhalle", opened just a short while ago.

Looking for designer fashions, ultra-modern fountain pens, vases made of chromium steel and candlesticks made of perspex? Go to "Rosselli" on the Habsburgerring. On the other side of the Ring, the **City-Treff**, belonging to the "Stadtsparkasse", is a place where anyone can relax, with its bistro and its reading corner.

Hohenzollernring, and **Kaiser-Wilhelm-Ring** in particular have been laid out very attractively with fountains, flowerbeds and groups of trees, creating a park atmosphere. There was a huge festival held in 1988 to mark the completion of the work. Insurance companies settled in the area a long time ago, alongside the numerous street cafés, cinemas, shoe-shops, record shops and smallish department stores. "Pesch" is still the number one address for all furniture enthusiasts, with its unique and highly impressive selection of cupboards, tables, armchairs and living accessories.

A dash of Turkey: The **Eigelstein** is a typical district of Cologne, and it also has a strong Turkish flavour to it. Anyone keen on lamb, mutton, veal or beef will find a fresh as well as comprehensive selection in the half-dozen or so Turkish butchers' shops here. Herbs and spices to go with the food, along with sheep's cheese and olives, good-value vegetables and fruit can be found in several shops. The delicious selection is complemented by Spanish, Italian and Greek shops, all selling products from their own countries, and of course there are also lots of restaurants and fast-food establishments ready to welcome the visitor.

Anyone keen on the "bazaar" atmosphere of fruit and vegetable stands, cheese and sausage stalls, flower stalls and knick-knacks in general would be very well advised to visit one of Cologne's many **markets** ("Wochenmärkte").

The ones in the Old City are of particular interest: there is one in the Alter Markt (Fridays, 8 a.m.– 6.30 p.m.) and at Apostelkloster (Tuesdays and Fridays, 7 a.m. – 1 p.m.), and there are also the markets at the Klettenberggürtel (Wednesdays and Saturdays, 7 a.m. – 1 p.m.) and in the Wilhelmplatz in Nippes (Monday – Saturday, 7 a.m. – 1 p.m.).

Form and function in the exclusive Olivandenhof shopping centre.

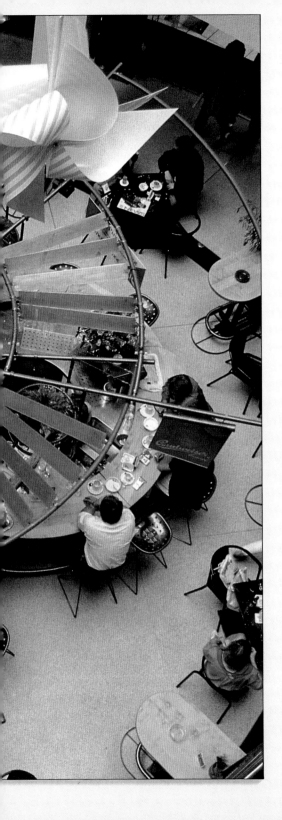

RHENISH GASTRONOMY

It's a known fact that the people of Cologne are full of *joie de vivre*. They love a good festival – and not just at Carnival time, either. They're very sociable, they enjoy a good laugh over their glasses of *Kölsch*, and are very keen on culinary attractions of all kinds. "*Jut esse und drinke hält Liev un Siel zesammen,*" as they say ("Good food and drink keeps body and soul together").

Anyone who doesn't believe this should take a look in the – by no means fully comprehensive – Cologne yellow pages. Over 1,800 breweries, restaurants and pubs, along with 80 cafés, can all be found jostling for the gourmet's attention, and these figures don't even include the establishments specialising in *Pommes Rut-Wiess* (chips with ketchup and mayonnaise) and *Rievkooche* (potato fritters) to take away.

A real beer-house atmosphere: Anyone who feels like trying out some of Cologne's gastronomic specialities should head for the city's **beer-houses**: the "Malzmühle" in the Heumarkt, for example, the "Pfäffgen" in Friesenstrasse, "Sion" in the Strasse Unter Taschenmacher or "Früh am Dom" (opposite the Cathedral) in the city centre. These traditional establishments, with their highly *gemütlich* and beery atmosphere, will serve you the kind of food every Cologne granny used to make: large helpings, very substantial, tasty and also good value for money. From midday onwards the wooden tables, scrubbed clean, are already packed with people of all ages.

At the centre of the crush you can see the *Köbes* (waiters) with their blue aprons and their stoic expressions, carrying plates piled high with steaming *Hämchen* (pork knuckle), *Rippchen Rut-Wiess* (cured loin of pork with red and white cabbage), and of course *Himmel un Ääd* (Heaven and Earth), that special Cologne mixture of mashed potato (earth), stewed apple (heaven) and fried blood sausage, also known as *Flönz*, the delicious aroma of which usually reconciles visitors to its questionable appearance.

In all the months with an "r" in, bright-red signs appear in the windows inviting one to sample *kutterfrische Muscheln* (fresh mussels). These can be served with onion rings in a pepper sauce, in wine or in a vegetable sauce, accompanied by delicious black bread with butter. The establishment known as "Bieresel" in Breite Strasse even cooks its mussels *à la provençale*, with garlic and herbs, and also "Vienna style", fried with a coating of breadcrumbs.

A taste of Cologne humour: Let the stranger be wary of such peculiarities as *Halver Hahn*, *Kölscher Kaviar* or *Flönz met Musik*, which actually seem to have been created expressly so as to lead *Immis* (the Cologne word for non-locals) and other unsuspecting individuals up the garden path. The "Halver Hahn" (the literal meaning is "half chicken"), for example, listed under "side dishes" on every Cologne menu, arrives looking very different from the marvellous and delicious bargain you thought it was going to be: it's just a simple roll of rye bread nestling under an enormous slab of Dutch cheese. "Kölscher Kaviar" is nothing more than a small pile of *Flönz* (see above) with a bit of mustard squirted on top, accompanied by a white bread roll. And as for "Flönz mit Musik", all that means is a few onion rings get plonked on top as a garnish.

To wash it all down there's "Kölsch", the city's famous top-fermented beer, which the *Köbes* slams down on the wooden table in small high glasses called *Stangen*. The worst thing you can do to your "Köbes" is to order a glass of Coke, let alone water. "*Jiddet nit*" ("There ain't none") is the usual gruff answer, before the gentleman in the blue apron slams yet another foaming

Preceding pages: a restaurant in the Olivanden-hof. **Below**, not only beer is consumed in Cologne's pubs.

glass of Kölsch onto his astonished customer's beer-mat.

Things are very different in the city's **elegant restaurants**, such as the "Goldener Pflug" in Cologne-Merheim, which has been the city's top address for years now, or Madame Rachel Silberstein's velvet-upholstered "Chez Alex" in the Old City. Kölscher Kaviar? *Jiddet nit*. Why not try *Jakobsmuscheln Noilly Prat*? With lobster parfait, perhaps? Cologne, with its "Halver Hahn" and its *"Hämchen"*, has a surprisingly large number of gourmet restaurants, but in the end it's all just *"jut esse un drinke..."*

Other top establishments include the Italian restaurants "Alfredo" in Tunisstrasse, and "Rino Casati" on the Ebertplatz; there's also the elegant "Wack", belonging to Romain Wack from Alsace, in Benesisstrasse, and the pigeon-grey "Ambiance am Dom". The people of Cologne certainly know how to eat well, and don't mind paying for it either. The main evening menu in the "Goldener Pflug", which has just enough room for 30 diners at any one time, can cost as much as DM 200 a head. Anyone who finds this too expensive just has to content himself with *Canard Nantais aux Raisins* for around DM 100, or a plate of *Turbot et Crème de Cellerie* for a modest DM 65.

Traditional food *à la maison*: If there's one thing common to all the top gourmet cooks in Cologne, whether they come from Italy, Belgium or Alsace, it's their love of consistency. They don't like to experiment. Indeed, why should they, if traditional food tastes so delicious anyway? *Babylotte* served with strips of zucchini, and fillet of sole with herbs have been firm favourites on the menu in "Alfredo" Carturan's 40-seat restaurant for years now, and fillet of beef *à la maison* is still an integral part of the menu at Madame Silberstein's. Quite different, though, is the "Graugans" restaurant in the Hyatt Regency Hotel in Cologne-Deutz. The chef de cuisine there has spiced up his

Kölsch **tends to level the social differences.**

dishes by borrowing heavily from Asiatic cookery, much to the astonishment of Cologne gourmets, and steams his strips of salmon on lemon grass.

Perennial favourites in Cologne are those living-room-sized French and Italian restaurants with seven or eight tables, house wine and a menu that changes daily, featuring such delicacies as Saddle of Lamb *à la provençale*, Fillet of Beef Strips in Gorgonzola Sauce or Quail in Port Wine Sauce. A main course like this usually costs no more than DM 35.

On Friday nights and at weekends these little rooms are packed to overflowing, guests can wear jeans if they like, and be prepared: when space is at a real premium you can often see right into the kitchen. And the cook at "Il Bagutta" on Heinsbergstrasse, in the student area around the Zülpicher Strasse which Cologne refers to as its "Kwartier Lateng", may even seat himself at the piano as midnight approaches and hammer out a few popular Italian tunes, making everyone's *Mousse au Chocolat* tremble in the process.

Fish soup and fried duck: A few streets further on, the "Tapabo" (Kyffhäuserstrasse), a small bistro with nine tables covered with paper tablecloths, hasn't changed its menu for years. The fish soup here is superb – at DM 10 a plate, too. And situated behind the railway embankment in Krefelderstrasse is "Moissonnier", an attractive restaurant with a very respectable wine-list. *On parle français.* The menu is also in French, but the waiters patiently explain to all the guests that a *Consommé de Queue de Boeuf*, at 8 marks a bowl, is oxtail soup, and that a *Parmentier de Canard* is actually a piece of fried duck.

There are several other similar establishments: the "Artischocke" on Moltkestrasse, for example, with its cosy, old-fashioned decor. Or there's the excellent "La Baurie" at the People's Gardens (Volksgarten). Not to forget "La Barrière", situated far out in Müngersdorf, where the sauces are as dark as the ink from octopus, and taste just as if one were seated somewhere deep within France, instead of next to a level-crossing on the Aachener Strasse.

There again, the astonished visitor really feels he is in Ankara, Istanbul or Anatolia when he enters the Weidengasse, a narrow street with quite a shady past, in the north of Cologne. Oriental music drones monotonously out of the open doors of the snack-bars with their huge pieces of meat revolving on spits, and a heavy aroma of garlic hangs in the air. The Weidengasse, not far from the Eigelstein and the city's Rings, has been taken over completely by the Turks.

The most popular restaurant in the street for years now has been the "Bizim", an elegant and rather cool, though still cosy establishment, where one can find the best in **Istanbul cuisine**: puff pastry rolls with sheep's cheese and parsley, for example, and saddle of lamb with aubergine rolls. To go with it, of course, there's Turkish coffee. On the opposite side of the street there's the "Bandirma", and also the "Baba" and the "Bosporus" a few houses further up.

A gastronomic trip round the world: Or how about a Burmese meal? Persian? Mexican? Cologne can provide you with a gastronomic trip round the world. Just a few tips as you go: Mexican food tastes best at the "Café Especial" Mexican restaurant on Neuhoffer Strasse, opposite the main station in Deutz. Fans of Asian food are recommended to eat at the "Mandalay" restaurant on Brüsseler Strasse. The menu at Cologne's only Burmese restaurant is enticing, and anyone who feels like it can eat his *Fisch à la Mandalay* with chopsticks. A few steps up the street, in the "Bali" restaurant on Brüsseler Platz, huge pieces of fried duck and strips of carrot cut incredibly thin are served on black plates. Haute cuisine, Indonesian-style.

A word about Cologne's **cafés**. They are at least as varied as the city's restaurants, if not more so. Some of them, full of knick-knacks and comfortable up-

When the weather's nice, the tables are put outside.

holstery, serve cream cake, and also *Gulaschsuppe* with a roll at lunchtime. One good example is the "Trödelcafé" (near St Agatha) opposite "Kaufhof". The tiny, comfortable interior is packed full of old pieces of furniture and antiques which can actually be bought on the spot by guests.

Others are very much in the good old coffee-house tradition. Their furnishings haven't changed for centuries: pastel-coloured walls, subdued lighting, tiny tables. Old ladies with blue rinses and housewives who've just completed their morning shopping tend to congregate in the "Café Franck" on the Rudolfsplatz, or in the "Café Schmitz" on Breite Strasse, for a slice of fruit cake with cream. Connoisseurs, however, patronise the "Café Reichard" (Unter Fettenhennen) next to the WDR, which is so luxuriously furnished that it's hard to believe you're not in Vienna, even though the spires of Cologne cathedral can be seen through the windows. The cake is incredibly delicious.

The alternative café scene: And of course there are also those unusual establishments which first started livening up the café scene here at the end of the 1970s, and now have absolutely nothing in common with the usual café image: "Café Fleur" (Lindenstrasse/Engelbertstrasse), "Café Krümel" (Zülpicherstrasse/Weyertal), "Café Moka" (Weyertal) and "Kaffeeböhnchen" (Kurfürstenstrasse), among others. They have a sort of ramshackle, comfy look to them, with a touch of Parisian bistro. Crowded into these places are students, schoolchildren, alternatives, painters, musicians and all those who simply appreciate a good cappuccino and fresh croissants for breakfast.

Which brings us to the "alternative" part of Cologne. For years, the "in" place to meet was the relatively run-down Südstadt area, around Chlodwigplatz and Bonner Strasse. That came to an end with the days of "Saturday Night Fever", when young people from out-side the city started making regular visits to the smoke-filled "Opera" and the no less tobacco-ridden "Spielplatz". Today, the Südstadt is certainly a lively area for pubs and clubs – but it's no longer "the in place to meet". The city's young artists, aspiring and otherwise, meet up in the "Broadway Café" on Ehrenstrasse. Dressed in black, and looking pale and serious, they spend the mornings there over a cappuccino before possibly switching later to the "Spitz" (Ehrenstrasse), a "cool", American-style bar with its shiny counter and pale green leather armchairs. And in the evenings they may show up at the "Königswasser" in Flandrische Strasse – if it's still "in", that is – or at the "Café Central" in the basement of the Chelsey Hotel on Jülicher Strasse.

Older boys and girls still swear by the "EWG" in Aachener Strasse, a very fifties-looking establishment, with its black-and-white tiled floor, and its rather miserable-looking rubber plants on the window-seats. On the other hand, everyone adores the "XX", or "Dos Eckies" in Friesenstrasse. Its design – red plush and subdued lighting – is a reminder of its original function: it used to be a "Kontakt-Café".

The most original place to meet: Anyone keen on seeing such Cologne greats as TV personality and talkaholic Alfred Biolek having his lunch should pluck up their courage and take a trip to the "Alter Wartesaal". Since its renovation, this former dining-hall at the main station, built in 1915, is now generally regarded as the most original place to meet in all of Cologne. Actors, journalists and artists jostle for a place at the counter, and the cuisine isn't bad either, while the younger generation leaps about in the disco of the same name next door.

It's also worth visiting the "Keule", too, at the Heumarkt, the No.1 meeting-place for Cologne's VIPs. "See and be seen" is the motto here in this restaurant with its black facade; Hans Dietrich Genscher is just one of many famous names to have downed a beer here.

The man who brings the beer is called the *Köbes*.

KÖLSCH

"Kölsch", Cologne's most famous beer, has been continually breaking its own records year in, year out. The breweries that produce it are in a totally unassailable position. Where draught beers are concerned, "Kölsch" has a market share of 90 percent, and the share in the bottled beer market is 70 percent. The 24 Kölsch breweries produce around 3.5 million hectolitres a year, and Cologne has long led the rest of Germany in per capita consumption of beer, as well as having more breweries than any other city in the country.

What is Kölsch exactly? Hard to say. Gustav Hamacher had this to say about it in dialect: "*Wenn su e Jlas Kölsch vör meer steit, dann jeit meer et Hätz op. Ich striche ens üvver et Jlas, hevven et andächtich an der Mungk – un dann läuft dat Kölsch wie jeölt durch der Stroß erav en der Mage.*" ("When a glass of Kölsch stands before me, my heart gives a leap and a bound. I run my hand across the glass, lift it reverently to my mouth – and then that Kölsch flows like oil down the passage leading to my stomach.")

Once it has reached the stomach it soon meets up with several others, for Kölsch is a sociable drink. Quickly consumed, it is swiftly followed by several more, and they all foster an atmosphere of togetherness: "*Mem Nohber am Desch fängk mer ne Verzäll an, un dann wedd dat esu jemötlich, als wammer uns allt johrelang kännte.*" ("My neighbour at the table starts talking to me, and then there's this cosy feeling that we've been friends for years.")

Kölsch is an exceptionally "fast" beer; it's ready the moment the glass has been filled, unlike a "Pils", which takes seven minutes. A Kölsch is there the moment you've ordered it – and in some of the beer-halls, even before you've done so. There it is sitting in front of you the moment you've emptied your glass.

In simple terms, Kölsch can be described as follows: it is a light and slightly bitter-tasting brew, very pleasant to drink, consisting of just water, barley malt and hops, like any other Ger-

man beer in fact. But Kölsch gets its unmistakable flavour from the fact that it is "top-fermented" (fermentation takes place at a higher than normal temperature, and a special yeast is also used, which rises to the top during the fermentation process, whereas with "bottom-fermented" beers such as Pils or Export, it sinks to the bottom).

Top-fermented beer was still the most common type of beer as late as the 18th century. It was only when Carl von Linde invented refrigeration towards the end of the century that beer could be produced at a lower temperature, which at the time also meant more hygienically.

Today, the higher sensitivity of top-fermented beer no longer poses any problems due to the cleanliness of the vats and pipes. And today no one, at least in Cologne, can stop the victorious advance of Kölsch. It scarcely has anything in common with 19th-century beer, though: it tastes different (the beer of the last century was "improved" via the addition of grated nutmeg); it doesn't have the same alcohol content (in those days beer was a basic source of nourishment and contained a lot less alcohol); and 19th-century beer wasn't even called "Kölsch" either (the name only appeared a lot later, probably in the form of a secret codeword like the "Halve Hahn").

The amount of Kölsch produced annually has increased 10 times over since 1960, despite the fact that the number of breweries has actually decreased. Even though the top breweries sell their beer in bottles these days, it still tastes far better on draught. And it's at its very best when it gets brewed and consumed under the same roof. There's just one place left in Cologne where this is still possible: "Pfäffgen", on Friesenstrasse.

Back in the 19th century Cologne was still considered very much a wine city: indeed – a fact that has been forgotten – it was north-west Europe's largest wine trading city next to Bordeaux, and the most popular drink here was wine from the Moselle region. With the triumph of Kölsch, Cologne has proved once and for all that, among the other records it holds, it also boasts the oldest brewing tradition in Germany – whatever boasts the Bavarians may make.

IN THE HEART OF THE CITY

The people of Cologne tend towards sentimentality. They're aware of the fact, and aren't in the least ashamed of it. The Old City (Altstadt) may thus be defined, without further ado, as "the heart of Cologne". Not in a hectic, big-city business sense, though; rather, it's the emotional centre of the city, the part of it which gives the people of Cologne the strongest sense of "home".

The term "Altstadt" is rather confusing, anyway. Many experts think it means the area bounded by the medieval city walls in 1180. It was over 400 hectares (1,000 acres) in size, making Cologne the largest city in Europe for much of the Middle Ages. If one subtracts the areas within this walled enclave that only properly became part of the city in the 19th century, the "Old City" notion is really almost reduced to the original Roman square between the Neumarkt and the Roman Tower on the one hand, and the Cathedral and the Capitol Hill on the other.

But even that is not what today's inhabitants have in mind when they refer to the Old City. The general opinion is that the Hohe Strasse and the Schildergasse, even though they symbolise the hectic, pulsating city centre, are not part of the "Altstadt" at all. Years ago, Cologne's famous actor Willy Millowitsch once tried to sing a song in praise of the Hohe Strasse ("*Wer eimol durch die Huhe Stroß jejangen is...*") – but it never caught on. No, these consumer thoroughfares have nothing to offer when it comes to defining the city's identity, and what life in Cologne is really all about.

The heart of Cologne: The Old City only really starts just beyond the Hohe Strasse, in the direction of the Rhine. Here we see the major showpieces of the city all clustered together in one small area: the Town Hall tower with its glockenspiel and its *Platz-Jabbek* (a

grotesque 15th-century figure which sticks out its tongue every time the hour is struck), the *Kallendresser* (a rather disrespectful-looking piece of sculpture in the Old Market) and the Jan von Werth Fountain; the magnificent panorama of the city; the "Martinsviertel" (the area around Great St Martin's), with the monument to those two legendary Cologne characters, Tünnes and Schäl, and the Schmitz Column; the Hänneschen Puppet Theatre, the Ostermann Fountain and all those picturesque little alleyways, filled with restaurants and bars, where business life in Cologne likes to wind down after a long day in an atmosphere of *Gemütlichkeit*.

All these attractions have the **Old Market** (Alter Markt) as their point of reference, with its colourful houses and those magnificent glimpses one catches of the Cathedral towers between them.

It is here that the Carnival reaches both its optical and its topographical climax every year. Here, we are at the true heart of Cologne.

Left and right, the people of Cologne are known for their *joie de vivre*.

This area has twice been the "cradle" of Cologne. In Roman times, an arm of the Rhine used to branch through here. Today's "Martinsviertel" was once an island. The Romans took advantage of this and used the area as a harbour, which must doubtless have affected daily life in Cologne even then. Harbours were always very lively places, full of hard work, hard trading, with colourful goings-on and generally loose morals.

Jupp Engels, a Cologne *Jrielächer* (a dialect word meaning "rogue"), whom the "Martinsviertel" has to thank for its **Schmitz Column**, claims in the inscription on the column that Roman legionaries met up with the beautiful Ubian (i.e. Cologne) girls on the harbour island and thus became the forebears of the noble Cologne family of Schmitz (the city's commonest name).

The Roman city wall passed below the city terrace, situated higher up, and still marked today by the Town Hall tower. The Roman **Praetorium** used to stand on this terrace, too. After the Romans moved out, only its ruins were left behind. Soon afterwards a Frankish princes' court was built a short distance away, on the site of today's Cathedral. In 1959, archaeologists made a sensational find below the Cathedral: the graves of a 6th-century princess and her son, lavishly equipped and completely untouched. Today the find is one of the attractions of the **Diocesan Museum** on Roncalliplatz, which also has a valuable collection of medieval religious art on display, best accompanied, for those interested in art history, by a walk through the Cathedral and its Treasury.

The Frankish princes provided little momentum as far as developing the city was concerned, but they did pave the way for the rule of the bishops.

The Jewish Quarter: Long after the Roman Praetorium had been reduced to ruins, however, it was the Jews who kept the final remnants of civic life together. The quarter of the city in which they lived was the chief centre of

Chilling reminder of the past: cells in the basement of the El-De-Haus, former headquarters of the Cologne Gestapo.

Northern European Jewry for centuries. In the 14th century, the number of pogroms practised by the Christian City Parliament began to increase, until the Jewish Quarter was mercilessly destroyed in 1424 and its final denizens driven out of the city without compensation. It was only in 1794, when the French had taken control of Cologne after the Revolution, that Jews were allowed back in the city.

The "**Jewish Quarter**" contained a "Burghers' House" – which later became the **Town Hall** – as early as the 12th century. Its site was probably chosen with conspiratorial care, for the Jews had their own area of jurisdiction, and the archbishop was unable to simply intervene whenever he wished. As the concept of a City Parliament gained in popularity, a palace-like structure developed from the initial hotchpotch of houses; much of it survives today in the shape of the **Hansasaal**, which is definitely worth a visit.

Self-confidence: Once the City Parliament had achieved its political aims it documented its triumphant self-confidence with the construction of the magnificent **Town Hall tower** (1407–14), visible from far and wide, still very much in the style of Gothic church towers. Inside it is the **Senate Chamber**, with seating and intarsia work by Melchior von Reidt, one of the artistic masterpieces of the Rhineland.

After the pogroms of 1424 the City Parliament, without any apparent scruples, extended its political centre to include the destroyed ghetto. The **Town Hall chapel** was built on the site of the former Synagogue directly opposite the Town Hall only two years later, in 1426, and given the tell-tale name of "St Mary's in Jerusalem". Stephan Lochner created his famous **Altar of the City's Patron Saints** especially for the chapel.

Fate smiled on the old City Parliament for quite a long time: however, 350 years later Lochner's altar had to be taken to the Cathedral – where it can still be admired today – in order to protect it from the French; and World War II destroyed the Town Hall chapel almost without trace.

It was only when the rubble was cleared away that deeper historic connections were laid bare: today the remains of the **Aula Regia**, which formed part of the Roman Praetorium, can be visited beneath the Town Hall (in the newer section known as the "Spanish Building"); the Jewish Quarter and the former positions of its various buildings can be made out via markings on the paving as well as the old street-names; and a glass pyramid marks the site of an ancient Ritual Bath known as the **Mikvah**, which still has a staircase leading down into it.

Those familiar with the origins of the Town Hall will realise why its actual facade faces the Town Hall Square (Rathausplatz) and not the Old Market (Alter Markt). All the important political decisions in the Free Imperial City took place in the Town Hall, one reason why one of the finest examples of Ren-

A detail of the bronze doors Ewald Mataré designed for the cathedral's south portal.

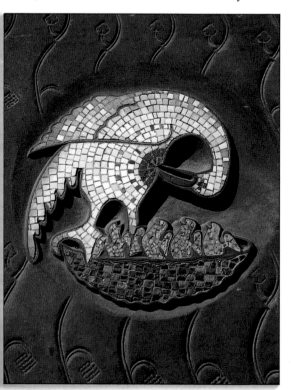

aissance architecture in all Germany can be admired here: Wilhelm Vernukken's **Loggia** (1569–73). By some miracle it was the only section of the building to survive World War II relatively unscathed. The Town Hall itself was rebuilt between 1966 and 1972 according to plans by architect Karl Band, and the tower was modelled on the old original one.

Cologne's industrial prosperity, on the other hand, began for different reasons. Its origins lie not in the Jewish Quarter but in the "Rheinvorstadt", or Rhine Suburb, the area between the old Roman walls and the river. In the 9th and 10th centuries, merchants and artisans settled on the former island, and grew extremely rich. Only one house dating from the 13th century bears witness to this period: the **Overstolzenhaus** in Rheingasse. Today it houses the recently-founded "College of Media Studies".

A trading suburb: Closer proximity to the Rhine as a natural supply route wasn't the only reason why the traders chose to settle between the old Roman city and the river; they also did so because they had turned the Rhine Suburb into their own area of jurisdiction, defying any and all encroaches by the archbishop, who had his residence in the upper part of the city. The *Schreinsbücher* of the Old City, the oldest land registers in the world, are still one of the most valuable assets of the city's archives, and have been kept uninterruptedly since the 12th century.

The former arm of the Rhine had silted up long before it was settled in medieval times. But the area contained no buildings. This link between the upper and lower part of the city became the cradle of newly-flourishing Colonia: the **Old Market** (Alter Markt). As a trading centre, it gradually supplanted the **Hay Market** (Heumarkt) further to the south, which according to reports from travellers in previous centuries used to be one of the largest and finest in Europe. Down by the Rhine lay the

The gables of the double-house "Zur Brezel" and "Zum Dorn" on the Old Market.

customs-houses and warehouses, and one of them, the **Staple House**, came to symbolise the independence of the Free Imperial City. Although only one of its towers – a later addition – survived the war, the Staple House itself has now finally been rebuilt. It forms an original addition, both in terms of its dimensions and its situation, to the line of buildings along the bank of the Rhine which, since their reconstruction, now make up one of the finest city panoramas in Europe (best appreciated from either the bridges or from the other side of the river).

Thus, not only the city's harbours but its markets, too, determined life in to-day's Old City for over a thousand years, since the 10th century. This lively and colourful mix of people – even more so than in Roman times – soon overflowed the narrow confines of the "Martinsvorstadt", which was swiftly incorporated into the city along with the former Roman boundary, and spread as far as the Neumarkt. Thus it

was that the whole area of the Roman city moved a few hundred metres in the direction of the new bank of the Rhine. The markets formed the heart of the city, and the river its main artery. And the situation remained like that all the way up to the last war.

Former focal points: The city's ancient parishes succeeded in retaining a large degree of independence for a long time, and originally even had a say in the appointment of the city's archbishops. Not much was left intact by the French and the Prussians in the 19th century, and World War II took care of the rest. There are only ruins left to remind us of the parish churches which, as former focal points, once played such an infinitely important role in the city's development: the tower of **Klein St Martin** at the "Heumarkt" tram stop; the church of St Columba, locally known as the "Madonna in the Ruins"; and Old St Alban's Church next to the Gürzenich, with its *Grieving Parents* by the artist and sculptor Käthe Kollwitz (1867–

Ewald Mataré's "Kallendresser" (gutter-defecator) squats over the Old Market.

1945), a memorial to the dead of the two World Wars. The only reminders of the former parishes of St Lawrence and St Brigida are street names.

In the ruins of Old St Alban's, by the way, one notices that the city so famous for its cheerful love of life also has an underlying awareness of suffering and injustice: the windows of the neighbouring Gürzenich, the banqueting hall where the Carnival reaches its climax, give a clear view of the ruins of Old St Alban's and of the *Grieving Parents*. The figures are actually copies, but they were created in the workshop belonging to the equally distinguished artist Ewald Mataré (1887–1965); Käthe Kollwitz considered the originals, which she created for the military cemetery in Roggevelde, Belgium, to be one of her greatest works.

And this is not the only piece of work by Käthe Kollwitz in Cologne by any means: the city contains an important collection of her art. One of Cologne's banks, the "Kreissparkasse", having

been both fortunate as well as wealthy enough to be able to do so, opened its own Käthe Kollwitz Museum in the Neumarkt quite recently. It contains what is probably the largest single collection of her graphics, and also features a few rare posters as well as several sculptures.

A memorial of horror: If this museum leaves its visitor a certain amount of room to reflect on social misery or on its portrayal in artistic form, another of the city's museum-like memorials will stun him with its reminders of human suffering as a result of merciless human cruelty: the former torture chambers in the basement of the building used as Gestapo headquarters during the "Third Reich", the so-called **El-De-Haus**, at the corner of Appellhofplatz and Elisenstrasse. No one can really say just how many people suffered and died here in these 10 cells. Twelve hundred inscriptions remain on the cell walls, hundreds of them in Cyrillic script as well as in many other European languages. Even those that are illegible still testify to the despair and suffering that has turned this place into a memorial, one from which it is all too difficult to return once more to the streets of light-hearted Cologne and its long history.

The Old City itself contains a lot of attractive details that are not simply there for show, but instead hint at deeper-lying associations. The boundaries between the mercantile "Martinsvorstadt" and the episcopal upper part of the city, between the religious foundations of the nobility and the parishes, were delineated by a complex network of regulations to which people must have been highly sensitive very early on. One instance of this has to be the **"Kallendresser"** figure up on the wall of house number 24, "Em Hanen", in the Old Market. Translated, this word actually means "the gutter-defecator", and the figure can be seen pointing its naked rear end at the square.

Of the many explanations in circulation as to the origins of this figure, the

Left, street performers. Right, these horses' heads are the subject of a popular Cologne legend.

one that comes nearest the truth is the one that treats it as an expression of civic protest. Legend has it that during the Middle Ages, a thief once took refuge from his municipal pursuers in Great St Martin's Abbey. The abbot there did not, however, grant him asylum under the law of that time, but instead handed him over to the patrician municipal council, whereupon the citizens of the Old City protested, both against the secular authorities and against the priests of Great St Martin's – at first via a rude gesture which then probably slowly fossilised into this small statue on the facade.

The fact that the old **Platz-Jabbeck** (derived from the verb *japsen*, meaning to gasp for air), under the clock on the Town Hall tower directly opposite, sticks its tongue out at the Kallendresser each time the hour is struck may just be coincidence, but there again one shouldn't put anything past the people of Cologne, then or now.

The original stone statue of the Kallendresser was lost beneath the rubble of World War II. When Jupp Engels, the "Jrielächer" mentioned earlier, rebuilt his "Em Hanen" house in the 1960s, he had the figure redone in bronze by Ewald Mataré. By the way, house number 24 itself is a listed building, certainly worth seeing for its consistent application of *Bauhaus* principles. Its external features (Kallendresser on the gable, mosaic above the main doorway, bronze plating along the pavement, grille and entryway at the rear next to Great St Martin's) are all the work of Ewald Mataré, whose most famous works include the bronze doors of the Gürzenich and those of the Cathedral's south portal.

Typical Cologne characters: The "Martinsviertel" and the city as a whole also have Jupp Engels to thank for his **statues of Tünnes and Schäl**. These figures, the work of sculptor Werner Reuter, are also among the most-photographed sights of the Old City. The statues refer to two puppets that origi-

nated in the 19th century, in the Hänneschen Theatre two blocks away.

Tünnes is a farm labourer from one of the farms that could still be found within the large city walls at the beginning of the 19th century. He can be recognised by his rural clothing, and particularly by his wooden clogs. His nose is unusually large and reddened by alcohol, and his red hair falls straight down. Schäl, taller and more gaunt altogether, is the epitome of elegance with his bow-tie and hat. He joined Tünnes only in the middle of the 19th century, and he symbolizes the city element which gradually took the place of the rural way of life in Cologne during those years. The feature of Schäl that strikes you immediately is his squint, which makes him look rather sly and is quite in character with him, in contrast to the harmless and amiable expression of his companion.

Another popular expression of collective identity is the statue of **Jan von Werth** on his fountain in the Old Market. Here, history and legend combine to produce a heart-rending story. First of all the historical side: the real Jan von Werth was a farmer's boy from the area around Neuss, who succeeded in becoming a famous mercenary leader and cavalry general during the Thirty Years' War. Cologne had him to thank for saving it from destruction, and acclaimed him as a war hero in the 1630s. The **Municipal Museum**, which after World War II was shifted to the medieval Arsenal on the street known as An der Burgmauer (north of the Roman wall), still has some of his original possessions on display.

The Legend of Jan and Jriet: The legend tells us more than the history books: apparently while still a young man, Jan von Werth once worked as a labourer on a farm near Cologne, and courted a pretty maid named Jriet (short for Margaret). She rejected his advances because she wanted to marry a rich farmer instead, whereupon he went off to war and made his fortune. Apparently they saw one another again as he was

THE CITY OF TOMORROW

After World War II, during which 85 percent of the city centre was destroyed, Cologne regained its identity only relatively late as city planners finally worked out their vision of the future. For a long time, the planners wandered aimlessly through a thicket of "pressing needs" and "functional requirements". They left the Heumarkt behind as a testimonial to just how confused they were. Here, one of the city's finest squares was mercilessly squandered on road traffic.

It was only in the 1970s that people began to realise that a city structure that had taken centuries to develop could not suit absolutely every modern traffic requirement, and that culture and commerce could actually co-exist quite happily. "A proper balance of the city's functions" has been the watchword of the city planners since then.

And their plans have worked, too. Despite the fact that Cologne is becoming increasingly prone to traffic congestion, more and more people are streaming into the city; despite the increasing number of shopping areas and recreation areas that are closed to traffic, business is really booming; and despite a strong concentration of "business" in the city centre, it still has 133,000 inhabitants – most of whom really enjoy living there.

The people of Cologne readily seize upon any excuse for a festival, and highlights in city planning over the past 10 years have provided ample opportunity: there was the restoration of the Romanesque churches, the redevelopment of much of the "Ring" system, the opening of several brand-new shopping arcades and above all, the redevelopment of the Old City (Altstadt). The focal point of all the efforts made here was the Cathedral/Rhine area with its museums, the Philharmonie and also the Rhine Gardens: the busy Uferstrasse was moved to a tunnel underneath them, at a cost of DM 120 million, which means that one can now take an unhindered stroll yet again between the Old City and the river, just like the good old days.

Work on the outward appearance of the city centre has not been completed yet, however. As a result of the general increase in traffic, the central U-Bahn network is having to be extended, and the area around the main station, as well as the Neumarkt, need basic redevelopment work too. Major traffic arteries, such as the "Nord-Süd-Fahrt" between the Schildergasse and the WDR, are to disappear inside underground tunnels.

A whole new section of the city has recently been under construction: the new "Media Park", on the site of the former Gereon freight depot. The aim behind this ambitious project is to secure for Cologne a key role in the fast-developing fields of information and communication technologies, while simultaneously contributing towards further revitalising the Inner City.

Two more highly promising projects are the redevelopment of the Heumarkt, and also of the city's harbour area. A cultural centre is planned for the site, one that will fulfil the expectations of the many artists living in the Südstadt section of the city, and that will also contain two new Cologne attractions: a "German Sports Museum" and a Transport Museum.

In the Heumarkt, the new building housing the Rautenstrauch-Joest Museum of ethnology is to fill the last remaining gap in the Old City panorama. The museum building will be constructed at the head of the Deutz Bridge, thus forming a link with the Heumarkt. The plans are the result of work by architect Gottfried Böhm. The new museum, with its 45-metre (150-ft) high tower above the ramp leading to the bridge, will provide the city with a whole new look.

The Heumarkt, too, is to be given a facelift. Gottfried Böhm has drawn up plans for this, too, and they include moving the traffic underground and putting a market back in the square – a solution to please motorists *and* pedestrians. After that, most of the damage Cologne sustained during World War II – apart from the area in front of the Town Hall, for which no plans exist as yet – will have been removed.

Considering the city's financial situation, though, it's still not certain whether these expensive plans can be realised. These visions of a more attractive Cologne may remain just that: visions, and nothing more.

being proclaimed a hero; she was still poor, and he said to her: "*Wer es getan hätte!*" ("If only you had married me, Jriet!"). She answered, quick as a flash: "*If only I'd known!*"

This famous Cologne scene has been immortalised in the relief beneath the statue, and also forms the basis of the annual Carnival play *Jan and Jriet,* performed on "Weiberfastnacht" (the Thursday prior to the seventh Sunday before Easter) by "Jan von Werth's Cavalry Troop" at St Severinus's Gate (Severinstor) in the Südstadt.

In 1884, a problem the city had been having with its identity ever since it had become Prussian in 1815 finally rose to the surface. The former Free Imperial City of the West was Catholic, but had now ended up under the authoritarian control of the Protestant state from the East. This naturally brought several economic advantages along with it, but unfortunately it also led to continual clashes in which Cologne's particular idiosyncrasies – above all Catholicism and the Carnival – became more and more pronounced.

In 1855, when a mayor of Cologne suggested that an equestrian statue should be erected in the Old Market in honour of the king during whose reign the city had been taken over by Prussia, the Roman-Catholic opposition became incensed, and immediately applied for permission to erect a column dedicated to the Virgin Mary in the Old Market instead. The Mother of God's Immaculate Conception had been made an article of faith in Rome only a short time beforehand.

A typical Cologne solution: Hefty disputes ensued, and it was actually decades later that a typical Cologne solution was finally devised: the **Column dedicated to the Virgin Mary** was erected in front of the archbishop's residence in Gereonsstrasse, where it can still be seen today; and the **equestrian statue** of Prussian king Frederick William III was erected in the Heumarkt in 1878 – and yet again in

1990 after its destruction in World War II. And in order to protect the valuable site at the "heart" of Cologne from any future intrusions, the decision was made to place the statue of Jan von Werth in the Old Market.

Another of Cologne's many legends has also been rendered in stone, in the shape of the two horses' heads visible on an old tower in the Neumarkt. Since every child always asks about them, just about everyone in Cologne now knows the legend of "**Richmodis of Aducht**". She was a woman who apparently died of the plague at an early age. However she had only been in a state of suspended animation, and at night she came back home and knocked on the door. When the butler brought the news to her grief-stricken husband, the latter is meant to have said that he thought it more likely that his horses would climb the steep staircase to his house than his wife would come back alive from the cemetery. Whereupon the horses actually did come up the stairs. Then he

Left, resting the legs after the bustle of the Schildergasse. **Right**, the statues of Tünnes and Schäl are among the most-photographed sights of the Old City.

believed it, ran to the door and put his arms round his wife, with whom he spent many more happy years.

One of the old buildings that has remained a firm favourite with the people of Cologne is the **Gürzenich**. The City Parliament built it here around the year 1440 as a "dancing-house". This is where the great banquets used to take place when emperors – the Holy Roman ones as well as the Prussian rulers many years later – were visiting the city. It is here that the proclamation of the Carnival "Prince" still takes place annually. In the 19th century, the Gürzenich was also turned into a concert hall, which is how the Gürzenich Orchestra got its name; and it has retained it, too, despite its move to the new Philharmonie next to the Cathedral in 1986.

Redevelopment of the Old City: The entire Old City, and not just the Gürzenich, has had quite a bit of redevelopment work done on it in the past. The most important restructuring activity took place in the 1930s, when new

squares were laid out. The Hänneschen Puppet Theatre was moved to the newly-created Eisenmarkt, and the **Ostermannplatz** received its large **fountain** with its stone figures immortalising the archetypal Cologne characters from the songs of Willi Ostermann (1876–1936), the city's most famous songwriter.

Back in the 1930s, the city's Rings, and its suburbs of Lindenthal, Rodenkirchen and Marienburg were already among the more desirable places to live for the middle classes. The Old City trod the thin line between popularity and social decline. And even after the almost total destruction wrought by the war and the subsequent reconstruction work, things didn't really get much better. Hardly anything was done to make the area any more useful or attractive. It was only in the early 1970s that a new generation began to rediscover the special attraction of the Old City.

Restaurants began to make use of the historic backdrop it provided. By the time the city planners decided they wanted to replace the rubble-strewn area around Great St Martin's with a large multi-storey car park, people had become so fond of the Old City that there was a wave of popular protest. The plans were thus altered, and one of the most delightful and internationally acclaimed inner-city residential areas in Germany was created instead: the **Martinsviertel**.

Old Cologne was thus gradually resurrected. The redevelopment work reached its peak in 1986 when the busy Uferstrasse was moved into an underground tunnel, the Rhine Gardens were laid out anew and the new complex containing the museums and the Philharmonie was opened next to the Cathedral. Since then, for natives of Cologne just as for visitors, even though the Old City's two-thousand-year history is really only fully documented in museums, it can always be experienced any day, and the citizens' emotional life has found a focal point once more.

Left, steps lead down to the Mikvah, or Jewish ritual bath, near the town hall. Right, witness to medieval prosperity: the Overstolzenhaus dates from the 13th century.

COLOGNE'S ANCIENT DISTRICTS

If Cologne draws most of its identity from its historic Old City (Altstadt), then the Cologne way of life and its unique qualities are primarily to be found in the so-called "Veedeln" (dialect form of the German word *Viertel*, meaning "districts") which form several circles around the Old City. The translation of the word simply as "districts", however, conveys very little of its real significance, and of the associations it evokes in its dialect form: it conjures up a sense of neighbourly belonging, a close-knit feeling of "one big, happy family", and it also conveys a sense of community not only as far as local life and local welfare are concerned, but also embracing beliefs and even destiny.

Life in the "Veedeln": Most of the "Veedeln" in Cologne were destroyed in World War II. What remains of them can hardly be traced to where the old streets used to run, but has instead survived in so-called "Veedel clubs" which were all founded back in the 1940s and 1950s, and whose members often live in widely separate parts of the city. Onlookers can get a good impression of them when they take part in the *Schull-und Veedelszöch* procession on Carnival Sunday.

The "Veedeln" that have been revived, and which are being celebrated today may be based to a certain extent on their historic forerunners, but in most respects they are a new development, dating from the 1970s or so. Since that time, the "Veedeln" have come to life again, and are developing their peculiar powers of integration, giving people a sense of belonging and giving Cologne – quite independent of the gloss of its Old City – that everyday, cosy, homely feel that ties people so strongly to their native city.

Absolutely typical "Veedeln" today are the "Vringsveedel" and the "Eigel-steinveedel". The former begins in front of the Roman southern gate, the "Hohe Pforte" at the Waidmarkt, and its name is derived from the early Christian bishop St Severinus, known in Cologne dialect as "Zinter Vring". The latter, the "Eigelsteinveedel", at the other end of the Hohe Strasse, gets its name from the eagle, a symbol of Roman domination, which used to mark the military road in front of the city's ancient northern gate.

Both "Veedeln" have several features in common: both are grouped around the former arterial roads of Roman Cologne, which today are among the liveliest, flashiest and yet still reasonably-priced supply centres of the city; both are bordered by the mighty gates of the medieval city wall which have been preserved to this day; both still contain monasteries that are still intact; both contain several Romanesque churches; both still have highly active Catholic communities, which celebrate their popular *Kirmesse* (fairs) every summer according to an ages-old, fixed tradition; and both of them are home to the oldest forms of Carnival celebration.

A mixed population: Alongside the "qualified minority" of old-established inhabitants here, there are also a lot of newcomers: the majority of them are foreigners, but there are also alternatives and artists, rich and poor, workers and intellectuals, famous people and not-so-famous people, believers and atheists, upright citizens and also several dubious individuals for whom the Cologne dialect has several drastic-sounding names. A distinctive feature of this community, however, is that the people here are all one colourful mix and that no one group dominates at the expense of the others; there's an admirable measure of mutual tolerance.

The topographical as well as emotional centre of any and all "Veedeln" is – as it has always been – a church. In the "Vringsveedel", this applies to **St Severinus's**, **St George's**, **St Mary's in Lyskirchen** and the **Church of St John the Baptist** (known as "Zint Jan"

A smile from Cologne city.

in Cologne dialect), and in the "Eigel-steinveedel", to **St Cunibert's** and **St Ursula's**. Even though the old popular piety has been somewhat diluted by secular developments these days, people do still go to these venerable churches for family celebrations and feast days, and continue to treat them with much familiarity; the heart of many an atheist has been known to beat faster at the magnificent sight of the procession of *heilije Knäächte un Mägde* ("holy farm hands and maids") at St Mary's in Lyskirchen.

These remnants of folklore within the city are clues to the strong traditions that the "Veedeln" still thrive on. From 1180 to 1815 there used to be a large rural area between the boundaries of the Roman city and the oversized medieval wall. This resulted in an unusual phenomenon: many farmers actually farmed within the city itself. They did not live in closed-off, conservative village communities, but instead in (relatively) broad-minded parishes, and were or-ganised into special unions, too, known as "Bauernbänke". They were therefore far more inclined to treat the city-dwellers, rather than the inhabitants of the surrounding rural areas, as their brothers.

Successful assimilation: As the 19th century progressed, industrial development began to spread across the fields: factories sprang up, and commercial enterprises were extended. This in turn swelled the ranks of the workforce, and during the course of only three generations, a massive population explosion took place, with the city gradually becoming more and more overcrowded.

Meanwhile, the original farming population had to assimilate a whole new social class made up of workers, with all the issues that entailed. The social misery that followed hot on the heels of this development, the cramped living conditions that forced many people to resort to refined techniques of survival, and group solidarity in the face of the unwelcome Prussian authorities

Left, the Ulre Gate (Ulrepforte), home of the "Red Sparks". **Right**, the Hahnen Gate on Rudolf-platz.

all combined to produce a remarkable human bond between people as they experienced joy and suffering together, helped one another or fell victim to baseness, dreamed sentimental dreams or had to learn to be tough to survive; and all of this has left its mark on the character of the city's "Veedeln" – on their dialect, their cuisine and their customs. Whatever its drawbacks, though, the assimilation has succeeded.

Love of life and a taste for festivals: The **"Stollwerck Girl"**, a statue by Sepp Hürten that has been standing at the fountain in front of St Severinus's Church since 1989, is a present-day reminder of this historical background. Stollwerck was once world-famous for its sweets and chocolates, and is still a big name in the business today.

In the second half of the 19th century, the Stollwercks built their factory in the "Vringsveedel", providing work and bread for the population. And since good capitalist exploitation of human labour went very much hand in hand with a patriarchal attitude where social and cultural welfare were concerned, the "Vringsveedel" found itself a lot better off than other sections of the city. The Stollwerck "upper crust" – as the firm's workers were referred to – radiated a straightforward love of life, an attitude that is still typical of the "Vringsveedel" today. It is here, on Carnival Sunday and on the Monday before Lent, that the city's Carnival reaches its climax.

The **Berbuer Fountain** opposite "Zint Jan" also testifies to the city's love of life and its taste for festivals. Karl Berbuer (1900–77) was Cologne's most important 20th-century songwriter, and gave a convincing account in his songs of life as seen through the eyes of the simple man in the street. His most famous one was the "Trizonesien Song", a cabaretist's comment on the situation facing the inhabitants of the three post-war occupied zones in West Germany. The song was even occasionally played as a substitute for the na-

Left, fruit seller in the Weidengasse. **Right**, detail of the famous Stollwerck chocolate factory.

tional anthem – because the state did not yet exist. Artist Bonifatius Stirnberg has decorated the fountain with motifs based on Berbuer's songs.

Distinctive-looking buildings: Despite having sustained much wartime damage, the "Vringsveedel" still retains several distinctive-looking buildings. The church and the gate have already been mentioned. Just in front of them is the **Balchem House** (Haus Balchem), Cologne's finest surviving Baroque mansion, with its picturesque oriel window. Halfway towards the Rhine, the **Bottmühle**, one of the four windmills built on the city walls in the 16th century, also provides a romantic sight; and right down by the harbour, the wall's southernmost corner tower, the **Bayentürm**, has been undergoing restoration work.

In the other direction, at the other end of the "Veedel", the **Ulre Gate** (Ulreporte) is also a picturesque sight. This old tower, once part of the city wall, is today the home of the descendants of the old city guard, the "Red Sparks", who have survived as a Carnival association. Between this tower and St Severinus's Gate (Severinstor), there is an impressive-looking assortment of sacred buildings on the site of the former Carthusian monastery, today serving as the administration centre of the city's Protestant community.

The "Vringsveedel" hasn't lost a trace of its vitality – despite the destruction wrought by the war, despite the fact that Stollwerck has now shifted into a brand-new, fully-automated factory out in the countryside, and despite the fact that the area experienced an enormous amount of redevelopment during the 1980s. The many bars which have survived in the area, however, bear eloquent witness to the close bond between life and pleasure here.

And the "Vringsveedel" has also been enriched by artists who have settled in the former "Cologne factory schools" area on the Ubier Ring during the last few decades. **St Severinus's**

Street festival and flea market in Severinsstrasse.

**Below,
Balchem
House,
Cologne's
best-
preserved
baroque
building.
Following
pages: St
Severinus's
Gate.**

Gate, which once marked the boundary of the "Vringsveedel", has thus become the centre of a new, extended "Veedel" which now includes quite a large chunk of the Bonner Strasse (i.e. the New Town): the Südstadt. The artists' dives and specialist restaurants in this area are even more popular with the people of Cologne than the various gastronomic experiences on offer in the Old City.

The Südstadt area is also a modern-day example of the integrating power that the former "Veedeln" used to have: many foreigners live here, and they have not only introduced a whole new range of goods and food to the city – their children also speak Cologne dialect, and they enjoy celebrating Carnival too. The city's traditional life is thus being carried on in new ways. Another example is the rock-group BAP, which became world-famous with its songs in Cologne dialect.

Flashpoints: Not quite as special as the "Vringsveedel", though just as lively, is the "Eigelsteinveedel". This area was a lot more miserable than the "Vringsveedel" during the 19th century, and social flashpoints developed which even today haven't quite been completely eliminated. The **Stavenhof** near the Eigelstein Gate once used to be a red-light district, and was not the subject of any polite discussion in the city until comparatively recently.

The trends of the times haven't been as kind to the "Eigelsteinveedel" as they have to the "Vringsveedel", either. The war destroyed as much on the outside as the aggressively ambitious Federal German mentality has on the inside; modern traffic, in the shape of numerous dual carriageways and railways, has carved up this formerly large "Veedel" quite a bit.

Large numbers of foreigners have filled the ensuing social vacuum, so much so that here – in the Weidengasse, for example – the concentration of Turkish inhabitants has reached almost ghetto-like proportions. They are valued by many of the locals, however,

because the food they provide has enriched the choice available to gourmets in the city. Others are afraid of the area, though, because Mediterranean male pride is easily injured, and problems here tend to get resolved permanently with the aid of knives and guns.

As far as buildings are concerned, it very much resembles the "Vringsveedel": Romanesque churches, the old City Gate, the **Weckschnapp**, a tower built into a house down by the Rhine, at the end of the old city wall; and at its centre, rather than drawings and paintings, it has music. The **State College of Music** is an important institution, even if its oversized dimensions have been plonked right in the middle of what once used to be an area full of small-scale workers' tenement buildings. One place definitely worth seeing is the **Ursuline Monastery Church** in Machabäerstrasse, a secondary school for girls founded by the Ursulines.

A picturesque backdrop: Despite its rather depressing history, much of the urbane charm of the "Eigelsteinveedel" has been rediscovered recently. It has provided a picturesque backdrop for many films – and detective films in particular. Redevelopment work is making visible progress here, too. The "Veedel" is once again in great demand as a place to live in the city, and a lot of the pubs here are a private tip for those in the know. Like the "Vringsveedel", the "Eigelsteinveedel", too, has already spread beyond its original borders: directly on the other side of the Ring, the equally lively "Agnesveedel" begins, with the Church of St Agnes, the second largest in Cologne, at its centre.

Just two of the city's most representative "Veedeln" have been described here. Anyone interested in them will certainly be able to find more. There's something rather jungle-like about them, which means it's a good idea to find someone who actually lives in one to show you around.

Fresh vegetables for sale.

THE RHINE

"To the north of Bonn, where the Rhine flows out of the narrow hills into the plain, it widens considerably as it rolls past frightened villages, threatening even Cologne, its secret queen" – thus did Heinrich Böll ruminate on the river upon whose left bank the Roman general Agrippa resettled the Germanic tribe of the Ubii more than 2,000 years ago, thereby laying the foundations of Colonia Agrippinensis, today's Cologne. The mighty river Rhine, 400 metres (1,300 ft) wide at this point, flows in a gradual arc up from the south and through the city, leaving it only 40 km (25 miles) further north.

Rather disrespectfully, the river here divides its "secret queen" into two different parts, which have never really made friends with one another. Traditionally, the left bank feels it is the "wahre Kölle" ("true Cologne") and looks across at the right bank, which it refers to by the rather nasty-sounding name of "Schäl Sick", with some degree of sympathy. Some of the sections of the city on the right bank, though, such as Deutz or Mülheim – once independent towns in their own right and retaining many individual features, despite having been incorporated into Cologne with its population of almost one million – look on their neighbours from the other side of the great river with a certain degree of condescension.

For centuries, only one ferry service connected the two sides of the river. Today, between Cologne-Rodenkirchen and Cologne-Merkenich, there are eight bridges. The first permanent bridge across the Rhine was only built as late as 1859, on the site of today's **Hohenzollern Bridge** between Cologne-Deutz and the main railway station. The high trussed arches of Germany's most often-used railway bridge can be seen from far and wide, and the trains come out of the darkness of the station straight onto the bridge. Pedestrians have to content themselves with a narrow walkway. The **Süd Bridge**, which also has impressive arches, is reserved for rail traffic too, while the **Rodenkirchen Bridge**, and the **Leverkusen Bridge** which was built in 1965 are both motorway bridges. Most impressive of all, though, is doubtless the **Zoo Bridge**, built in 1966, the most recent as well as the longest (1,300 metres/4,200 ft) of all the eight bridges. Designed by Gerd Lohmer, this bold, box-girder construction held up by heavy cables seems to be hovering above the water.

The pedestrians' favourite, however, is probably the **Deutz Bridge** leading from Cologne-Deutz directly into the Old City (Altstadt). Originally, it was meant to be a suspension bridge, but World War II robbed it of that honour. Instead it was resurrected between 1947 and 1948 as a plate girder bridge with box-girders, over 400 metres (1,300 ft) in length. From here, one gets what is easily the best view of the left bank of the Rhine: the narrow houses of the Old City in the foreground, and behind them the pointed silhouette of the Cathedral and the massive towers of Great St Martin's church.

On New Year's Eve thousands of the city's inhabitants congregate here on this gently sloping bridge to see in the New Year with plenty of fireworks: a festival which has long since become a Cologne institution.

Heinrich Böll called the Rhine "both filthy and majestic". River traffic never stops in Cologne. Up to 300 ships pass the city every 24 hours, and traffic on the river is only stopped when the water level is too high. Around 4½ million tons of goods are handled annually in Cologne's five harbours – oil and petrol in the **Niehl II** oil terminus, general and bulk cargo at Niehl I, Cologne-Mülheim, Cologne-Deutz and the **Rheinau Harbour** opposite.

The people of Cologne refer to their river affectionately as "Father Rhine", and it plays an important role in their

Preceding pages: the Rhine is Europe's busiest waterway. **Left,** making fast: a statue in the harbour area. **Following pages:** pleasure cruise on the Rhine.

lives. There is scarcely a single person in Cologne who has not spent at least one hot summer afternoon in the **Rhine Gardens** between the Hohenzollern and Deutz bridges. This long-neglected area at the foot of the Old City was transformed only a short while ago into an attractive park, with flower borders, trees and bizarre-looking fountains. Broad flights of steps lead up to Heinrich-Böll-Platz and to the ultra-modern Wallraf-Richartz Museum/ Ludwig Museum complex, while enticingly narrow alleyways lead off into the Old City.

Another attractive place for a stroll is along the river-bank in the chic suburb of Rodenkirchen, a few kilometres upriver. There are also several restaurant-ships on the river, the best of which is the *Alte Liebe*, as well as a large number of restaurants and bars along the river bank with their inviting terraces affording fine views of the Rhine.

The best way of discovering Cologne from the river is to take a trip on one of the "Köln-Düsseldorfer" excursion boats. The boat known as the *MS Domspatz*, based at the Frankenwerft (the embankment by the Old City between the Deutz and Hohenzollern bridges), also does hour-long trips, several times a day, from April onwards. First it goes past the houses in the Old City and the tall buildings of the Rheinau Harbour, then under the Süd Bridge and along the length of the Oberlander shipyard, and all the way up to the Rodenkirchen Bridge, where it does a huge turn. The way back leads past the meadows and fields of the right bank, past the vast Rhine Park and as far as the Mülheim Bridge, where the *Domspatz* then makes another turn.

There are also "coffee cruises" that go further upriver as far as Porz, and take roughly two and a half hours: they leave from the Frankenwerft every afternoon at 3.30 p.m. And during the journey, the loudspeakers on board keep booming out the famous song *"Warum ist es am Rhein so schön?"*

COLOGNE'S
NEW TOWN

In the 1870s, Cologne was on the point of bursting out of its tight girdle of medieval walls. Just how crowded the city had become is clear from the statistics: in 1870 there were 345 people per hectare of land in Cologne. In Paris at that time there were more than 100 fewer, and in London the figure was 96 – not even a third.

A century of expansion: Cramped living conditions are by no means foreign to the Cologne lifestyle. But those who wanted to live well, and who thought ahead, were forced to expand – and it was a century of expansion. The city's time-honoured wall stood in the way, however, and eventually, it fell – the victim of extensive town-planning and an accompanying lack of insight into the significance of a monument that was unique in all Germany. All that was spared were a few grandiose gates.

There again, only two decades later the people of Cologne – who had all previously been in favour of the wall being removed in order to usher in a supposedly better, more open and freer future for their city – were already ruefully singing the praises of the "*ahl schön Stadtmur*" (fine old city wall) they had sacrificed to the ideal of progress.

But once it had been removed there was certainly a lot more space, for the area that had previously been occupied by the wall was now turned into a broad boulevard called the **Ringstrasse**, with trees and colourful flowers. Starting off as the Ubierring in the south, the "Ring" extends in a broad arc around the Old City today just as it did then.

The city's rings have historical names: first there is the Karolinger Ring, followed by the Sachsen, Salier and Hohenstaufen Rings. Then the Habsburg and Hohenzollern Rings lead on to the Kaiser Wilhelm Ring, which forms a transition to the Hansa Ring and the Theodor Heuss Ring (formerly the Deutscher Ring).

The city's new Ring of those days was only the beginning, and today it is still the most obvious symbol of the expanding city of Cologne during the 1880s and 1890s. For since that time, the New Town (Neustadt), the first ever thoroughly-planned urban extension on German soil, has been nestling close by the "Ring". Joseph Stübben was the chief architect behind the New Town area, which lay like a broad belt around the city's old medieval core.

Whether the much-vaunted "chain of festive spaces", made up of streets, squares, apartment blocks and fountains, ever became reality, or whether it ever has to this day, is doubtful. Not all that much is "festive" these days between the northern and southern part of the Rhine, the Rings and the inner "Green Belt" with its railway ring. But the region is lively all the same, with its active "Kwartier Lateng" between the city centre and the university, its innumerable

Preceding pages: a work of art: hydrokinetic sculpture on the Ebertplatz. **Left,** taking in the sun. **Right,** St Agnes, the second largest church in Cologne.

private theatres and art galleries, discotheques and pubs, and last but not least, its two parks: the People's Gardens (Volksgarten) and the Municipal Gardens (Stadtgarten).

A home from home, out-of-doors: The **People's Gardens** aren't all that large, nor are they what one would usually call "elegant", though of course that doesn't mean they're "vulgar" at all either. It's just that people here do whatever they want: in the company of their families, over a drink, out in a boat, playing out on the meadows or breaking open their *Pittermännchen* (small beer barrels) beside the pond. In brief, the place smells of Eau de Cologne and dogs, and contains a mixture of Cologne's young, would-be yuppies and people from the "Vringsveedel", students and tramps, all of them peacefully coexisting in a small area.

The idea of these gardens glowing with health and being a fine example of a well-kept municipal park is one that nobody would ever seriously entertain –

and therein, perhaps, lies their charm and the secret of their success.

Joseph Stübben described the gardens while they were still being laid out in 1888: "This area, almost rectangular in shape, is 590 metres (2,000 ft) in length, 285 metres (900 ft) wide with a total surface area of 15.3 hectares (38 acres)." The gardens contained all the best features of parks laid out in the 1880s: a place where beer was served, a children's playground, a rose garden, and the groundwater level was also artificially raised so that it seemed to be gushing out of a grotto and flowing into a pond.

These days the gardens still contain the pond, the fountain, the playground and the place that serves beer. However, the racetrack, the concert hall beside the restaurant and the ice rink have long since vanished. The fine street that runs north-east of the People's Gardens, and which contains some of the finest examples of buildings dating from the *Gründerzeit* (the period of rapid indus-

Newly redeveloped, the city's "Rings" are once again an inviting place for a stroll.

trial expansion at the end of the 19th century) is named after the gardens: the "Volksgartenstrasse".

What the People's Gardens are to the south-western part of the New Town, the **Municipal Gardens** (Stadtgarten) are to the north-western section of it. In fact they are and they aren't: they're smaller, closer to the least industrialised section of the Ring system and the Old City, and also a great deal older than their Südstadt counterpart, the People's Gardens. The Municipal Gardens were out in front of the city walls 50 years before Stübben's plans were drawn up. Originally planned as a nursery, they were enlarged in 1865 before being cut back by more than 50 percent in the 1880s to make way for the planned railway.

Cool and cosmopolitan: The gardens were given a facelift and totally altered at the same time, and with the addition of a new restaurant – on the Venloer Strasse side – they also gained some cosmopolitan flair. This is even more true today, because ever since the "Kölner Jazzhaus" began here – between the railway, Venloer Strasse and Spicher Strasse – the atmosphere's been cool and highly international.

On 22 April 1882, the foundation stone for the first house in the New Town was laid, at No. 60 (today No. 58), Hohenzollern Ring. This Ring later became a magnificent boulevard, then after the war it deteriorated into a cinema, fast-food and junk-shop area; it was only at the end of the 1980s that the whole region, which had seen its first house (of what would eventually be a total of 4,000) completed only 100 years previously, was reasonably spruced up once more.

If the area's construction was unique over a century ago, so was its destruction during – as well as after – World War II. One quarter of the buildings were destroyed in the bombings, and just as many were destroyed by the pickaxes of enthusiastic property developers in the 1950s and 1960s. The stucco

A popular meeting-place in the New Town: the municipal gardens.

on the facades was all too often smashed, and figures and projections vanished – along with much of the character of this part of the city.

Nevertheless, over 2,200 of the original buildings are still standing, and what remains still gives one a good impression of what the New Town must originally have looked like.

New Town Renaissance: Had the 1970s not witnessed a reappraisal of the architectural achievements of the "Gründerzeit", Stübben's work might have been further "modernised" out of all recognition. But after having been long scorned, if not rejected out of hand by modernism, the old buildings changed for the better again and their "Renaissance" began.

Stucco was in demand once more, the facades were painted new colours, and came to life. And it hasn't stopped since. These days, many sections of the New Town contain magnificent town houses – especially those in the west, in what was once called the "west end" – that

look much as they did at the turn of the century when the area to the north and the south of the New Town, near the Rhine, was still very much the home of "upright citizens". In between, in the south-west and north-west, the atmosphere was a good deal rougher, and the buildings were more modest – these areas were mostly populated by working-class people.

There's one thing Stübben would never have suspected back then, though: the university, which was later built away to the west, directly behind the railway line and thus outside the New Town, has given the area its own very special "student" flavour.

The most unusual and original pubs in the city can be found here around Zülpicher Platz and Zülpicher Strasse, between the Ring and the railway. You can find everything here, from every conceivable kind of pub, serving all manner of food, to beer halls that offer a lot more than just Kölsch; from student bars filled with deafening heavy

Left, the "Colonius" telecommunications tower. Right, the synagogue on Roonstrasse.

metal music all the way to "in" discos. Anyone who considers Cologne a lively place must have paid at least one visit to the "**Kwartier Lateng**".

Right at the centre of the student area lies Walter Bockmayer's "Filmdose", a fun pub which also shows films. Indeed, most of the city's innumerable free theatres and miniature cabarets can be found here in the New Town.

Good food, good art, good pubs: The New Town is more than just an attractive collection of late 19th-century buildings between the eastern, medieval, Cathedral section of the city on the one hand and the western, "Green Belt", suburban section on the other. It also contains numerous art galleries, which have made Cologne the artistic metropolis it is today.

But is the New Town stylistically coherent? – it was designed by one man, after all, and completed within 20 years. Hardly: even Stübben had to make compromises, and World War II as well as the post-war period left deep scars. It was only at the end of the 1980s that streets like Volksgartenstrasse and Moltkestrasse were once again transformed into avenues that were to some extent worthy of their name. And the Ring itself, run-down and sacrificed to traffic long since, is also more reminiscent now of the magnificent boulevard it once used to be – especially along the 2-km section between Kaiser Wilhelm Ring and Barbarossa Platz, with its shops, banks, cinema and pubs. Traffic-free zones have also gone some way towards restoring some of the area's former dignity.

But a lot of scars still remain, many of them deep: the Aachener Strasse and the Richard Wagner Strasse, for instance, the roads leading to and from the western part of the city, have degenerated into overcrowded traffic arteries. To sum up the problem, it is the squares, avenues and open spaces that have suffered the most. It's a painful realisation, and one that is not only true of Cologne and its New Town.

Curious shop-window display in a side-street.

EXCURSIONS ON THE LEFT BANK

As far as most tourists are concerned, Cologne is generally limited to the area between the Rhine and the Ring, though perhaps the New Town (Neustadt) area, and Deutz on the right bank of the Rhine also receive a certain amount of attention as well. Nevertheless, there's also a lot to be discovered in Nippes and Ehrenfeld, and in Lindenthal and Rodenkirchen too.

Riehl-Niehl-Nippes: One of the biggest attractions on the left bank of the river, outside the city centre, is the **Cologne Zoo**. Founded in 1860, it is the third oldest zoo in Germany. Despite heavy bombardment during World War II, some of its former buildings have still survived: the elephant house, built in the "Moorish" style, dates back to when the zoo was founded. Around 1880, the cattle house was erected in log-cabin style, and the "South American House", modelled on the city's Russian church, was built in 1899. In 1914, the huge island for the apes was built, and even at that time, modern methods of animal-keeping were being applied: first of all, lemurs were successfully bred, and only recently, a modern house for primates was opened. Another big attraction is the aquarium, which contains not only exotic species of fish but insects as well.

If you cross the old Stammheimer Strasse you reach the so-called **Flora**, and also the **Botanical Gardens**. For its 125th anniversary in 1988 the Flora was – almost – restored to its former splendour. In 1862, a dozen rich burghers of Cologne decided to create an "ornamental pleasure garden", and in 1863 the king of Prussia gave permission for it to be constructed. No less a person than master landscape architect Lenné was responsible for planning the garden, and the "conservatory" was based on Paxton's Crystal Palace at the World's Fair in London. The Flora landscape garden blends into the Bo-

Preceding pages: flea-market knick-knacks. Below, a touch of personal grooming at the Cologne Zoo.

180

tanical Gardens, which were laid out alongside it in 1914.

Church-building in Cologne is not only a medieval affair: the 20th century, too, has its share of important edifices. One extremely talented family of architects, already in its third generation, is the Böhm family. The eldest member was Dominikus Böhm (1880–1955). In 1931 he built **St Engelbert's**, a mighty brick building on the Riehler Gürtel (beyond the Flora), with its eight parabolic conches arranged in a circle.

If you take the Amsterdamer Strasse out to the Niehler Damm you will find a small and very old Romanesque church on the bank of the Rhine: **Old St Catherine's** (Alt St Katharinen). The building was mentioned as belonging to the religious foundation of St Cunibert in 1238; its choir was consecrated in 1260, and the nave was later given another storey and a vault.

Anyone who feels like a swim can make a detour from here to the lake **The good life.** known as the **Fühlinger See** in the dis-

trict of **Chorweiler**. A few attempts have been made recently to improve the appearance of the area surrounding the skyscrapers here. One delightful place, though, is the **Casimir Hagen Collection** (Sammlung Casimir Hagen) on Pariser Platz. Hagen, a simple post office employee, collected a great deal of ancient artefacts, but also made his rooms available to progressive Cologne artists. Much of the collection was donated to the city in 1957.

From Niehl to Nippes: Another Cologne churchbuilder is Rudolf Schwarz. He designed **St Christopher's**, on Waldfriedstrasse (reached via Königsberger Strasse), a strictly Cubist church, with a free-standing bell-tower.

Cologne also achieved much in the field of housing development in the early part of this century. If you take the Neusser Strasse to Friedrich Karl Strasse and travel along it, on your left you will see the housing estate built between 1922 and 1924 known as **Mauenheim**, designed by Cologne ar-

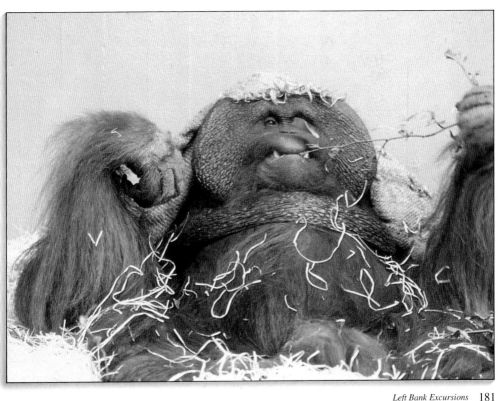

chitect Wilhelm Riphahn. It has a large courtyard area in the middle and is based on Dutch models.

Nippes is a typical Cologne district, with its own shopping centre on the Neusser Strasse and also a daily market on the Wilhelmplatz, with its happy mixture of German and Turkish lifestyles. There are some fine houses on the Erzberger Platz, dating from the years of rapid industrial expansion at the end of the 19th century. Something else that shouldn't be missed is the "Goldener Kappes", a popular beer-hall at the entrance to Florastrasse.

Ehrenfeld: A trip to Ehrenfeld should be either started or finished off with a ride up to the top of the **Colonius**, Cologne's telecommunications tower. Once you're up there you can take a seat in the revolving restaurant, and enjoy the panorama of the city below. In good weather the view stretches as far as the Ville chain of hills, and the Bergisches Land. One also gets a very good impression of how Cologne is laid out.

The Cologne suburb of **Ehrenfeld** was founded in 1845, and it quickly developed into a flourishing industrial centre. It has always been an industrial suburb, something that still has an influence on its layout even today. The Neo-Gothic **Church of St Joseph**, one of the first churches in Ehrenfeld, is situated on the Venloer Strasse, the main shopping street. If you take Neptunstrasse opposite you'll reach the recently restored *Jugendstil* glory of the **Neptune Swimming Baths** (only club members can swim there, but visitors are allowed). The square in front of the building is where Ehrenfeld's colourful weekly market takes place.

To the right of the baths is the **Friedenskirche**, rather a rare piece of churchbuilding in Cologne, with its brick walls and semicircular arches, very much in the Berlin style. If you take Vogelsanger Strasse towards the town centre you'll come to **St Mechtern's Church**, a rival of St Gereon's for the city's roll of holy martyrs. The

The "Uni-Center", the highest apartment building in Cologne.

church was badly damaged in World War II, and rebuilt between 1953 and 1954 by Rudolf Schwarz. Nearby are the **4711 factory buildings** (Wilhelm and Rudolf Koep, 1950), fine examples of the city's first period of reconstruction. And a particularly delightful part of town is the area around **St Anna's** (Eichendorffstrasse, Försterstrasse and Ottostrasse) with its fine late 19th-century residential buildings, some featuring luxurious *Jugendstil* decoration.

Lindenthal: Lindenthal (which also includes Sülz, Klettenberg, Braunsfeld and Müngersdorf) is a place that should really be discovered in several stages.

The best place to begin is the **Museum of East Asian Art**. After you've taken your trip through the ancient cultures of China, Korea and Japan, follow the magnificent avenue of chestnut trees along the Lindenthal Canal until you reach Brucknerstrasse. Towering above you at the end of the canal is the **Church of the Resurrection**, a concrete and brick structure built between 1967 and 1972 by Gottfried Böhm. Its interior is an example of the almost brutal sparseness of decoration and that concentrated spatial and spiritual intensity that is so characteristic of much of Böhm's work.

The Brucknerstrasse takes you northwards, straight to the **Melaten Cemetery**, founded by Napoleonic decree in 1810. The cemetery lies on the site of a former leper asylum, which was mentioned as far back as the year 1180. This is also clear from the cemetery's name: it was the *Maladen*, the sick people, who used to live here. The existence of a chapel on this spot was mentioned as early as 1245; it stood on the site of the small church (in use today as a Greek-Orthodox church) set against the wall that separates the cemetery from the Aachener Strasse.

After its destruction in 1474 it was rebuilt as a hall basilica ("Hallenkirche") with two naves of equal height (no entry to the public). The Melaten Cemetery is neoclassical in design, and

Car manufacturing at the Ford works in Niehl.

laid out in a strict grid pattern; the tombs of the great Cologne families can be found along the main axes. Today, many of the gravestones are under preservation order.

Our second tour also begins at the Museum of East Asian Art. To the south of it lies the **university**. Various institutes are dotted along the Universitätsstrasse: next to the museum there is the Japanese Cultural Institute, with the Italian one over the road (built by Hans Koerfer between 1954 and 1955), and also the first major extension to the university after the war: the Faculty of Economics, built by Wilhelm Riphahn.

The university itself was newly founded in 1929, and opened in 1935. The main building, designed by Adolf Abel, has a massive portal in its facade, with the institutional buildings fanning out behind it across the "Green Belt". The artificial lowering of the road in front of the entrance has created a small forum. The bronze statue of **Albertus Magnus** (Albert the Great) by Gerhard

Marcks (1956) is a monument to the famous theologian. The new university library and the auditorium were built on the other side of the forum in the 1960s by Rolf Gutbrod.

Our trip takes us past the library to the **Geusen Cemetery** (Weyerthal). This is where the city's Protestants were buried, and it was first mentioned in 1576. "Geusen" is an old word for "beggar", and was a name once given to the Protestants, many of whom had fled here from the Netherlands. The sign of the cross is absent from the gravestones; instead we see familial coats-of-arms, often surrounded by symbols of death: hourglasses, skulls, and oil-lamps.

Something else not to be missed is the **Church of St Lawrence** (reached via Gyrhofstrasse) by Emil Steffan. Built out of broken bricks, it is a unique example of the modest style of much post-war architecture. The small courtyard, enclosed by the church's outbuildings, is an oasis of tranquillity (closed between midday and 3 p.m).

The Albertus Magnus memorial in front of the University's philosophical faculty.

The next trip begins at Decksteiner Strasse. Right at the beginning of it is the church of **St Thomas More**, built by Fritz Schaller between 1962 and 1963. Now turn off into Werthmannstrasse, and you'll reach **St Elizabeth's Hospital**. Dominikus Böhm built the church here, a mighty, triple-naved structure, between 1930 and 1932, and sick patients are allowed onto its upper balconies during services. In the ambulatory is the simple tomb of prelate Johannes von Acken, with the impressive Man of Sorrows created for it in 1939 by Ewald Mataré.

Decksteiner Strasse leads past the **Jewish Cemetery**, with its beautiful old trees, to the Deckstein Mill, a popular excursion destination in Cologne as early as the 19th century, and today a much-frequented garden pub, especially in the summer.

If you take Gleueler Strasse in the direction of the town centre you'll reach the **Krieler Dömchen** and the **Church of St Albert the Great**. The latter was rebuilt after the war from the rubble of its former basilica, and the paintings in the choir were created in the early 1960s by Peter Hecker. The "Krieler Dömchen" of St Steven nearby is a real jewel. Built on the site of a Carolingian wooden church, the present structure was built between the early 10th and 12th centuries, originally with just one nave. It is a magnificent example of a harmoniously-proportioned Romanesque village church.

Following the Mommsenstrasse will take you to the **Municipal Forest** (Stadtwald), the starting-point of your tour. On the way there you'll pass several large, handsome-looking town houses dating from the early part of the century.

Castle route: Lindenthal is also the best place to begin a real live castle route: start off from Barbarossaplatz and follow Luxemburger Strasse as far as **Schloss Weisshaus** (car parking is in Leybergstrasse), mentioned as early as 1145. This delightful little Baroque cas-

Boat-house in Roden-kirchen.

tle, with its extensive grounds, served as a summer residence for the abbots of St Pantaleon's. It changed ownership several times after secularisation. The castle is closed to visitors, but there's still a fine view of it to be had from Luxemburger Strasse.

Further out of town, the **Komarhof**, which also used to belong to St Pantaleon's, can be most easily reached via Geisbergstrasse. This well-preserved building is open to visitors from Monday to Friday.

On the Militärring, change over to Berrenrather Strasse and you'll reach **Burg Efferen**, which was once used by the city of Cologne to defend itself against an archbishop it had expelled. The facade, with its seven windows, faces the street, and the gable bears the coat-of-arms of the Bourscheid family. The side with the castle gate facing the town has a mighty tower above it, capped by a slightly wonky-looking Baroque dome.

Continue driving out of town, following signs to Hürth-Gleuel. Opposite the church is the painstakingly restored **Burg Gleuel**. It is now surrounded, along with its outbuildings, by a modern housing estate.

The route continues to Frechen-Bachem, and if you turn into Mauritiusstrasse just before reaching the church you'll see **Haus Bitz** directly in front of you. Unfortunately, the Baroque manor-house is all that remains; today it contains an art gallery.

Follow the road a bit further and soon you'll come face to face with **Burg Bachem**, which dates back to the Hohenstaufen period. This elegant Baroque building, and especially its interior, underwent generous extension work in the 19th century, and restoration work has been going on since 1970 (no entry to the public).

Take the 264, and you'll reach **Haus Forst**, a magnificent, privately-owned manor-house. Then, between the two autobahns, a road signposted to "Horbell" branches off to the left. In a wooded area (follow the sign saying "Autobahnmeisterei") can be found **Burg Hobell**, the last castle on our route. The inner courtyard of this castle, with its wooden galleries, is particularly charming.

Rodenkirchen and Marienburg: You can reach Marienburg by taking the Bonner Strasse. In front of the roundabout stands the Anglican **Garrison Church of All Saints**, built between 1951 and 1952 by Rudolf Schwarz for the English occupation forces. The high, austere brick building is supported on all sides by buttresses. Here, Schwarz has adapted Romanesque formal elements to match modern requirements.

On the northern side of the Südpark lies **Maria Königin**, the last work to be completed by the great churchbuilder Dominikus Böhm (1853). Rather inconspicuous when seen from the outside, the structure possesses a surprising lightness and brightness inside. The south wall consists of almost nothing but window, and floral motifs form a strong connection between the sacred room and the natural scenery surrounding it.

Marienburg has successfully managed to retain its character of an elegant suburb filled with villas (Leyboldstrasse, Marienburgstrasse, etc.), even though much of the building space here was filled by large residential blocks in the 1980s.

On the Rhine Embankment, drive straight under the motorway bridge to **Rodenkirchen**, and turn off down the Rathausstrasse in the direction of the Rhine. The way leads along the embankment past artists' villas from the 1920s (Richard Seewald, for example, used to live in No. 11), and up to the picturesque part of town around **Old St Maternus's**. The chapel, which dates back to the 11th century, lies high above the Rhine and is surrounded by some very smart-looking half-timber buildings that also double as restaurants – a favourite destination with the people of Cologne.

**Right,
Memento
Mori: in the
Melaten
Cemetery.**

THE RIGHT BANK
OF THE RHINE

Since 1888, the Rhine has flowed through Cologne. Up until then it actually flowed past the city. In the summer of 1888 Cologne decided to finally loosen its tight belt of fortifications in order to keep step with the increase in its population, and later on in the same year, the city incorporated the municipalities outside its gates.

Cologne grew rapidly in all directions, also eastwards for the very first time, across to Deutz and Poll on the right bank of the Rhine. The city was now almost 11 times its original size. As businesses established themselves in the newly-acquired regions, the standard of living in the outlying areas rose considerably.

In retrospect, this incorporation certainly seemed to have been justified, and it also seemed the best argument in favour of further ones: at the beginning of 1919, Vingst and Kalk, on the right bank, were swallowed up, and in 1914, after Mülheim and Merheim with all their territory had also been incorporated, Cologne was the largest city in the whole empire, with 20,000 hectares (80 sq. miles) of land.

In 1975 the city expanded once more, this time swallowing up a large area of the right bank yet again: Porz, Cologne's former neighbouring city on the Rhine. More than 40 percent of Cologne's entire surface area (40,000 hectares/160 sq. miles) is now on the right bank of the river.

Wrong side of the river: Of course, statistical harmony conceals the true relationship between the two sides of the Rhine that has developed over the years, best summed up in the nasty-sounding expression "Schäl Sick", which literally means "squint side", though that gives one no clue as to its real meaning: it means the "wrong" side of the Rhine, and originated on the "correct" one i.e. the left one. Indeed, animosity is so widespread that Adenauer used to claim that Walachia began on the other side of the Rhine, and once when plans were made to shift some people from some slums on the left bank across to much more attractive housing on the opposite side of the river, the cry went up and promptly became famous: *"Mer wolle nit no Yokohama!"* ("We don't wanna go to Yokohama!")

Whatever unpleasant things are attributed to the Deutz side of the river, the fact remains that people there don't squint any more than anywhere else. Indeed the phrase itself, and not only its slanderous intention, originated on the Cologne-city side: in the old days, ships going up-river had to be towed, and each horse used for the purpose had its eye facing the river blinkered, which made it *schäl* (squint), and the side of the river it could no longer see was the *schäle Seite* i.e. Deutz.

However, the people of Deutz have learned to live with their reputation, and in 1952 they self-confidently referred to their own Carnival society as "Schäl Sick". In 1990–91 the Carnival's "big three" ("Dreigestirn") was composed exclusively of Deutz inhabitants.

Barbarians: The right bank of the Rhine at Cologne has had rather a bad name in historical times, too: under the emperor Constantine, around AD 310, the Romans built a military camp on the opposite bank in order to secure their bridge over the Rhine and their "Colonia". The camp was known as *Castrum Divitium* (today's Deutz), and measured less than 150 sq. metres. Beyond it lay the land of the Franks, whom the Romans regarded as barbarians.

In the year AD 700 or thereabouts, St Boniface complained that the "town opposite Cologne" was still a pagan stronghold, and in the 16th century the Cologne City Council lamented the immoderate amount of "drunkenness" among "the foreigners of Deutz".

Finally, perhaps it is best to content oneself with what Victor Hugo felt while he was staying in Deutz in 1838,

Preceding pages: Rhine bridges; at a riflemen's meeting in Deutz. Left, mother and child in the Rhine Park.

and later recorded for posterity: "The windows of Cologne face Deutz, and those of Deutz face Cologne; and it is better to live in Deutz, with a view of Cologne, than vice versa." So it's all a question of how you look at it! At that time the Prussians had already been in charge for quite a while, and Deutz was a fortified city just like Cologne, both of them together forming the country's strongest bastion against the French enemy. In 1817 almost every third inhabitant of Deutz was employed by the *Preussen* ("Prussians") – the rather disrespectful term applied since then, by Cologne's older inhabitants, to the military as a whole.

It was in Deutz, in 1840, that the founder of German social democracy, August Bebel, was born. The house at No. 8 Kasemattestrasse still bears traces of this opponent of Bismarck's, whose reference to Cologne in a speech in 1893 probably gave many people more than they had bargained for: "If any city in Germany… can claim the honour of considering itself the birthplace of socialism, then that city is certainly Cologne."

A fortified city: Deutz even has a "Bebelplatz", though it's pretty hard to find. Far more noticeable, even from as far away as Cologne, is Deutz's military past. The tall **Equestrian Statue** beside the river was erected in memory of the Deutz cuirassiers from the 8th "Graf Geller" regiment, who had to draw their sabres more often against revolutionaries and rioters than against enemy soldiers during their time in Deutz, and more of whom were killed by disease, between 1870 and 1871, than by the enemy.

Over here, on the "Kennedy Embankment" with the world-famous panorama of the Old City opposite, the history of Deutz is concentrated into quite a small area. The site of the Roman fort during the emperor Constantine's time has been occupied since 1970–78 by the 20-storey **Lufthansa Building**. The Roman remains were sifted through one

Equestrian statue of the Deutz Cuirassier in front of the Lufthansa Building.

last time during the construction of the 95-metre (300-ft) high building, and some Roman remains survive: the east gate of the fort, for example, situated between the Lufthansa Building and the old people's home inside the restored monastery walls, on the way to Old St Heribert's church.

A permanent bridge used to lead from here across to the left bank. Later, small boats, barges and ferries had to be relied on, and it was only in 1959 that another permanent Rhine bridge, the "Dom Bridge", was built, which because of its box-girder construction is also known as the "Muusfall" (mousetrap).

After the decline of Roman rule, their fort became part of the Crown lands of the Franks, and Otto III presented it to Cologne archbishop Heribert, who subsequently founded a Benedictine monastery within its old walls in 1002. In 1816, after secularisation and the Wars of Liberation, Prince Augustus of Prussia considered the fact that the royal artillery had settled within the monastery walls and turned St Heribert's church into their smithy as an expression of his "goodwill" towards Cologne.

The church's outer walls have meanwhile been reconstructed, after its destruction during World War II. The church's greatest treasure, the magnificent reliquary of St Heribert, was transferred in 1896 to the neo-Romanesque New St Heribert's church, situated at the entrance to the busy shopping street of "Deutzer Freiheit". It dates from 1160 and is the best-preserved reliquary of that time in Germany.

A greenhouse with a view: We continue on down the Rhine, along its embankment, past the less obtrusive "**Landeshaus**" belonging to the Rhineland Landscape Association (1957–58), and next to it, the **Hyatt Regency Hotel**, built in 1988. Its colourful granite-and-glass facade reflects the cityscape opposite for passers-by, and inside, the whole place is rather like a greenhouse – indeed, one of its restaurants is called

Kite-flying on the Rhine Meadows.

exactly that. "Belle Vue" was the name of the hotel in which Victor Hugo so enjoyed the panorama of the city, and this luxury hotel now provides just the same *belle vue* for its guests.

Beyond the Hohenzollern Bridge and north of the Trade Fair Complex is the **Rhine Park** (Rheinpark), originally called the "Kaiser Wilhelm Park" when it was first laid out in 1913, but fully democratic these days; it is the largest park area in Cologne, one that everyone can enjoy, with its unspoilt Rhine meadows, its sculpture parks and its flower borders.

It's possible to travel round the large meadows by narrow-gauge railway, or admire the shrubs and flowers from above on the chairlift. Best of all, though, is the trip across the Rhine and high above the Zoo Bridge inside the gently rocking cars of the **Rhine cable railway**, 900 metres (2,950 ft) long with a 45mm thick cable, and originally opened in 1957. In the summer, one cable car leaves every minute. On the

other side of the river the same ticket allows the passengers a trip to the zoo, naturally without any parking-space problems. A footpath leads from the Rhine Park along the harbour and all the way to Mülheim; otherwise the path leads back to Deutz, past the railway station building dating from 1914.

In front of it, on the Ottoplatz, a four-stroke motor on a pedestal (1931) stands as a reminder of its inventor Nikolaus August Otto, whose "Gas-motoren Fabrik Deutz AG" of 1872 later became the famous firm of "Klöckner-Humboldt-Deutz AG". One can gain some inkling of the great importance of that Deutz factory when one considers that its employees included a certain Gottlieb Daimler as well as a Karl Benz.

Jewish tradition: In 1907 the fortifications at Deutz were dismantled, and in front of the defensive installations the street known as Gotenring emerged. The zig-zag course of the Wallstrasse, today known as the "Helenenwall-

A popular place to meet in Zündorf: the island of "Groov".

strasse", is the only reminder of the strategists' former layout. The police station that stands at the end of this street where it broadens out into the Reischplatz once used to house the Deutz Synagogue. Deutz had had a strong Jewish tradition ever since the 15th century, largely due to the restrictive policies in Cologne.

The main synagogue on the Rhine Embankment was torn down in 1914 to make way for the construction of the "suspension bridge", and the premises on the Reischplatz were destroyed during "Kristallnacht" under the Third Reich. Since then there has been no Jewish community in Deutz.

The Nazi plans for the reconstruction of Deutz after the war were, thank God, never realised: a "regional Forum" was to have been built here, a massive deployment zone on Cologne's east-west axis. Cologne of all places, where the Nazis couldn't even get a majority in March 1933, a bastion of Fascism. These plans luckily only got as far as the

Nature still has a chance to shine in this park landscape.

drawing-board. Today, Deutz, so close to the heart of the city, is having a huge sports and leisure centre planned for it, which will regularly make the headlines.

Once the fortifications had been taken down there was also room for a new harbour. Industrial settlements grew up along the Schnellert, a disused arm of the Rhine. The entrance to the harbour is still spanned by a swing bridge from that time. The long, lime-tree-lined Rhine Embankment adjacent to it is named after the tool factory in the background: "Alfred Schütte Allee".

Poll: Poll, formerly a fishing village, and the same size as Deutz, contributed a lot to the growth of Cologne. The winding streets around the church still contain several clues to this suburb's rural past: many streets are named after fish, such as "Salmstrasse" and "Maifischgasse", and people still refer affectionately to "Poll fisher boys" and "milkmaids".

A favourite meeting-point on Sun-

days in the summertime is the **Poll Meadow** ("Poller Wiesen"), along the embankment, with its many sports facilities; shepherds can often be seen tending their flocks here. And in autumn, young and old frequently meet here to fly their kites, too, because the wind blows at its strongest down the Rhine itself.

Kalk: Kalk, together with its neighbouring districts of Buchforst, Vingst and Höhenberg, is an industrial suburb, and the fact that a farmstead is documented as having been on this very spot as early as 1003 is all too easily overlooked. Yet Kalk only became a parish, town and mayoralty in its own right at the end of the last century. Growth at that time was unbelievably rapid: it was transformed from a Sunday picnic destination into Prussia's largest industrial centre within less than a century. It also received a suitable coat-of-arms: an anvil, a hammer, a cog-wheel – and a chapel, too.

The chapel's successor still stands today, in Kalk's main street. The 15th-century Pietà inside it had turned Kalk into a place of pilgrimage. In 1941 the **Chapel**, built in 1704, was destroyed by an air raid during the course of a single night, but no one believed that except the Nazis: with its 30,000 pilgrims a year, the chapel had always been a thorn in their side anyway, symbolising as it did not only piety but also resistance – so much so that it is widely believed that they blew up the chapel themselves during the bombardment.

Many of Kalk's original factories still survive: the "Chemische", the local name for the Kalk Chemical Factory ("CFK"), still puffs its white smoke into the sky, and even if the odd factory here is forced to close down now and then, its buildings are usually kept preserved.

Buchforst: Until 1932, Buchforst (the name means "beech forest") was known as "Kalkerfeld". It then decided to bask in its own past glory, even though the people of Mülheim had chopped down all the vast beech forests in the south of

their city as long ago as 1797 in order to help repay their war debt to France.

A market here on Wednesdays and Saturdays in the Waldescher Strasse livens up this suburb, and from here, on sunny days, one can see the shining contours and cubic structures of the still very modern-looking "**White City**", built between 1929 and 1932 by Wilhelm Riphahn (who later built the Opera House) and Caspar Maria Grod.

Mülheim: For centuries, Mülheim was the mainstay of the pastoral region now known as the "Bergisches Land", which was formerly the Duchy of Berg. The inhabitants of Mülheim erected a monument in their Municipal Gardens (Stadtgarten) in grateful memory of the most popular of their regents, "Jan Wellem", who as Johann Wilhelm II became Elector Palatine and Duke of Jülich Berg, and in so doing seem to have forgotten all about the stiflingly high taxes they had to pay in order to finance the Baroque splendour of the court in Düsseldorf.

There again, they were probably in a much better position to pay than their neighbours. An edict of toleration proclaimed by its Catholic rulers had made Mülheim an attractive destination to believers suffering persecution elsewhere – believers who were not only pious but also very industrious.

"The industrious one" ("Die Fleissige"): This was also the epithet given to the tiny river Strunde, which used to turn several mill-wheels on its brief journey from Herrenstrunden, near Bergisch Gladbach, to the Rhine. Indeed, it was the mills along the banks of the Strunde that first gave the town its name: mention was first made of "Mulenheym" in the year 1098.

Just as with Deutz, Mülheim's proximity to Cologne forcibly hindered its urban development for a long time. Civic autonomy and a civic constitution in 1322 were very little help either, since there were no town walls. Fortifications were planned on several occasions only to be blocked by Cologne

COLOGNE'S TRADE FAIR CENTRE

Even though Konrad Adenauer liked to close the curtains of his compartment just after the train had pulled out of the main station in Cologne and crossed the Hohenzollernbrücke, there was still one thing on the right bank of the river he was eager to keep: the "Messe", Cologne's Trade Fair Centre, near the station in Deutz which is now known as "Messebahnhof". The Rhineland was still under British occupation, and most people in Cologne probably had more urgent things on their minds when their mayor first began making the idea of a "Rhine Trade Fair" in Cologne sound attractive to the members of the City Council.

It would mean continuing an old tradition that had its roots in the 14th century. The trade fair association was founded on 1 April 1922, and construction work based on plans drawn up by Hans Verbeek began soon afterwards on the right bank, on the site formerly used for the 1914 Werkbund (Craft Union) exhibition. On 11 May 1924 Cologne's first ever Spring Trade Fair, with 2,800 exhibitors occupying more than 65,000 sq. metres of space, opened its doors. There were more than 600,000 visitors, including the President of the German Reich, Friedrich Ebert.

Similar trade fairs elsewhere during the postwar era were relatively short-lived, but the "Kölner Messe", as it was now called, very soon developed into an economic enterprise of immense European significance.

Soon it had to be divided up into subsidiary trade fairs, and the original plan is still faithfully adhered to today: there are separate exhibitions of furniture, household goods and clothing; "food, beverages and tobacco", better known as "Anuga", takes place every two years in the autumn, alternating with the famous "Photokina" trade fair. Confectionery and sports goods are other important branches, and there are also two art fairs: the rather classically oriented "Kunstmesse", and the art market, known as "Art Cologne".

The Trade Fair Centre assumed its present-day appearance in 1928, when it was re-designed by Adolf Abel for the "PRESSA" exhibition. Since then it has been characterised by its vertical brick facades and its austere expressionism. The five million visitors to the international press exhibition were also most impressed by the new symbol on the Rhine, the 85-metre (280 ft) high trade fair tower, which is still referred to today by the city's older inhabitants as the "PRESSA tower". It was in the restaurant up here that Oskar Kokoschka painted his "View of the City of Cologne" in 1956 (on display in the Ludwig Museum).

Today, the Trade Fair Centre is one of the most important in the world. Cologne is now the leading trade fair metropolis for over 20 different branches and sectors of the economy; 37 international trade fairs and exhibitions every year attract up to 29,000 firms from over 100 countries, along with 1.8 million buyers and trade visitors from all over the world. Annual turnover has been galloping ahead, reaching DM 250 million. To ensure things stay that way, a lot of investment activity is taking place which will soon turn the Trade Fair Centre in Cologne into one of the world's largest, with 260,000 sq. metres (311,000 sq. yards) of exhibition space.

However, the darkest chapter in the history of the Centre, during the "Third Reich", should not be forgotten. An "SS construction brigade" was stationed here, and more than 1,000 of the prisoners in it had been sent to Cologne and to the industrial areas of the Rhineland for bomb clearance and bomb disposal, and then on to France to build the starting-ramps for the new "wonder weapon", the V2 rocket. Gipsies, above all, were deported from the "Messelager", as were roughly 12,000 Jews, to concentration camps in the east.

Finally, the buildings also served as a so-called "re-education camp" in which the politicians of the Weimar Republic – the ones who could still be hunted down, that is – were held after the attempt on Hitler's life in 1944. Among them was the city's mayor, removed from office long since, whose far-sightedness had originally made the construction of the Trade Fair Centre possible: Konrad Adenauer.

each time, and whatever walls were already in existence were razed to the ground by imperial decree. Flooding and drifting ice were just a few of the resulting problems. It was only in the 18th century that prosperity finally reached the town; the grand-looking burghers' houses on "Mülheimer Freiheit", some of which can still be seen today, bear witness to those times.

In those days, when Mülheim was still a small barge town, the church of St Clement's used to be at its centre. And it was here, where the white excursion boats still moor, that the holy custom of the *Mülheimer Gottestracht* first began.

A pilgrimage on the Rhine: If one is to believe the legend, it all started with a miracle: after stealing some chalices from the church, a thief had attempted to flee down the Rhine. But in the middle of the river his boat suddenly failed him and remained perfectly still: there was still a Host inside one of the chalices. The chalice was brought back again to the church in a solemn procession, and

ever since then, on Corpus Christi Day, the barges leave one by one from the embankment in front of St Clement's. The procession, complete with firecrackers and rifle-bearers, is a mixture of seriousness and fun, a pilgrimage on the Rhine that has become a real Rhenish spectacle.

The barges of Mülheim (*Müllemer Bötche*) have long been featured in Cologne songs: Just say "*Heidewitzka, Herr Kapitän*" – everyone'll sing along immediately. For a long time the barges provided the only means of access to the left bank.

Mülheim also had a pontoon bridge as long ago as 1888, of course: the mayor had acquired it second-hand in Mainz, and it did its duty until 1926, by which time it had become more of a traffic hindrance than anything else. In 1925 the bridge had to be opened roughly 31 times a day, and was thus open for a total of five hours a day altogether. That was the most important argument in favour of a new, artistic bridge which – restored after the war – still spans the Rhine near Mülheim. At its opening in 1929 it was the largest cable suspension bridge in the world.

Flittard: If one follows the course of the Rhine along the Stammheimer Embankment (Stammheimer Ufer) one eventually reaches Flittard, a town continually threatened by flooding (its name is derived from the German verb *fliessen*, to flow, referring to the mud there). Here, at number 152, Egonstrasse, one can admire a monument to 19th-century communications: the "optical telegraph", one of the final traces of a signalling system that once used to extend through the whole of Prussia. After it was completed, in 1833, it passed on signals from Schlebusch to St Pantaleon's in Cologne.

When visibility was good, the stretch from Berlin to Koblenz was quickly covered by 55 such stations. The electric telegraph, however, was significantly faster, and also operated independently of daylight, and so this opti-

Left, the main thing is, it tastes good! **Right**, burning the "Nubbel" – an old Carnival custom.

cal connection with Berlin was finally abandoned in 1849.

Merheim: When it was incorporated into the city in 1914, Flittard, along with all the other parishes between Dünnwald, Brück and Rath, belonged to the mayoralty of Merheim, a vast rural region with farmsteads and country houses, many of which – including Burg Herl, Haus Mielenforst, Haus Thurn and others – are still in good condition.

Although in those days the mayor actually had his headquarters in Holweide, the central town was Merheim. And while Holweide and Dellbrück, along the road to Bergisch Gladbach, developed into closely-knit settlements, Merheim – at least the very heart of it around the church of St Gereon – has largely retained its village character. The old "Fronhof", built in 1775, and the restaurant opposite, "**Em ahle Kohberg**", built in 1665, both still nestle among its meadows.

Another part of Merheim runs along

the length of the major A-road in the area, and here, quite unexpectedly, at No. 421, Olpener Strasse, we find the "**Goldener Pflug**" restaurant, one of the top gourmet establishments in all of Germany. The Merheimer Fliehburg extends away eastwards like a peninsula in the middle of a former arm of the Rhine; from the Stone Age until the Middle Ages, the inhabitants used it as a place of refuge whenever danger threatened.

Rath: One of the castles in the region on the right bank of the Rhine, Haus Rath, had an entire suburb named after it. Rath, on the edge of the Kings Forest (Königsforst), and united with the suburb of Heumar, has retained quite a lot of historical interest despite its swift development.

Porz: Porz, too, has been part of Cologne since 1975. This town on the Rhine, with its highly cosmopolitan centre, has also brought Cologne two very attractive excursion destinations: the **Leidenhausen Estate** (Gut Leidenhausen) with its Forest House ("Haus des Waldes"), and the **recreation island of "Groov"** (Freizeitinsel Groov), at Zündorf. The Forest House is a remarkable nature museum, with a game park as well as a bird of prey reserve in which several rare birds can be observed at close quarters. Anyone who finds the place too much of a crush at the weekend can wander off to the "Wahner Heide" nature conservation area nearby; on weekdays it is used as a military training area.

Zündorf is the most attractive part of Porz. This town, with its old Rhine island of "Groov", was mentioned as far back as the Middle Ages, and even today many medieval buildings, spruced up affectionately for the visitors, still remain between its church and its market. Zündorf's **fortified tower** (Wehrturm) still looms above the town; it was built during the 13th century out of basalt, a substance that medieval weaponry had not yet found a way of destroying.

Left, the Rhine cable car. **Right**, the Trade Fair Tower.

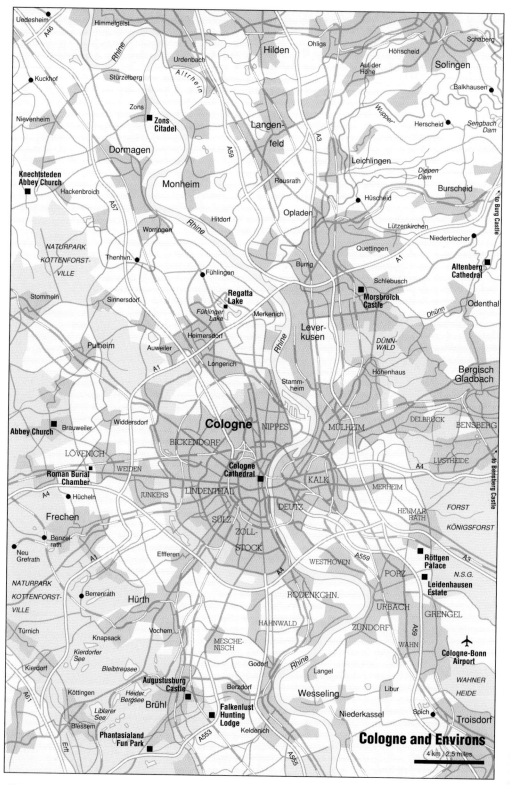

Uedesheim

A46

Himmelgeist

Hilden

Ohligs

Höhscheid

Schaberg

Solingen

Kuckhof

Rhine

Stürzelberg

Urdenbach

Auf der Höhe

Balkhausen

Nievenheim

Altrhein

Zons

Langen-feld

Wupper

Herscheid

Sengbach Dam

Zons Citadel

Dormagen

Reusrath

Leichlingen

Diepen Dam

Burscheid

to Burg Castle

Knechtsteden Abbey Church

Monheim

Hackenbroich

Hitdorf

Opladen

Hüscheid

Lützenkirchen

Niederblecher

A57

Worringen

Rhine

Burrig

Quettingen

A1

Altenberg Cathedral

NATURPARK KOTTENFORST-VILLE

Thenhvn.

Fühlingen

Merkenich

Schlebusch

Morsbroich Castle

Odenthal

Stommeln

Sinnersdorf

Regatta Lake

Fühlinger Lake

Lever-kusen

DÜNN-WALD

Dhünn

Pulheim

Auweiler

Heimersdorf

Rhine

Höhenhaus

Bergisch Gladbach

A1

Längerich

Stamm-heim

Widdersdorf

Cologne

NIPPES

MÜLHEIM

DELBRÜCK

BENSBERG

Abbey Church

Brauweiler

BICKENDORF

LÖVENICH

WEIDEN

Cologne Cathedral

KALK

MERHEIM

LUSTHEIDE

A4

to Bensberg Castle

Roman Burial Chamber

JUNKERS

LINDENTHAL

DEUTZ

HEUMAR RATH

FORST

Frechen

Hücheln

A4

SÜLZ

ZOLL-STOCK

KÖNIGSFORST

Benzel-rath

Neu Grefrath

A1

Effferen

WESTHOVEN

A559

PORZ

Röttgen Palace

A3

N.S.G.

NATURPARK KOTTENFORST-VILLE

Berrenrath

Hürth

Vochem

RODENKCHN.

URBACH

Leidenhausen Estate

Türnich

Knapsack

MESCHE-NISCH

HAHNWALD

ZÜNDORF

GRENGEL

A59

Kierdorfer See

WAHN

Kierdorf

Bleibtreusee

Godorf

Rhine

Langel

Cologne-Bonn Airport

Augustusburg Castle

Berzdorf

Libur

WAHNER HEIDE

Köttingen

Heider Bergsee

Brühl

Wesseling

Spich

Troisdorf

Liblarer See

Falkenlust Hunting Lodge

Keldenich

Niederkassel

Blessem

Phantasialand Fun Park

A553

A555

Cologne and Environs

4 km / 2.5 miles

A61

Erft

THE CITY'S GREEN BELTS

Inhabitants of Cologne in search of rest and relaxation were still having quite a hard time of things as early as the beginning of the 19th century: apart from a few tree-lined squares, the city, enclosed in its Prussian fortifications, had no parks to speak of at all. Today, however, Cologne is one of the "greenest" cities anywhere in Europe. The two so-called "Green Belts" that run through it are an unmistakeable feature, and were the inspiration of the city's former mayor Konrad Adenauer. A total of 8,700 hectares (21,000 acres) of parkland can now be found within the city's borders.

Unlike many other cities in the last century, Cologne never possessed a royal residence of its own, surrounded by parkland. There were only a few orchards and stretches of farmland just beyond the gates of the medieval city, which were hardly suitable for country walks. This made the creation of various park areas within the city virtually essential. Cologne's first and oldest park – the Municipal Gardens (Stadtgarten) – was laid out across an area measuring 11 hectares (30 acres) between 1827 and 1829.

It was only 40 years later, in 1863, that an attractive new destination for excursions and relaxation came into being with the Flora, which in those days was far outside the city gates, and to which the Botanical Gardens were annexed in 1914. But after this, progress was rapidly made because of the need to extend the city boundaries. From 1881 onwards, further areas of green were added: the Ringstrasse and the People's Gardens (Volksgarten), as well as the Municipal Forest (Stadtwald), impressive for its sheer dimensions.

The Municipal Forest: With its large pond (where boats can be hired), its game enclosure and its old trees, the Municipal Forest, situated between Dürener Strasse and Aachener Strasse near the suburb of Lindenthal, is a favourite hiking area. Around the turn of the century, horticultural director Kowallek had over 300,000 trees, plants and bushes planted, and also laid out various winding paths, ponds and meadows.

Today the Municipal Forest, extended several times (it measures around 200 hectares/500 acres), is an integral part of the city's Outer Green Belt. Avenues of chestnut-trees and mixed forest alternate with areas of pine and birch. Extensive meadows and forests, numerous lakes and ponds with rowing-boats, café-restaurants and small kiosks add variety to this recreation area. The Cologne F.C. football ground here is a big attraction for the fans, and the professional players can often be observed training.

The Inner and the Outer Green Belts: It was largely thanks to the Treaty of Versailles that Cologne's Inner and Outer Green Belts were created at all. Under its provisions, the ring of military fortifications around the city had to be dismantled after 1919, and this was a good opportunity to gain valuable land close to the city for town planning purposes.

Konrad Adenauer, who was mayor at that time, made use of this opportunity and had several large areas (11 large farms, to be precise) of the outer fortifications and the field of fire cleared and turned into parks, despite hefty opposition from the families who owned the land. The work was carried out according to plans drawn up by the landscape architect Fritz Ecke, and his successor Josef Giesen.

The **Inner Green Belt** runs along the Inner Kanalstrasse, past the Aachener Weiher (pond), the Museum of East Asian Art (well worth a visit) and the university area, all the way to the People's Gardens (Volksgarten) and the Hindenburg Park. The **Outer Green Belt** extends for nearly 30 km (18 miles) from the Fühlinger Lake (Fühlinger

See) water sports area north of Cologne, near Chorweiler, right down to the Forstbotanischer Garten south of the city on the Rhine near Rodenkirchen.

The sections of the Outer Green Belt on the right bank of the Rhine begin at the river itself, at the Poll-Westhovener Rheinufer and the Gremberger Forest. Some way past the Severinus Bridge, the Rhine meadows begin, and here one can often see shepherds grazing their sheep in the summer. Tennis courts and football fields border on a hiking trail which leads via two campsites, and one or two interruptions, all the way to Porz-Zündorf and the Groov peninsula.

The Fühlinger Lake: As the city was extended further to the north towards Volkhoven and Chorweiler, it became necessary to create parkland for recreation purposes in this region too. The Fühlinger Lake region, with its mixture of woods, meadows and its man-made lake area (with seven lakes) is an all-year-round attraction. This local recreation area, which covers nearly 300 hectares (700 acres), was completed in 1982. The region formerly contained gravel and sand quarries for use in industry.

Those keen on water sports certainly get the best deal here on the Fühlinger Lake: it has a 2,000-metre (6,500-ft) long regatta course for canoeists and rowers. Riding stables, a tennis hall and outdoor barbecue areas are also available. In the summer, surfers and swimmers throng in their hundreds alongside the lakes, and this is not doing a lot to help the ecological balance. Nature-lovers and those in search of peace and quiet will only feel really at home here outside the swimming season. That's when the extensive network of footpaths and trails, and benches to relax on around the lakes are at their most inviting for people looking for quiet walks.

The Beethoven Park: The green finger of the Beethoven Park stretches from the Outer Green Belt into Sülz, a part of the city much favoured by the student community. It ends up at the Auerbach- **A field of poppies.**

platz, where flea markets take place regularly (except in the winter months). Broad meadows, shady trees and enchanted footpaths make the Beethoven Park an idyllic place, in which everyone can find what they are looking for, whether it's somewhere to daydream, play or stroll. There's also a popular beer garden (the "Birkebäumche") situated in the middle of some allotments separating the Outer Green Belt from the city.

A particular attraction for children is the **Children's Zoo** in Sülz, which belongs to the Association of Aquarium and Terrarium Owners. The area once only contained a few ponds; today even such exotic animals as apes, chinchillas, raccoons and porcupines, as well as many varied species of birds, can be observed at close quarters.

The Forstbotanischer Garten: To the south of Cologne, near the suburb of Rodenkirchen, lies the Forstbotanischer Garten, well worth an excursion, with its wealth of rare plants, trees and bushes. It lies on what actually used to be an old rubbish-tip, and it was opened in 1964. Over 3,000 different types and species of trees from Japan, China, America, the Balkans and the Caucasus have made their home here, along with roughly 550 conifers, 2,000 deciduous trees and over 500 different types of rhododendron.

The focal points of the garden are the Rhododendron Ravine, the Japan Park and the Peony Meadow. But the Heather Garden is also worth a visit with its dwarf shrubs, most of them evergreen, which bloom at every season of the year in some form or another. There is also a 10-km (6-mile) long network of footpaths for walkers.

The special theme park known as the **Friedenswald**, in the southern part of the Forstbotanischer Garten, was added in 1979. Across an area of 26 hectares (65 acres) trees have been planted symbolising all the countries with whom Germany has diplomatic relations. The colourful mixture of different types of

Free-time fun on the Fühlinger Lake.

wood makes the park an exciting experience the whole year round. Red maple from Canada, weeping birch from Finland, wild pine from Sweden or the gingko tree from China are just a few examples. The entire park can be walked around along a 4.5-km (3 mile) long footpath. Roughly 100 different kinds of shrub roses and climbing roses can be enjoyed along the park's inner footpath.

The King's Forest (Königsforst): The King's Forest, on the right bank of the Rhine in Cologne, is a fine example of an area of green which, though very close to the city itself, features an impressive variety of possibilities for hikers, walkers and cyclists. The King's Forest is one of the most attractive forest regions of the Lower Rhine basin. It covers an area of 3,000 hectares (7,500 acres) and was originally a part of the crown lands of the Frankish kings. In the year 958 the emperor Otto I gave the forest to his brother, archbishop Bruno of Cologne, as a present. Later on, the abbeys of Deutz and St Pantaleon shared in its ownership.

During the Napoleonic era, the forest was badly damaged: most of its ancient oak trees were felled and the wood taken to France. It was only in 1815, when the Rhineland was retaken by the Prussians, that the area could be properly reafforested. Swedish fir, Japanese larch and Douglas pine were planted. Today, native coniferous and deciduous trees are preferred.

Numerous hidden ponds, long paths through mixed woodland, and groves of pine and oak provide something for everybody in search of rest and relaxation. The footpaths can be walked or cycled along for hours, right up to Bensberg in the north or to Rösrath in the east.

The Brück game preserve: The Brück game preserve lies to the west of the King's Forest, near the suburb of the same name. The preserve, which covers an area of 50 hectares (120 acres), is open until dusk every day of the year.

Wild boar and Dybovsky deer in particular can be observed roaming wild here in their natural habitat. A 700-metre (2,000 ft) long **nature trail** at the main entrance to the preserve (on Flehbachmühlenweg) provides visitors with information via notice boards about more than 100 different kinds of trees and shrubs. Picnic tables, shelters and benches are spread about invitingly. In the Erkermühle area, idyllic footpaths lead along the edge of the Flehbach pond.

The Dünnwald game park: The Dünnwald game park, roughly half the size of the one in Brück, lies to the north. Wild boar predominate here, too, as well as fallow deer. One can also go for a refreshing dip nearby in the delightful Dünnwald open-air "forest swimming pool", and nearby there is also a mini-golf course as well as a restaurant.

The Leidenhausen Estate (Gut Leidenhausen): Situated to the south of the King's Forest, the Leidenhausen Estate is definitely worth a visit. At the **bird of prey sanctuary**, which by the way is only open to visitors on weekends, one can see eagles, falcons, buzzards, capercaillie and also pheasant. Injured animals are cared for here and then set free again. In the adjoining Forest House ("Haus des Waldes"), the history of the forests in the Cologne area and their ecology is graphically described with the aid of slides, models and original exhibits.

And since 1989, the estate now has a further attraction: a **fruit museum** has been set out on a stretch of open land. It is a living museum in which different varieties of fruit have been planted which are no longer available from the usual fruit-growing industries.

Even further to the south of the King's Forest is the **Wahner Heide State Forest**. This military training area is, however, only open to the public at weekends. Here, the sandy heathland with its many pine-trees as well as mixed forest creates an interesting contrast to the King's Forest.

Autumn in the municipal woods.

INTO THE COUNTRY

The countryside outside Cologne is attractive and varied. To the east are Burg Castle, Altenberg Abbey and Bensberg with a fascinating combination of modern and historic architecture, and to the west are the monastery churches of Knechtsteden and Brauweiler, as well as the medieval walls of Zons. To the south lies Brühl with its castles and its large amusement park.

Burg Castle, Altenberg Abbey and Bensberg: Our first trip takes us into picturesque rolling countryside of the "Bergisches Land" to the east of the city. Take the A1 motorway as far as the turn-off to Wermelskirchen/**Schloss Burg**. The castle's history goes back as far as the 12th century: Count Adolf I of Berg handed over his ancestral seat in Altenberg to the Cistercians in 1133 and built a new castle on the plateau above the **River Wupper**, which is surrounded by steep slopes on all sides and can only be approached on the castle entrance side.

Between 1218 and 1225, the castle was considerably extended during the rule of Cologne archbishop Engelbert II, who was also the closest adviser of Hohenstaufen emperor Frederick II. A particularly impressive feature dating from this period is the castle hall; its sheer size (10 metres/30 ft wide, 25 metres/80 ft long) is also a telling symbol of the power wielded by those who had it built. Towards the end of the 14th century the Von Berg family stopped using the castle as a family seat, and from then on it was used only for banquets, and as a hunting lodge. Düsseldorf, then a small village on the Rhine, had become more important and this duly became the capital of the new Duchy of Berg. The old castle was besieged unsuccessfully on several occasions during the Thirty Years' War, but was only actually fully destroyed after the war was over, by imperial troops.

The castle then fell into disrepair, and was dismantled and sold in 1850.

But then in 1887 the "Society for the Restoration of Burg on the Wupper" was founded, and reconstruction work began under the supervision of the head of a weaving factory from Wermelskirchen. In 1914, the work was completed. Famous painters from the Düsseldorf Academy were invited to do the magnificent historical frescos. The "**Bergischer Museum**", which moved to the castle in 1904, features various interesting aspects of local history.

Even though very little remains of its original walls, Burg Castle is still definitely worth a visit, with its picturesque setting, its various gates, its battlements and its keep, and especially because of the magnificent view across the Wupper Valley.

Should you be interested in monuments to technology, take the road in the direction of Solingen as far as the **Müngsten Bridge**. This railway bridge was built as a cantilever steel construction between 1894 and 1897. It spans a distance of 160 metres (520 ft) and the summit of the arch lies at a height of 107 metres (350 ft) above the valley below. Technically speaking, this daring construction is considered a pioneering achievement.

Our next destination is **Altenberg Abbey**, also known as the "Bergischer Dom" (cathedral). The landscape is far more attractive if you go via Wermelskirchen instead of via the motorway (Burscheide exit). As you enter Wermelskirchen the road forks off to Dabringhausen, then it's signposted. About 20 km (12 miles) further on the valley starts to widen, and then the mighty Cistercian Gothic abbey towers among the green meadows.

The abbey is also connected with the Counts of Berg: when they handed over their old ancestral seat to the Cistercians in 1133, the monks, who busied themselves with reclaiming swampland, fishing and agriculture, and led lives of austerity, devoid of all show, decided to

Augustusburg Palace in Brühl.

build their church and their monastery somewhat further down the Dhünn Valley. The first Romanesque pillared basilica was started on as early as 1135, the choir was consecrated in 1145, and the nave in 1160. Thanks to generous donations, the monastery, known by historians as Altenberg I, flourished.

Then, in 1222, an earthquake shook the monastery and caused considerable damage. Construction work thus began in 1259 on what was to be an even more magnificent church, one which would also serve simultaneously as a burial-place for the Dukes of Berg.

As early as 1276, the choir, with its corona of chapels and 11 altars, built according to plans by the monk Walter, was ready to be consecrated. The transept was completed by the end of the 13th century, but then construction work came to a standstill, and the nave was only consecrated in 1379. After secularisation in 1803, and a fire in 1815, the building fell into disrepair, and in the following year parts of the

cathedral and the monastery caved in. It was only in the mid-19th century that reconstruction plans were drawn up. The abbey was reconsecrated in 1847, and since that time has served as a church for both confessions: the restoration work lasted until the 1970s.

The building is impressive for its simple clarity of design; any extra ornamentation has been dispensed with, thus allowing the magnificent space and its architecture to have its full effect. The mighty nave has no bell-tower, only a modest roof turret containing a small bell to summon the monks to prayer. A distinctive feature is the leaf ornamentation on the capitals, based on plants native to the Rhine region.

The stained glass windows still survive, and are unusually beautiful. The ones in the choir chapels employ geometric motifs; the large window in the northern transept is decorated with stylised floral patterns in grisaille and already contains a small amount of colour; it is only the massive west window (dating from the end of the 14th century) with its tracery and gold-tinted glass, that is resplendently colourful. This results in a bright, clear light, made even more intense by the limewashed stone of the walls. The Baroque additions to the cathedral have been lost, but the tombs of the abbots and dukes of Berg still survive.

Little remains of the monastery. The Baroque entry gate and the outbuildings opposite the western portal, however, have been preserved, and there is still a charming bar-restaurant there today, the "Küchenhof", with St Mark's Chapel, one of the oldest buildings, on its southern side. The chapel's exterior walls date from the time the monastery was founded, and after the earthquake of 1222 it was given a new vault – a particularly fine example of Early Cistercian Gothic architecture.

A **Fairytale Forest** ("Märchenwald"), in which the tales of the Brothers Grimm come to life at the touch of a button, is a few minutes' walk away.

Keeping old traditions alive in front of Altenberg Abbey.

Bensberg rounds off our trip into the Bergisches Land. Anyone interested in modern church architecture should make a detour to Schildgen (in Odental, turn right in the direction of Cologne) and visit the **Church of the Sacred Heart** there, designed by renowned Cologne architect Gottfried Böhm. One of his first ever buildings, it was consecrated in 1960, and its six conical towers make it easily recognisable. The interior is successful both in terms of its simplicity and its spiritual tranquillity.

The road to Bergisch-Gladbach forks off just beyond the church. It leads past the red Burgher's House – also by Böhm, though designed in 1970 – and then on to Bensberg. The first street signposted to the town centre (Zentrum) leads straight up to Elector Johann Wilhelm's Baroque **Hunting Lodge** (Jagdschloss), built between 1700 and 1716 by Matteo Alberti. Now that the rubble masonry has been whitewashed once more, the edifice has regained something of its Mediterranean grace.

The generously laid-out building, with its three wings, today houses a boarding school (no entry to the public).

Off to one side lies the **Goethe House**, with a good view of the Rhine Valley from its terrace, and only a few steps away from here is the **Town Hall**, a daring exposed concrete structure built by Gottfried Böhm between 1965 and 1970. It has the basic shape of a historic round castle, and aspects of Romanesque architecture have been incorporated into its modern structure.

Brauweiler, Knechtsteden and Zons: Our second trip takes us to the Lower Rhineland. Anyone keen on visiting the abbey church at Brauweiler should make sure he chooses either a Thursday morning or a weekend to do so, because those are the only times it's open. **Brauweiler Abbey**, dedicated to SS Nicholas and Medardus, is best entered via the door beneath the mighty westwork, which is flanked by two towers.

The abbey's history dates back to the year 1024, but nothing remains of the

Clear proportions give the interior of Altenberg Abbey its special atmosphere.

original building. A second building, which included the church's magnificent crypt, was started in 1048, and consecrated in 1061. The church then underwent several alterations until 1226; the westwork dates from the first half of the 12th century. The Late Romanesque nave with its fine niched triforium was given a Gothic ribbed vault in 1514. The building features several interesting examples of different styles, from Romanesque all the way to Baroque.

The abbey has had quite a changeable history. In its structure, the "Marienhof", situated near the back of the building, dates from as long ago as the end of the 12th century. The capitals in the cloister are particularly fine, and there is an important cycle of Romanesque wall-paintings in the chapter house.

The front courtyard, the "Prälaturhof", was built in the mid-18th century and in the following century another storey was added. A very fine imperial hall in the rococo style still remains (all the inner chambers can only be entered on guided tours). In 1809 Napoleon decreed that the abbey should be used as a doss house, and then in 1811 it fell into the hands of the Prussians, and was used for a long time as a prison, eventually by the Gestapo. After a brief and inglorious spell as a mental hospital, the abbey was then thoroughly renovated by the Rhenish Office for the Restoration of Public Monuments.

To reach Knechtsteden, travel via Geyen, Pulheim and Rommerskirchen, and then turn off towards Neuss. It's signposted at Frixheim.

Knechtsteden Monastery was founded in 1132 and handed over to the Premonstratensian Order. Construction work on the eastern end of the church began in 1138; between 1151 and 1162 the nave and the western apse were built, and the crossing tower as well as the towers flanking the choir were extended. In 1477, the east choir was redone in the Gothic style. After flourishing for a brief period, the abbey then

Entrance lodge to the monastery at Knechtsteden.

sank into obscurity. Construction work only began again in the 17th century: the church was given a new roof and the monastery buildings were extended considerably. In 1802 the monastery was dissolved, and both church and monastery were destroyed by a fire in 1869. Reconstruction work began again in 1878. Since 1895, the building has been used as a missionary training school by the Congregation of the Holy Ghost. Restoration work began on the church at the end of World War II.

The building, with its two choirs, conveys a strong feeling of tranquillity. It has two distinguishing features; one is the way the buttresses alternate in the nave. Here, the vault is not only held in place by several main supports but also by a series of small intermediate pillars. The cupolae are also unusual: they finish off the crossing and the transepts in place of the usual vault. The western apse is dominated by the 12th-century fresco of *Christ as Pantocrator*, and the font also dates from the same period. There is also a 14th-century Pietà.

From the abbey, turn left in the direction of Strabag, and when you get there follow signs to Dormagen. Beyond the motorway, keep on going straight ahead until you reach Zons.

Zons, sometimes known as *Feste Zons*, and originally a fortified customs post, was built by Cologne archbishop Friedrich von Saarwerden between 1373 and 1400, after the Rhine customs post had been moved there from Neuss. But after mismanagement by archbishop Dietrich von Moers, the fortified post had to be pawned off to the chapter of Cologne Cathedral. In 1620 the town was destroyed by a major fire, then in 1794 Zons became French and was confiscated from the Cathedral chapter. The castle, the customs tower and the customs house itself were all then sold in the following year. Today Zons is a part of Dormagen.

Large sections of wall, as well as many gates and defensive towers still survive from this fortress, which was

originally constructed on an almost rectangular ground-plan measuring 300 metres (980 ft) by 250 metres (820 ft). After the fire, the houses were rebuilt, and since 1908 the town has undergone elaborate restoration work. Today it is a popular tourist destination, with all that that entails, including good food.

Friedenström Castle is largely in ruins, but some of its buildings have now been restored, and the handsome manor-house ("Herrenhaus") contains the **local museum**, with its impressive specialist collection of *Jugendstil* art. Fairy-tales are performed on an open-air stage here in the summertime.

Brühl: Our third excursion leads to Brühl. To get there, take the Luxemburger Strasse. Then follow the signs beyond Hürth. This route first takes you to **Schloss Augustusburg**.

There was another building on the site before this magnificent palace was built: in 1284, Archbishop Siegfried von Westerburg began building a moated castle, which was completed in

A matter of taste: Gottfried Böhm's Town Hall building in Bensberg.

1298. For the archbishops, the castle served both as a magnificent country seat – the area was very good for hunting, with plenty of game nearby – as well as a fortress. Louis XIV then captured Cologne and Brühl, but it was only when the fortress was recaptured by troops from Holland and Brandenburg, in 1689, that it was blown sky-high.

Elector Joseph Clemens already had plans for its reconstruction in the French style as early as the beginning of the 18th century, but it was his successor Clemens August, from the Wittelsbach family, who began the work in earnest. He was most impressed by the suggestions he received from Westphalian architect Johann Conrad Schlaun, and the latter went on to complete the initial shell construction between 1725 and 1728.

After that, French architect François Cuvilliés was entrusted with the construction work; he removed the final traces of the original moated castle and shifted the state rooms to the southern wing of the building. In front of the new palace, an elegant parterre was laid out according to a design by Dominique Girard. The stairwell was also shifted to suit this, and in 1740 no less a person than Balthasar Neumann was successfully enlisted to design it. In 1768, after 40 years' construction work, the palace was completed.

In 1794 French troops occupied the palace and its magnificent contents were sold off cheaply; the palace and its surrounding gardens then fell into disuse for many years. In 1815 the palace became Prussian. Renovation work took place between 1876 and 1877, and renowned garden architect Lenné was enlisted to remodel and to extend the palace gardens. During World War II the palace was badly damaged, but over the years it was restored once more, and has now regained its former splendour.

The guided tour takes three-quarters of an hour (it's impossible to get into the palace without going on it) and starts off in the north wing. After going through the well-preserved winter rooms one reaches the generous stairwell, which separates off into two flights of stairs on the central landing, leading up to the state-rooms on the upper floor. After the "Gardesaal" and the music room one then reaches the audience chambers on the south side, with their magnificent view of the park. Luxuriant and elegant stucco, magnificent painted ceilings and richly ornate wood panelling lend the whole place a festive atmosphere. The summer rooms on the ground floor, with their blue-and-white "de Bloempot" Dutch tiles, are somewhat more austerely furnished.

Close by is the **palace church**, connected to the palace itself via an orangery; the church is a simple Franciscan Gothic structure, with a magnificent Baroque altar by Balthasar Neumann in its choir.

Only a few kilometres from here – and well signposted, too – is **Schloss Falkenlust**, a rococo jewel that is not to be missed. The house was built according to plans by Cuvilliés – and also commissioned by Clemens August – between 1729 and 1733 as a *maison des plaisances*, and its tastefully laid-out rooms have a very intimate feel to them. The decoration in the rooms is both more reserved and more delicate than that of the larger palace.

After the revolutionary troops had retreated, this small palace fell into private hands and was only acquired by the German state of North Rhine-Westphalia in 1960, before being brilliantly restored.

On the way to Schwadorf it's also worth taking a look at the **Schallenburg**, a well-preserved 12th-century fortress in the form of a moated castle.

Take the autobahn to Brühl-Süd, and you'll come to **Phantasialand**. Go through the "Brandenburg Gate", and you've reached Europe's largest amusement park, with mountain railway, white-water rafting, cable-car rides and Wild West attractions. The park is closed from 1 October to 1 April.

A nice day out: the fortified medieval town of Zons.

TRAVEL TIPS

Getting There

BY AIR

The Cologne/Bonn Airport is organised on the drive-in principle and has the reputation of being an airport of conveniently short distances. It is situated about 17 km (10 miles) from the city centre and is easily accessible by motorway. Due to its sophisticated safety equipment and extensive landing facilities, during especially troublesome and unfavourable weather conditions it is frequently used as an alternative airport for Düsseldorf and Frankfurt. All large airline companies offer flights into the Cologne/Bonn airport and there are a number of non-stop connections to various other cities, for example to New York.

The Airport Information Office is open 24 hours a day; its telephone number is (02203) 400. Independent airline companies maintain business hours between 8am–6pm Monday–Friday and 8am–noon on Saturday.

BY RAIL

The main railway station is centrally located right next to the Cologne Cathedral. During peak traffic periods there have been as many as 100,000 passengers counted on any one day. This particular railway station is the busiest traffic junction in all of Germany and its main terminal is classified as a historical monument. Trains operated by both the Deutsche Bundesbahn (German Federal Railways) as well as those run by other large international lines pull into the main station. The shops, restaurants and International Press Agency located in the main terminal remain open quite late. The Tourist Information Office is only about 200 yards away from the main station.

BY BUS

Numerous tour buses make stops in Cologne for one or even several days. The main bus station for regular public buses is located between the main railway station and Rheinuferstrasse.

BY ROAD

A circular motorway with seven major intersections makes it relatively easy to leave Cologne in just about any direction. There are two motorways which lead directly into the city itself, thus helping to relieve the congestion on general inner-city traffic. The best routes to take into the city if you're driving in from the circular motorway are as follows:

If you're coming in **from the North** (A 3), turn off at the motorway intersection Köln-Ost and head in the direction of Cologne. Drive over the Zoobrücke until you reach the exit marked "Rheinuferstrasse" (get into the right lane after going over the bridge), and continue driving south until you reach the cathedral.

If you're coming in **from the East** (A 4), drive across the motorway intersection Köln-Ost in the direction of Cologne and continue over the Zoobrücke. Keep going until you reach the Rheinuferstrasse Exit (get into the right lane as soon as you leave the bridge), and continue in a southerly direction until you reach the cathedral.

If you're coming in **from the South** (A 3), at the Dreieck Heumar (Heumar intersection) take the A 4 in the direction of Aachen. At the very next motorway intersection (Köln-Gremberg) turn onto the A 559 and head towards Köln-Deutz. From here, follow the signs which will lead you over the Severinsbrücke into the city centre. The first exit after the bridge will bring you to Rheinuferstrasse. From here the cathedral lies to the north.

If you're coming in **from the West** (A 4), at the motorway intersection Köln-Süd turn onto the A 555 and continue in the direction of Köln-Süd. At the next roundabout take the first exit towards Rheinuferstrasse and follow this northwards until you reach the cathedral.

A computerised parking system informs car drivers as to the current situation in the car parks located within the inner-city area. Fifteen multistorey car parks are open 24 hours a day including the Parkhaus am Dom (an underground car park located beneath the cathedral square), the Aral-Parkhaus Augustinerplatz (close to Neumarkt), the underground car park situated beneath the Hotel Intercontinental (Helenenstrasse) and the Parkhaus at the corner of Hohenzollern-ring and Maastrichter Strasse. As not all car parks remain open at night it's a good idea to keep the aforementioned in mind before setting out for an evening stroll or bout of entertainment.

The same laws apply to foreigners (if they have not been living in Germany for more than a year) as to German citizens with regards to driving: both are required to be in possession of a valid driver's licence and car registration papers.

TRAVEL ESSENTIALS

VISAS & PASSPORTS

Citizens of the following countries (amongst others) are required to have a visa: Eastern European countries (with the exception of Poland, Hungary and Czechoslovakia), China, Turkey, the Near East, many countries in Africa, Thailand, the Philippines, India and Vietnam. As current policies pertaining to obtaining a visa are subject to change at short notice, it's wise to check first with the German Consulate in your own country.

MONEY MATTERS

Many hotels, restaurants and larger shops accept credit cards. Due to sliding work schedules, banks often maintain different business hours. However, it is pretty safe to assume that banks are generally open from 9am–4pm Monday–Wednesday, 9am–6pm Thursday and 9am–3pm Friday. The ex-

change offices located in the main railway station are open daily 7am–9pm.

HEALTH

On the whole the standard of hygiene is good and you can drink the water without giving it a further thought. Be that as it may however, *Kölsch* (lager beer) tastes better and *Kölnisch Wasser* (Eau de Cologne) smells sweeter.

WHAT TO WEAR

When packing your bags keep in mind that it can get quite hot in summer and very cold in the winter (with temperatures sinking to as low as minus 15°C/5°F), so choose your wardrobe accordingly.

GETTING ACQUAINTED

GOVERNMENT

Since the end of World War II the city of Cologne has nearly without exception been governed by the SPD (German Social Democratic Party). The very first chancellor of West Germany, Dr Konrad Adenauer (a member of the Christian Democratic Union [CDU], was not only the mayor of Cologne from 1917 to 1933, but also held this office from 4 May to 6 October 1945. Norbert Burger (SPD), the 1991 successor to this position, is assisted in his office by Hans-Josef Blum (CDU) and Renate Canisius (SPD). The city council is composed of 84 members. In 1991, 41 of these belonged to the SPD, 30 to the CDU and six to the FDP (Free Democratic Party). In addition to these there are three members belonging to "Die Bürger" (The Citizens), three from the Republican Party (the far right-wing party), and one independent member.

In Cologne the City Council and Administration are separate entities. The mayor presides over the former while the town clerk is in charge of the latter. He is assisted by 11 town councillors, each of whom is responsible for a different department.

Since the beginning of 1975 Cologne, like many other large North Rhine-Westphalian cities, has acquired yet another division of local administration, the District Government. Cologne is divided into nine districts; the very first district representative were elected on 4 May 1975. The districts have the power to make decisions concerning matters of local importance.

ECONOMY

Cologne has been a significant economic and trading metropolis (with an emphasis on the latter attribute) ever since the Middle Ages. This has been mainly due to the city's fortuitous geographical position at the intersection of European traffic routes and the Rhine. Today Cologne boasts a ring motorway, unlike any other to be found in Europe, with 10 major intersections leading off from it into all four directions, a city motorway, eight bridges spanning the Rhine, the busiest railway junction in Germany, an intercontinental airport as well as the biggest river port in Europe. Around 1,100 trains pass over the Hohenzollernbrücke each day, making it the most frequently travelled railway bridge in Europe and the Cologne/Bonn Airport is the veritable centre of air freight transport in Germany. At the present time the airport is under construction, which will increase its passenger traffic capacity. The Rhine has always been a vital European economic thoroughfare. It is therefore no wonder that Cologne has developed into an important trading and economic centre.

The Cologne Trade Fair can be described as the "turntable" of foreign trade. Altogether 37 international trade and specialised fairs take place regularly in the city. Many of these specialised fairs are the largest of their kind in the world, for example ORGATEC, PHOTOKINA, IFMA (International Bicycle and Motorcycle Exhibition), ANUGA (Nutritional Foods and Luxury Edibles), the Furniture Fair and Confectionery Fair. The exhibition centre comprises 14 different halls, the dimensions of which taken together add up to a total of 150,000 sq. metres, plus a further 52,000 sq. metres of open space. In addition

to all this, two convention centres provide the framework for the 1,100 exhibitions put on as part of the annual Cologne Trade Fair. Around 29,000 exhibitors, hailing from 102 different countries, and 1.8 million visitors – about a third of them from foreign lands – congregate every year at the Cologne exhibition grounds.

Cologne is ranked third (after Hamburg and Munich) as the city with the highest number of insurance companies. There are about 60 insurance agencies maintaining offices here and many important companies have made the city their main headquarters.

In the realm of automobile manufacture Cologne occupies the Number One position in Europe. Since the year 1931 the Ford factory situated in Niehl on the left bank of the Rhine has been producing cars. Today 1,200 completed vehicles leave the assembly line per day. In addition, the car manufacturers Citroen, Mazda, Toyota and Renault have all established main German branches in or around Cologne.

A momentous event in the city's history took place in 1876 when Nikolaus August Otto developed the internal combustion engine, which was later named after him. His memorial is located in front of the Deutz Railway Station. And in Deutz, located on the right side of the Rhine, the firm Klöckner-Humdoldt-Deutz continues to manufacture diesel engines of every shape and size, as well as tractors for export throughout the world.

Numerous retail trade and speciality associations maintain headquarters in Cologne and the some 6,500 different trades businesses are based here. Last but certainly not least, Cologne is proud of Glockengasse No. 4711, home of the world-famous eau de toilette of that same name.

GEOGRAPHY

Cologne is situated at an altitude of 55 metres (183 ft) above sea level and is almost completely flat. The only visible waterway is the mighty Rhine, which makes an enormous curve to the left through the middle of the city. All other waterways are contained within subterranean channels and are thus more or less hidden from sight.

POPULATION

According to a census taken in 1991, Cologne numbers about 1 million inhabitants. Of these 524,000 are Catholic and 215,000 Protestant. The remaining quarter of the population is divided into adherents of the Moslem, Jewish or Old Catholic faiths. Approximately 16 percent of the total population is composed of foreigners, the highest percentage of these being Turkish, followed by Italians and Yugoslavians.

TIME ZONE

The time in Cologne corresponds to Central European Time. Daylight Savings Time is in effect from the end of March until the end of September.

ELECTRICITY

The electrical supply in Cologne is AC 220 volts and 50 Hz. Outlets are designed to accommodate three-pronged safety plugs.

BUSINESS HOURS

Due to sliding work schedules, office hours vary. However, generally speaking, the core time falls between 9am and 4pm. In the city centre shops are open from 9am to 6.30pm except on Thursdays, when most remain open until 8.30pm. In the suburbs stores are usually closed for lunch in the afternoons from 1pm to 3pm. On the first Saturday of every month during Daylight Savings Time shops in the city centre stay open until 4pm; at all other times of the year they are open until 6pm. Beginning four weeks prior to Christmas, stores in the city centre remain open every Saturday until 6pm. In the suburbs many shops close for the day at 1pm on Mondays or Wednesdays.

Official buildings and offices are open to the public only until noon and are always closed on Saturdays.

Shops located in the main railway station and airport stay open later than others.

HOLIDAYS

In addition to the federal holidays celebrated throughout all of Germany, public officials in Cologne are also given a break on the Feast of Corpus Christi (held on the Thursday in the second week following Whitsun) and on All Saints' Day (1 November).

During the peak periods of Carnival in Cologne there isn't much going on in the way of official business, but this lack is more than made up for by the enthusiasm of celebrating civilians. The Thursday before Shrove Tuesday is *Weiberfastnacht* – the day during Carnival when the women take control of things. On this day many offices and shops close around lunchtime. Work also comes pretty much to a standstill on *Rosenmontag* (the Monday before Lent) in both the city itself and in the surrounding countryside. When the regional parades take place on Shrove Tuesday (in most suburbs), you can count on the shops and offices in the city being closed.

EVENTS

Each month the Tourist Information Office issues a list of all up-coming events. The Cologne Carnival Festival Committee publishes a calendar of festival events at the beginning of every year.

RELIGIOUS SERVICES

CATHOLIC

The Cathedral: Masses are held at 6, 7, 8, 9,10 (High Mass), and 11.30am. Evening masses take place at 5 and 6.30pm. The well-known cathedral choir, the only boys' choir in Cologne, usually sings at the High Mass.
St Columbia, Kolumbastrasse 4: Masses are held Saturday at 6.30pm and on Sunday at 8 and 9.30am.
Minorite Church (Minoritenkirche), Kolpingplatz: Masses are held on Sunday at 9 and 11am.
Great St Martin's (Gross-St-Martin), An Gross-St-Martin 9: Mass is held on Sunday at 11am in Portuguese and again at 12.30pm in Spanish.

PROTESTANT

Antonite Church (Antoniterkirche), Schildergasse: Services conducted on Sunday at 10am and 6pm. At 6pm Monday–Friday "10-minute devotionals" are held.
Church of the Cross (Kreuzkirche),

Machabäerstrasse 26: Service conducted on Sunday at 11am.
Church of Jesus Christ (Christuskirche), Werderstrasse 16: Service conducted on Sunday at 11am.

COMMUNICATIONS

MEDIA

Cologne is home to three radio stations (Westdeutscher Rundfunk, Deutschlandfunk, Deutsche Welle), two TV stations (Westdeutscher Rundfunk, RTL plus) and many studios.

Print media are represented by the daily newspapers:

Kölner Stadt-Anzeiger, Breitestrasse 70, tel: 2 24-0.

Könische Rundschau, Stolkgasse 25–45, tel: 16 32-0.

Express, Breitestrasse 70, tel: 2 24-0.

POSTAL SERVICES

The big post offices located in the city centre are open throughout the day 8am–6pm Monday–Friday and on Saturday 8am–noon. The post office in the main railway station is open on weekdays 7am–10pm and on Sundays and holidays 10am–10pm. In the suburbs most post offices close for lunch between noon and 3pm.

TELEPHONE & TELEX

Local calls cost 30 pfennigs; for long-distance calls 0.10 DM, 1 and 5 DM coins may be inserted. You'll find a number of yellow, public pay-phone booths located at various places throughout the city. Round telephones can only be operated with telephone calling cards. For information on calls within Germany dial 11 88; for calls placed to countries outside Germany the number for information is 0 11 88. The dialling code for Cologne

is 0221. It is possible to send a telegram 24 hours a day. If you want to send one from within the city limits dial 11 31; if you're placing the telegram from any adjoining area, the number is 0 11 31. At many post offices there is a public telefax service.

EMERGENCIES

SECURITY

Several car parks provide parking places near the exit which are especially reserved for women. They are usually well-lit and monitored by video cameras.

LOST & FOUND

The Lost and Found Office located at Herkulesstrasse 42 in Cologne-Ehrenfeld can be reached by dialing 221 63 12. It is open 7.30am–noon Monday–Friday and can be contacted by phone between 7.30am and 3.45pm Monday–Thursday and 7.30am–noon on Friday.

MEDICAL CARE

There is a University Clinic, three municipal and 18 private hospitals in Cologne. In exchange for a special health insurance paper, patients from other European Community countries are given a certificate necessary for obtaining medical treatment at no extra cost. It is recommended that visitors hailing from non-EC countries get medical insurance from their private insurance agency before leaving home. The telephone number for emergency medical aid is 72 07 72. Under the number 1 15 00 you can find out which dentists, vets and chemists are currently open for emergency duty.

GETTING AROUND

AIRPORT TRANSFERS

The number 170 bus leaves at 20-minute intervals to transport passengers between the Cologne/Bonn Airport and the city. (Departures from behind the main station and from the Deutzer Station.) A taxi ride from the airport to the city centre takes about 20 minutes and will cost around 30 DM.

ORIENTATION

Because the streets of Cologne are laid out in the form of five concentric rings, getting oriented is a relatively easy process. The innermost ring is called simply the "Ring", the middle one "Innere Kanalstrasse", the next the "Gürtel", which is followed by the "Militärring" and, finally, the Autobahnring (the aforementioned circular motorway).

Main arterials radiate outwards in a star shape along both the right and left sides of the Rhine from the city centre.

On the left side of the Rhine Neusser Strasse leads towards the north (Neuss-Düsseldorf), Venloer Strasse towards the northwest (Grevenbroich, Venlo), Aachener Strasse towards the west (Bergheim), Luxemburger Strasse towards the southwest (Hürth, Zülpich), and Bonner Strasse towards the south (Wesseling, Bonn).

On the right side of the river Siegburger Strasse heads towards the southeast (Troisdorf, Siegburg), Olpener Strasse towards the east (Bensberg, Bergisch Gladbach), and Bergisch-Gladbacher-Strasse towards the east (Bergisch-Gladbach, Wipperfürth).

CITY MAPS

Large maps of the city are provided at prominent points throughout the city centre. They are often displayed on the back of advertisement billboards.

PUBLIC TRANSPORT

Well-developed bus, tram and subway systems make it fairly convenient to get around in Cologne. The subway includes sections which run at street-level. As there are no conductors present on any of the various forms of local transport operated by the Köln Verkhersbetriebe (KVB) (Cologne Transport Services), tickets must be purchased before boarding – at ticket machines, from the special counters located at subway stations, or from the vehicle driver. At some specially marked stops and in the subway trains, however, drivers are not permitted to sell tickets. Tickets must be cancelled just prior to or after boarding (either before leaving the platform or actually in the vehicle).

An all-day ticket costs 8 DM and is valid for a full 24 hours. Single-journey tickets are 1.50 DM for shorter distances and a three-day pass is available for 14 DM.

TAXIS

You can find a taxi parked at any of the taxi-stands located at all the particularly busy places in Cologne. Other alternatives include hailing one on the street, or ordering one by calling 28 82. Taxis are usually beige in colour. The base rate is 3 DM with each kilometre thereafter costing 1.80 DM.

RENTAL CARS

The following is a selection of regional and international car rental agencies:
Avis: City office. Tel: 23 43 33
Airport office. Tel: (0 22 03) 40 23 43
International reservations. Tel: (0 130) 77 33
InterRent: City office. Tel: 13 20 71
Airport office. Tel: (0 22 03) 5 30 88
Hertz: City office. Tel: 51 50 84
Airport office. Tel: (0 22 03) 6 10 85
Reservations. Tel: (0 130) 21 21 or (0 69) 73 04 04
Braun: Open day and night. Tel: 32 20 32
Colonia: Open 7.30am–6pm Monday–Friday and 8am–noon Saturday. Tel: 25 30 28

Cologne Public Transport

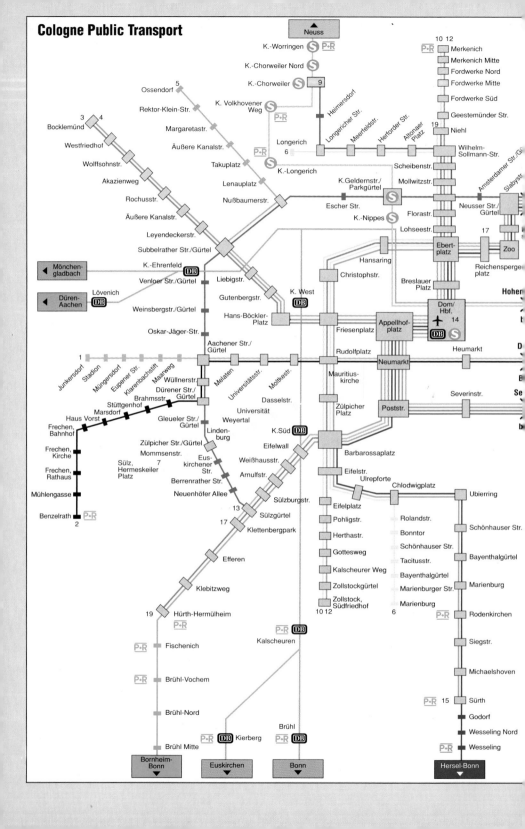

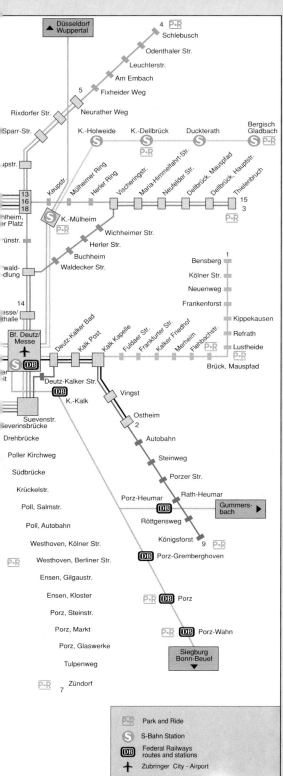

RHINE CRUISES

If you're planning on visiting Cologne during the summer, don't miss the opportunity to take a boat trip along the Rhine. There are several different types of cruises available, including short trips which take place within the space of an afternoon or evening and longer voyages which may last all day, for instance the journey to Koblenz. The hydrofoil *Rheinpfeil* (a member of the Cologne-Düsseldorf German Rhine Steamer Company) provides a speedier means of boat travel and will even take you as far as Mainz (a mere four hours). The return trip to Cologne via the German Federal Railway takes a good two hours.

Day excursions, for example one that ferries you by Bonn and past the Siebengebirge ("Seven Hills"), or even one that just cruises within the Cologne city limits, are quite worthwhile. The boats are in operation from Easter until October. Tickets can be purchased at the mooring located between Hohenzollernbrücke and Deutzer Brücke.

Köln-Düsseldorfer Deutsche Rheinschiffahrt AG (Cologne-Düsseldorf German Rhine Steamer Company): Tel: 21 13 25
Steamboat Colonia: Tel: 21 13 25
Passenger Boat Linden: Tel: 38 47 38
Rhine-Mosel Passenger Boat: Tel: 12 16 00

ON FOOT/BY BICYCLE

The numerous sightseeing attractions in Cologne's city centre can be explored conveniently on foot. There are three pedestrian zones located in the very heart of the city: Hohe Strasse, Schildergasse and Breite Strasse. Roncalliplatz (situated next to the cathedral) and the Rheingarten (adjacent to Roncalliplatz) are also devoid of car traffic, as are many streets and alleys in the old part of the city.

The paths running along the banks of the Rhine are especially suitable for cycling, as is the outer green-belt containing the city forest. The following touring maps are recommended for those wanting more extensive bike riding excursions both in and around Cologne:

Radwanderkarte Stadt Köln (Cologne Bicycle Touring Map), published by Landkartenhaus Gleumes, 1:50,000.

Rad-und Wanderkarte Köln/Bonn (Bicycle and Hiking Map for Cologne/Bonn), published by RV-Verlag, 1:50,000.

Radtourenkarte Nr. 40 (Bicycle Touring Map No. 40): around Cologne and Bonn, 1:100,000.

WHERE TO STAY

Lodgings in Cologne run the gamut from simple youth hostel quarters to luxury-class hotel suites. There are over 16,000 beds available in more than 200 different hotels. When the huge international trade fairs take place in Cologne in the spring and autumn, it's a good idea to book accommodation well in advance. If you want to make a reservation by mail, make sure you send in your request sufficiently far in advance to receive a written confirmation. If you're in need of help or advice in the matter of finding a hotel room, contact the Verkehrsamt der Stadt Köln (the City of Cologne Tourist Information Office), Unter Fettenhennen 19, D-5000 Cologne 1. Tel: 221 33 45. They're open from 1 May–31 October on regular working days 8am–10.30pm and from 1 November–31 April on workdays 9.30am–7pm.

HOTELS

UPPER PRICE CATEGORY

Double rooms starting at 300 DM:
Dom-Hotel, Domkloster 2a. Tel: 20 24-0
A first-class hotel enveloped in a wealth of old tradition located directly across from the cathedral. It's quiet, lavishly decorated and contains 181 beds.
Excelsior Hotel Ernst, Trankgasse 1–5. Tel: 27 01
Another top-class hotel of long-standing located right by the cathedral. It's quiet, exclusively furnished and contains 255 beds.
Holiday Inn Crowne Plaza, Habsburger Ring 9–13. Tel: 20 95-0
A luxury-class hotel housed in what used to be an administration building. It's situated just a few short minutes away from the cathedral, has a swimming pool, sauna and 420 beds.
Hyatt Regency Köln, Kennedy-Ufer 2a, Deutz. Tel: 82 81 234
Located as it is on the right bank of the Rhine, not far from the Trade Fair Centre, this hotel provides its guests with the most superb view of Cologne. It was first opened in 1988, has a swimming pool, sauna and 614 beds.
Hotel Im Wasserturm, Kaygasse 2. Tel: 20 08-0
An old water tower, extensively renovated in 1989 and located just a few minutes away from the cathedral, is the site of this top-class hotel. It boasts a modern French interior, a roof-top restaurant with an all-around view and 170 beds.
Inter-Continental Köln, Helenenstrasse 14. Tel: 22 80
Situated directly in the city's historical centre, the Intercontinental is furnished to please those with the most discriminating of tastes and is well-suited for accommodating conferences and conventions. It has a swimming pool, sauna and 530 beds.
Maritim, Heumarkt 20. Tel: 20 27-0
This noble hotel, opened in 1989, is located directly along the Rhine in the old part of Cologne. Its enormous, glass-ceilinged atrium housing a variety of shops and eating establishments is unique in Germany. Within the hotel is a large hall suitable for both celebrations and conventions, a swimming pool, sauna and 900 beds.
Ramada Renaissance Hotel, Magnusstrasse 20. Tel: 20 34-0
First opened in 1989, this hotel is situated right next to the recently renovated Friesen Quarter and boasts a swimming pool, sauna and 300 beds.

MIDDLE PRICE CATEGORY

Double rooms starting at 200 DM:
Altea Hotel Severinshof, Severinsstrasse 199. Tel: 20 13-0
Located right by the Severinsbrücke about 10 minutes from the centre of town. Both the bus and subway stop nearly at the door. Long-term guests are given the option of having a room fitted with a tiny kitchen. There's an atrium beer garden in the inner

courtyard and the hotel contains 519 beds.

Ambassador, Barbarossaplatz 4a. Tel: 23 51 81

This hotel is located just on the edge of the old part of the city. The windows are made of special noise-prevention glass and the hotel boasts high-quality service, is furnished quite comfortably and has 70 beds.

Consul, Belfortstrasse 9. Tel: 77 21-0

Despite being only 10 minutes away from the old part of the city, the Consul is exceptionally quiet. It is ideal for both conventions and large celebrations, has a swimming pool, sauna and 230 beds, 20 percent of which are reserved for non-smokers.

Dorint Hotel Köln, Friesenstrasse 44-48. Tel: 16 14-0

Although this hotel is located right in the middle of the lively Friesen Quarter, it is nevertheless quiet and comfortable. Decor is modern and there are 213 beds.

Pullman Hotel Mondial, Kurt-Hackenberg-Platz 1. Tel: 20 63-0

A hotel recently renovated in a way that will please even the most discriminating of guests. It was built in 1963 and is located just opposite the Philharmonie. The Symphony Restaurant provides exactly the right ambience in which to meet with friends after a concert and wind down the evening over a quiet drink. There are 350 beds.

Viktoria, Worringer Strasse 23. Tel: 72 04 76

Just a few metres from the Rhine in the new part of the city, this Art Nouveau-style villa, which is officially under protection as a historical monument, possesses a wonderful atmosphere. Breakfast is included in the room price and the hotel has 75 beds.

LOWER PRICE CATEGORY

Double rooms starting at 100 DM:

Hotel am Augustinerplatz, Hohe Strasse 30. Tel: 23 67 17

A comfortable hotel with good service located in a shopping centre. It has 105 beds.

Coellner Hof, Hansaring 100. Tel: 12 20 75

This well-known establishment is located at the edge of the old part of the city and boasts comfortable rooms and a good cuisine. There are 110 beds.

Domgarten, Domstrasse 26. Tel: 12 03 03

A small hotel with a nice atmosphere situated along a quiet street in the old section of Cologne. There are 22 beds.

Haus Marienburg, Robert-Heuser-Strasse 3. Tel: 38 84 97

This peaceful hotel is housed in an old Art Nouveau-style villa with a lovely garden in the distinguished suburb of Marienburg. It has 22 beds.

Hotel Rheingold, Engelbertstrasse 33–35. Tel: 23 65 31

A well maintained hotel which has a sauna and bar. It's located quite near to Rudolphplatz and contains 130 beds.

Stapelhäuschen, Fischmarkt 1–3. Tel: 21 21 93

This simple, homey hotel is in an old medieval house which is classified as a historic monument. It is located directly on the banks of the Rhine in the old part of the city and has 57 beds.

PENSIONS

There are several pensions that offer single rooms with running water in them starting at 25 DM per night. Two of these are the "Jansen" (Tel: 25 18 75) and "Kirchner" (Tel: 25 29 77), both located near Rudolphplatz at Richard-Wagner-Strasse 18.

YOUTH HOSTELS

Probably the most inexpensive overnight arrangements to be made in Cologne are at its youth hostels. The only prerequisite for staying here is a valid Youth Hostel Membership Card.

Jugendgästehaus (Guest House for Young People), An der Schanz 14. It's located in the suburb Riehl (on the left-hand side of the Rhine) near the Mülheimer Brücke.

Jugendherberge (Youth Hostel), Siegesstrasse. This hostel is located in Köln-Deutz at Hohenzollernbrücke. Tel: 81 47 11.

CAMPING

Municipal family camp site in Poll, Weidenweg. Open: 1 May–30 September.

Young peoples' camp site in Poll, Alfred-Schütte-Allee. Open: only during the summer holidays.

Campingplatz Berger in Rodenkirchen, Uferstrasse 53a. Open: 1 March–30 October.

Campingplatz Waldbad in Dünnwald, Peter-Baum-Weg. Open: all-year round.

FOOD DIGEST

CUISINE

Cologne natives prefer good, substantial fare when it comes to dining out and in many restaurants you'll find a number of regional dishes on the menu including:

Rheinischer Sauerbraten mit Klössen (braised beef with dumplings in the traditional Rhine style). Though this dish was originally prepared with horsemeat, nowadays it is almost always made of beef. However, there are some places which still serve it in its original form.

Himmel un Ääd (Heaven and Earth). Stewed apple (heaven) and mashed potatoes (earth) are mixed together and eaten with fried blood sausage (called *Flönz* or *Bloodwoosch* by Cologne natives).

A dish that frequently serves to confuse many out-of-towners is *Halve Hahn*, which is assumed by most to refer to half a fried chicken. Contrary to expectations, however, what will actually be brought to your table is a *Röggelchen* (a roll made from dark rye flour) with butter and some aged Dutch cheese. The history of the "Halve Hahn" can be traced back to the 19th century and is as follows: Parsimonious businessman invited some friends over for a "Halve Hahn" (half a chicken), but, unbeknown to his guests, he gave instructions to the innkeeper that the aforementioned rye roll, whose dark, crispy surface is faintly reminiscent of a fried chicken, should be served with cheese instead. At first his guests were, understandably enough, disappointed, but in no time at all the the culinary invention caught on throughout the entire city. The "Halve Hahn" tastes especially delicious when accompanied by *Kölsch* (the local beer) and is frequently consumed as a snack rather than a full meal.

Rievkoche, a kind of potato pancake, are sold by the threes with or without apple sauce at snack bars and are also served in restaurants at special times during the year. The fragrance alone emanating from these little pancakes made of freshly grated potatoes and fried in oil with a generous amount of onions is irresistible. At the very least, every tourist will be confronted with these savoury morsels on the square just outside the railway station; in one of the pavilions here *Rievkoche* are prepared according to an original recipe.

Hämmche met suure Kappes refers to pork knuckles served with sauerkraut and mashed potatoes. This is the ideal dish if you've got an especially hearty appetite, even taking into account that the bones contribute significantly to the size of the portion.

Ääzezupp is the code word for a tasty pea soup which is cooked with onions, lamb or rendered bacon. There are still many families in Cologne that maintain the tradition of serving *Ääzezupp* on Saturdays. It is also a very popular dish at street and folk festivals.

BEVERAGES

All of the aforementioned specialities have something in common; they all taste best when washed down with the national beverage *Kölsch*. In Cologne Kölsch is the Number One beverage. Every year about 3.9 million hectolitres of this delicious brew are poured down thirsty throats. Cologne natives prefer to swill a glass down while standing at the counter in a favourite bar, and of course, as one thing often leads to another, a second (or third or fourth) glass frequently follows. Because this fermented beer must be as fresh as possible, it is typically served in tall, narrow glasses which, although swiftly emptied, can be just as quickly refilled. This "liquid bread" is also said to be quite healthy as it purifies the body, normalises blood pressure and aids the digestive process. There are even some people with kidney stones who swear that drinking *Kölsch* prevented them from needing an operation.

In the Cologne breweries *Kölsch* is brought to you by a waiter called *Köbes*, wearing black trousers, a blue cardigan and blue apron made of linen. His purse is generally concealed under the apron, and usually under his overhanging belly as well.

Of course there are also other beverages available in Cologne. Those who prefer drinking good wine have a number of different and excellent wine bars to choose from. The proximity of the city to the wine-growing area that begins 30 km (19 miles) to the south beyond Bonn, is an advantage. At one time grapes were also cultivated in Cologne itself. Today, all that's left of this heritage is a tiny vineyard located near the government buildings.

RESTAURANTS

For a really superb dining experience, choose one of the gourmet temples that have been awarded either stars, chef hats, or spoons. There are more than two dozen of these fine eating establishments in Cologne.

Keep in mind, however, that an exceptional meal is enjoyed at a characteristically exceptional price.

EXPENSIVE

As a rule, you can expect to pay at least between 40 and 50 DM for a main dish at the following restaurants:

Chez Alex, In der Mühlengasse 1. Tel: 23 05 60
Fine French cuisine served in an elegant atmosphere.

Ristorante Alfredo, Tunisstrasse 3. Tel: 24 43 01
A small restaurant serving Italian cuisine. Specialities include fish and pasta in a multitude of variations.

Bastei, Konrad-Adenauer-Ufer 80. Tel: 12 28 25
Excellent French and international cuisine. A splendid view over the Rhine.

Em Krützche, Am Frankenturm 1. Tel: 21 14 32
A restaurant with over 600 years of tradition behind it. Specialities are based on traditional Rhineland cuisine, and include brain of calf, sweetbread and game.

La Poele d'Or, Komödienstrasse 50–52. Tel: 13 41 00
French cuisine prepared with a light, fine touch. The specialities of the house are based on different kinds of top-quality fish.

Goldener Pflug, Olpener Strasse 421. Tel: 89 55 09
French cuisine at its finest. The speciality is the "menu surprise".

Rino Casati, Ebertplatz 3. Tel: 72 11 08

This restaurant is known for its imaginative Italian cuisine and top-quality wines. Homemade pasta dishes are the speciality.

Restaurant Wack, Benesisstrasse 57. Tel: 21 42 78
An especially noble dining establishment which specialises in fine Alsatian cuisine.

Weinhaus Im Walfisch, Salzgasse 13. Tel: 21 95 75
This restaurant, located in a house dating from the year 1626 which has been classified as a historical monument, is known for its exquisite international cuisine. The wine list contains more than 300 different kinds of wine. Fish dishes are the speciality.

Bergische Stube, (Hotel Inter-Continental), Helenenstrasse 14. Tel: 22 80
Excellent French and international cuisine are served here amidst classy surroundings.

Dom-Hotel Restaurant, Domkloster 2a. Tel: 20 24-0
High-quality international cuisine served in exquisite surroundings. The menu boasts a wide assortment of different kinds of fish; in the evenings diners are entertained with live piano music.

Hanse-Stube (Excelsior Hotel Ernst), Trankgasse 1–5. Tel: 27 01
This subtly and tastefully decorated restaurant serves creative international cuisine. The wine list is truly outstanding.

MODERATE

Due to the fact they haven't been honoured with any particular badge of culinary distinction, the following restaurants of the middle-class price range are less expensive than the aforementioned ones. A main dish in one of these eating establishments will cost between 25–35 DM.

Amabile, Görrestrasse 2. Tel: 24 60 17
This restaurant serves gourmet French food. The speciality of the house is lamb filet in a basil-garlic crust.

Artischocke, Moltkestrasse 50. Tel: 25 28 61
A cosy restaurant well known for its fine French cuisine and in particular for its raw salmon marinated in raspberry vinegar and olive oil.

Colonius Turmrestaurant, Innere Kanalstrasse 100. Tel: 52 20 61
While enjoying their meal, diners have a view of Cologne and the surrounding countryside. International cuisine is served here.

Daitokai, Kattenbug 2. Tel: 12 00 48
Gourmet Japanese restaurant where the specialities are prepared at your table.
Haus am See, Bachemer Landstrasse 420. Tel: 43 43 21
A much-frequented restaurant located on Decksteiner Pond in the Stadtwald (City Forest), a short drive beyond the city. Both international cuisine and regional specialities are available here.
La Baurie, Vorgebirgsstrasse 35. Tel: 38 61 49
A small, French restaurant. The house speciality is potato pancakes served with marinated salmon.
Le Bouquet (Holiday Inn Crowne Plaza Hotel), Habsburger Ring 9–13. Tel: 20 95-0
A light-filled, friendly restaurant with excellent French food and a diverse wine list.
Le Moissonnier, Krefelder Strasse 25. Tel: 72 94 79
Lovely Art Nouveau-style restaurant. The tasty French cuisine is complimented by an outstanding selection of wines.
L'Osteria De Donatis, Eigelstein 122. Tel: 12 33 73
This small Italian restaurant specialises in pasta made on the premises.
Maharani, Komödienstrasse 40. Tel: 13 76 52
A well-known Indian restaurant which has recently moved from the Ring to premises near the cathedral. Tandoori specialities cooked in a real Tandoori oven are served.
Marienbild, Aachener Strasse 561. Tel: 49 31 66
An elegant dining establishment specialising in "New German Cuisine".
Poncho's, Salzgasse 9–11. Tel: 24 65 65
Here you can sample Argentine dishes of the finest quality. It specialises in huge steaks that melt in your mouth.
Ratskeller, Alter Markt. Tel: 21 83 01
German cuisine served in surroundings with a markedly historical ambience. Fish and game are the specialities.
Restaurant Der Messeturm, Kennedy-Ufer. Tel: 88 10 08
This restaurant offers fine French and international cuisine and a splendid, panoramic view out over the old section of the city.
Wirtshaus Schwejk, An Gross St Martin 2. Tel: 21 67 30
An eating establishment known for its Bohemian specialities including Prague ham in bread dough and Pilsener Urquell on tap.
Zorba the Buddha Oscho Restaurant, Brüsslerstrasse 52. Tel: 57 40 745
Diners can enjoy exquisite vegetarian specialities from all over the world here. There's a vegetarian pizzeria adjoining the main restaurant.

INEXPENSIVE

It is also quite possible to eat well and relatively cheaply in the breweries where traditional Cologne specialities are served with *Kölsch*. Tasty fare both here and at numerous other restaurants serving foreign cuisine will cost about 10 DM per main dish.
Bier-Esel, Breite Strasse 114. Tel: 24 85 59
Cologne's oldest mussel house. During the summertime instead of mussels a large assortment of salads are offered.
Bizim, Weidengasse 47. Tel: 13 15 81
A small restaurant specialising in fine Turkish cuisine, in particular lamb and fish dishes.
Brauerei zur Malzmühle, Heumarkt 6. Tel: 21 01 17
An old and venerable brewery serving traditional Kölsch cuisine.
Brauhaus Päffgen, Friesenstrasse 64–68. Tel: 13 54 61
A restaurant rich in tradition specialising in fare indigenous both to Cologne in particular and the Rhineland in general.
Consülchen-Pub, Belfortstrasse 9. Tel: 77 21-0
"New German Cuisine" served here. The house specialities include homemade brawn served alongside potatoes fried with bacon and potato pancakes with pickled salmon.
La Barrière, Aachener Strasse 569. Tel: 49 32 56
French cuisine with an emphasis on vegetarian dishes.
La Fattoria, Severinstrasse 8–10. Tel: 32 72 43
This Italian restaurant offers a large selection of pasta dishes and delicious antipasto.
La Lavallier, Am Hof 20–26. Tel: 23 38 91
A bistro serving international cuisine. There's a great view of the cathedral from the terrace and a good bar.
Früh am Dom, Am Hof 12–14. Tel: 21 26 21
This cosy brewery serves Kölsch specialities, its own home-brewed schnapps and, of course, *Kölsch* on tap. They also have a beer garden.

Früh em Veedel, Chlodwigplatz 28. Tel: 31 44 70
Typical Kölsch dishes such as "Halve Hahn" and lamb.
Mandalay, Brüsselerstrasse 53. Tel: 52 74 73
An Indonesian restaurant where many dishes tend to be piquant and spicy. Specialities include "Fire Pot" and "Shanghai Duck".
Oasis, Kennedy-Ufer 1 (in the Lufthansa building). Tel: 81 44 41
From this Greek restaurant diners have a lovely view of the old part of Cologne and the cathedral.
Osho's Place, Venloerstrasse 5–7. Tel: 57 40 745
This vegetarian restaurant is a congregating place for friends from all over the world.
Spaghetti-Palast, Hahnenstrasse 37. Tel: 21 17 09
The specialities here are spaghetti dishes. Guests are entertained by a pianist.
Stadtgarten-Restaurant, Venloerstrasse 40. Tel: 51 60 37
This Italian restaurant has a large beer garden and puts on well-frequented jazz concerts. Specialities here include salads, pasta and, in summer, fare grilled on the barbecue.
Taj Mahal, An St Agatha 27. Tel: 24 11 12
An Indian restaurant where vegetarians are well catered for. Curries are the speciality.
Theatre-Schänke, Schwertnergasse 1. Tel: 21 57 31
Both actors and audience of the nearby theatre meet after performances in this small Greek restaurant.
Tchang, Grosse Sandkaul 19. Tel: 21 76 51
A cosy Chinese restaurant of long-standing tradition.
Zum Treppchen, Kirchstrasse 15. Tel: 39 21 79
A popular restaurant with a large beer garden located some distance away from the centre of things in the suburb Rodenkirchen. Specialities include Mainzer Käse (Mainz Cheese) and Cologne liver sausage.

PUBS

When the conversation turns to pubs in Cologne, the historical breweries are generally the first places that come to mind. However the usual place to down a beer after a long day's work is at one of the corner pubs located in the middle of just about every neighbourhood. If you stand at the counter, it probably won't take long before you get into a conversation with one of the many regulars.

Things tend to get a little more lively in the pubs located in the old part of the city. Starting from the posh pub **Keule**, Heumarkt 56, you wil find drinking and eating establishments in just about every building. **Papa Joe's Biersalon Klimperkasten**, Alter Markt 50–52 is especially worth mentioning. The pub houses a valuable collection of musical instruments, one of which is played every hour. Between these special performances jazz bands play live music.

A number of different jazz musicians take turns playing daily at **Em Streckstrump**, Buttermarkt 37. On Sundays at 11am, there's a *Jazzfrüschoppen* – the first beer(s) of the day accompanied by jazz and free peanuts.

Mostly students tend to congregate in the area around Zülpicher Strasse in Sülz, with its picturesque ensemble of pubs and cafés. People associated with the radio and television business meet at the **Orgelchen**, An der Rechtschule, while the clientele frequenting the **Kleinen Glocke**, Glockengasse 58–60, tends to be members of the literary guild.

Directly opposite the cathedral is **Alt Köln** with its splendid facade and carillon. Moving figures strike the hour throughout the day. Inside you'll find a veritable warren of cosy rooms, corners and balconies.

The **Alte Wartesaal**, located in the main railway station, is a real original. Predominantly journalists and artists congregate here.

CAFES

Cafés, both those where you can and cannot dance, have a long tradition in Cologne. Nowadays however, the *Tanzcafé* is pretty much extinct. At the head of the list is the place with the very best view of the cathedral, **Café Reichard**, Unter Fettenhennen. During summer it seems as though the whole world meets on the terrace here; during the winter months guests can enjoy a view of the west facade of the cathedral from inside a glass pavilion. Violinists and pianists playing discreetly complete the atmosphere of grandeur. Other cafés include:
Café Jansen, Obermarspforten 7
Café Riese, Schildergasse 103
Café Zimmermann, Herzogstrasse 11. The speciality here is Havannatorte.

Café Fassbender, Mittelstrasse (in the Bazaar de Cologne)
Café Cremer, Breite Strasse 54
Café Schmitz, Breite Strasse 87. The specialit is *Printen* (a type of gingerbread). (You can also get a replica of Cologne Cathedral made from the same dough.)
Café Wahlen, Hohenstaufenring 64. The speciality is *Baumkuchen*.
Café Steudter, Kaiser-Wilhelm-Ring
Café Füllenbach, Ebertplatz
Café Eigel, Brückenstrasse. The speciality is *Pilztorte* (mushroom pie).
Café Franck, Rudolphplatz.
Trödelcafé, near St Agatha. Doubles as an antique shop.

NIGHTLIFE

Cologne is neither Hamburg nor Las Vegas when it comes to nightlife. Nevertheless, there are several streets in the city where night owls can enjoy themselves until dawn.

DISCOS

Alter Wartesaal im Hauptbahnhof
Coconut Grove, Salzgasse 5
Lord's Inn, Roonstrasse 7
Omas Schnapshaus, Alter Markt 36–42
Wicküler im Römer, Kleine Budengasse 1
Show-Boat, Hohenzollernring 16–18
Clou, Hohenstaufenring 58
Ekkstein's, Ubierring 24
Zorba The Buddha Osho Diskothek, "die Grosse", Hohenzollernring 90
Zorba The Buddha Osho Diskothek, "die Kleine", Brabanterstrasse 15

NIGHT CAFES & BARS

A substantial part of Cologne's nightlife takes place around Friesenplatz on both sides of the Hohenzollernring. Very few of the night cafés and bars open before 9pm, but they compensate for this fact by staying

open until the small hours of the morning.
Blue Night, Im Klapperhof 48
Chez moi, Palmstrasse 38
Chez Nous, Große Budengasse 13
Kokett, Altenberger Strasse 11
Intermezzo, Unter Käster 5
Karibik, Gereonshof 36
King George, Sudermannstrasse 2
Apropo, Im Dau 17
Tiffani, Venloer Strasse 19
Bonotel, Bonner Strasse

GAMBLING CASINOS

Although Cologne has its own gambling casino, the roulette balls roll in a more fashionable atmosphere in Bad Neuenahr 45 km (28 miles) to the southwest and in Aachen 80 km (50 miles) to the west.

THINGS TO DO

SIGHTSEEING

At numerous places scattered throughout the city centre you can see a variety of sights attesting to Cologne's 2,000-year-old history. New evidence of both the Roman and medieval cultures emerges with each excavation. Many of these finds have been integrated into the surroundings, for example in the Parkhaus am Dom (the multistorey car park located beneath the cathedral).

Any sightseeing tour through the city should be devised with the specific interests of its participants in mind. The emphasis of such a tour might be archaeological sites, or sacred medieval or modern architecture. The following are a few suggestions.

The area around the cathedral has changed quite a bit over the past few years, especially when the Wallraf-Richartz and Ludwig Museum, Philharmonie and Rhine Garden came into being. This complex has created a car-free network of pedestrian zones running from the cathedral to the Rhine. As a result of the Rheinuferstrasse being lowered and routed through a tunnel between the cathedral and Heumarkt, Cologne is once again actually situated "on the Rhine".

The first stopping point of nearly every tour is, naturally, the **Cathedral** itself. Its High Gothic architecture alone is enough to mesmerise just about every out-of-town visitor. A number of remarkable sights are also to be found inside the cathedral, for example the Shrine of the Three Magi, the Altar of the City's Patron Saints by Stephan Lochner, the modern painting beneath the organ gallery by Peter Hecker, and the Treasury. A truly panoramic view of the city and surrounding countryside can be had by climbing the 504 steps leading up from the visitors' floor. On the way up take a minute to catch your breath by looking in the belfry where you'll see the "decke Pitter", the biggest bell in the world. The tower is open from 9am to 5pm.

If you continue on your way over the cathedral plaza and Roncalliplatz, you'll pass the venerable Dom-Hotel and the fascinating Roman-Germanic Museum before entering the **Altstadt** (the old part of the city) with its many historical houses, cafés and restaurants. This particular section of Cologne extends all the way to the Rhine where a number of boats are moored.

Hohe Strasse, the most famous shopping street in Cologne and the very first pedestrian zone in Germany, can likewise be reached from the cathedral plaza. Here you'll find boutiques, speciality shops and restaurants strung like a row of beads, one right after the other. Street musicians, wandering salespeople and fruit vendors serve to make the already colourful scene even more brilliant. At the point where the attractiveness of Hohe Strasse dwindles, the wider **Schildergasse** begins. In this street there are a number of giant department and clothing stores as well as speciality shops, a butcher's and a church.

Schildergasse ends at **Neumarkt**, a large square surrounded by surging traffic. One of the 12 Romanesque churches in the city, **Church of the Holy Apostles** (St Aposteln), is situated on the west side of the square. This also marks the start of yet another shopping area full of exquisite boutiques, jewellery shops and the **Bazaar de Cologne**, an especially classy shopping arcade.

Mittelstrasse runs into Rudolphplatz, where you'll see the **Hahnentor**, one of the three preserved medieval city gates in Cologne. Heading off to the right is Pfeilstrasse with its many galleries and trendy shops. This street leads right to St-Apern-Strasse, where you'll find quite a few good antique stores.

Rudolphplatz is bordered on the west by **Ringstrasse**, called here Hohenzollernring and a bit further on Hohenstauffenring. This street follows the course of the former medieval city wall and thus encloses the oldest part of the city centre. The biggest cinemas in Cologne are mostly concentrated north of Rudolphplatz. This particular boulevard is a real promenade where people stroll with the intention of seeing and being seen. Along the northern part of Ringstrasse, in front of Ebertplatz, and along the southern part, in front of Chlodwigplatz, you can see preserved sections of the city's medieval fortifications. **Eigelstein-Torburg**, the northern city gate, is located at Ebertplatz and the **Severinstorburg**, its southern counterpart, is situated at Chlodwigplatz. At one time there were no fewer than 12 fortified major and minor gates built into the city wall. These served to protect the 40,000 citizens living within and constituted one of the largest medieval fortifications. Of all the smaller gates, the Ulrepforte is the only one still in existence today. Currently, the Carnival society "Rote Funken" (Red Sparks) has set up its domicile there.

If you head out in a westerly direction from the cathedral, you'll pass a number of different buildings which are all affiliated with Westdeutscher Rundfunk (West German Broadcasting). Continuing along this route will lead you by the **Kunstgewerbe-Museum** (Museum of Arts and Crafts), which was formerly the home of the Wallraf-Richartz Museum, over busy Tunisstrasse to the **Opera House** with its own theatre. To the right of this is the reconstructed original factory **Glockengasse 4711**, the famous eau de Cologne company established by Ferdinand Mülhens.

By going over the cathedral plaza and Roncalliplatz, you'll get to the **Alter Markt**, characterised by narrow houses with pointed gables, the **Jan-von-Werth-Brunnen** (Jan von Werth Fountain) and the **Rathaus** (Town Hall). It's here at the Alter Markt at 11.11am on 11 November, in what's known as the fifth season in Cologne, that the Carnival period is officially opened. Stairs lead to the Rathausplatz and to the front side of the Town Hall where there's an exquisite Renaissance gazebo and, inside, the sumptuous Hansesaal, dating from the year 1349. The carillon in the Town Hall Tower can be heard daily at noon and again at 5pm. A ritual Jewish bath, the **Mikwe**, has been unearthed in front of the Town Hall. It dates from the Middle Ages and can only be reached by going down through a 15 metre (50 ft) shaft. This bath, which is now filled with ground water, was at one time used for ritual ablutions. The bath is open for public viewing during Town Hall working hours; the key can be obtained from the gatekeeper in the Town Hall gazebo.

The **Gürzenich** is about 100 metres (335 ft) further to the south. The citizens set up this building as a dance hall between 1437 and 1444 and it is still used today in its original capacity. Celebrations, dance events, conventions and Carnival activities all take place in what's fondly referred to as "Cologne's living-room". Behind the Gürzenich are the ruins of **St Alban's Church.** In the nave is a copy of the sculptural group by Käthe Kollwitz entitled *Grieving Parents.* There is, moreover, an entire museum in Cologne devoted to Kollwitz where many of the artist's sketches, sculptures and printed graphics are on display. (Neumarkt 18–24, in the Neumarkt Passage.)

As far back as the Middle Ages Cologne was described as "hillige Cöllen" (holy Cologne). Doubtless contributing to this reputation is the fact that there are **12 unique Roman Romanesque churches,** all located in quite close proximity to one another within the medieval city's perimeters. These churches are considered to be 12 of the most important in all of Western Europe. Nearly all the holy edifices are closely tied to the names of the city's archbishops. The oldest of the garland of Romanesque churches is **St Pantaleon's,** which was consecrated in the year 980 and contains the gravestone of Kaiser Theophanu. **St Andrew's** (St Andreas), situated directly to the northwest of the cathedral, houses the tomb of the Doctor of the Church Albertus Magnus and **St Ursula's,** located a bit further to the north, holds the relics of the city's patron saint and her 11,000 madonnas, whose memory has been preserved for ever by the 11 flames visible on the city's coat of arms. The other churches attesting to the magnificence of Romanesque architecture include **St Gereon's,** the **Church of the Holy Apostles** (St Aposteln), **St Cecilia's, St George's, St Cunibert's, St Mary's in the Capitol, St Mary's in Lyskirchen, Great St Martin's** and **St Severinus's.** It was through these 12 churches that Cologne gained the reputation of being the "Rome of the North". All were badly damaged during World War II and it was only with great effort that their reconstruction was completed by the year 1985. Only the west tower of St Cunibert is still under construction at this time.

There are other churches of significance in Cologne in addition to the aforementioned Romanesque churches and the cathedral. These include the Gothic places of worship, the **Minorite Church,** containing the tomb of the "father of apprentices" Adolf Kolping, the **Antonite Church** (Antoniterkirche), which houses Barlach's *The Angel of Death,* and the **Church of the Assumption** (Maria Himmelfahrt), erected by the Jesuits between 1618 and 1678. The latter is located in Marzellenstrasse, not far from the cathedral and main railway station.

The **Church of Mary in the Kupfergasse,** which sustained serious damage during the war, has been restored in its original Dutch Baroque style. Cologne natives have grown especially fond of the scaled-down reproduction of the Holy House of Loretto and its "Black Madonna", a statue attributed with miraculous powers.

A sacred jewel is the **Chapel of St Columbia,** located on Brückenstrasse. The chapel was erected from within the ruins of the parish church by Professor Gottfried Böhm in 1950. The windows were made by Georg Meistermann. The chapel is popularly referred to as the "Madonna in the Ruins".

TOURS

City Tours: Further information and exact times are available directly from the Tourist Information Centre near the cathedral, tel: 221 33 32.

Cathedral Tours: Weekdays at 10am, 11am, 2.30pm and 3.30pm. During the summer there is an additional tour offered at 4.30pm. Tours are conducted Saturdays at 10 and

11am, and on Sunday and holidays at 2.30 and 3.30pm. Occasionally, due to special circumstances, these tours begin a little later. **Town Hall Tours**: Monday, Wednesday and Saturday at 3pm.
Ubii Monument: near der Malzmühle 1; Thursday 4.45pm–6pm.

CITY SIGHTSEEING TOURS

Throughout the entire year the Tourist Information Centre organises city sightseeing tours. During the winter these tours commence at 11am and 2pm; during the summer they begin at 10 and 11am, 1, 2 and 3pm. Each lasts approximately two hours and includes all the major sights of Cologne. There is a 20-minute stop planned in either the Schnütgen or Municipal Museum.

Explanations of what you are seeing are given in German, English and French. Tickets can be purchased directly from the driver for 20 DM per person. The bus departs from the southern side of the Tourist Information Office.

In the months of July and August additional **Abendfahrten** (evening tours) are also on the agenda. These begin with a bus tour of Cologne by night, followed by a boat trip along the Rhine and take in two short detours to see the Dance Fountain and TV Tower "Colonius", which affords the most beautiful view by far over the twinkling city. The evening tour is concluded with a glass of *Kölsch* or wine, a bite to eat and some lively entertainment in a restaurant or bar. This particular variety of evening pleasure lasts about 3½ hours and costs 45 DM (subject to change).

Taxi-Guide is a special taxi service which can be ordered by calling the number 28 82. It has 25 taxi drivers who, after having been especially trained to be city tour guides and passing the necessary test, have received a licence permitting them to guide tourists round the historical sights of Cologne. Visitors interested in hiring this service can request that their driver speak German, Italian, Dutch, English, French or Turkish. A tour lasting just short of two hours will cost you about 60 DM. Taxi drivers are also happy to fulfil any special sightseeing wish. Naturally, these out-of-the-ordinary requests will cost you a bit more. Air Service Teuberg, tel: (0 22 03) 40 24 53, offers **City Sightseeing**

Tours by Plane. These tours take about 15 minutes and cost 160 DM for up to three persons.

EXCURSIONS

Whether you choose to travel by bus, tram, rail or by boat along the Rhine there are several interesting excursions which will lead you into the surrounding countryside.

Brühl lies to the southwest between the cities of Cologne and Bonn. The main attraction here is the **Augustusburg Castle**. Hours: 9am–noon and again 1.30–4pm every day except Monday. Closed: during the months of December and January. Guided tours of the castle are available on the hour or half-hour, depending on demand. For further information tel: (02232) 42 471. In the summer the castle provides an elegant backdrop for the well-known **Brühler Castle Concerts**, conducted by Helmut Müller-Brühl. It is necessary to reserve tickets for the concerts in advance; they are also available at the usual ticket outlets in Cologne.

Other attractions in Brühl include:
Falkenlust Hunting Lodge. Hours: 9am–noon and 2–4pm. Closed: Mondays. For further information tel: (02232) 121 11.
Phantasialand, the biggest recreational and adventure park in all of Europe. Hours: 9am–6pm daily from 1 April–31 October. Tel: (02232) 361 01.

Bensberg lies to the east just short of Cologne's city limits and can be easily reached via the A 4 (motorway), or by tram in about 20 minutes. Today a part of Bergisch Gladbach, this little town became famous throughout the world for its modern **Town Hall** built of concrete and glass by Gottfried Böhm. The remains of the old castle on the site have been integrated into the new construction. From a good distance away you can catch a glimpse of the mighty **baroque hunting lodge**. Unfortunately the building is not open for public viewing as it now houses a boarding school.

If you continue on beyond Bergisch Gladbach you'll come to the **Altenberg Cathedral**, an immense Cistercian abbey situated in the heart of the picturesque Bergisches Land. Some of the cathedral's stained-glass windows are over 700 years old and the western window with its brilliant colours and beauty is especially breathtaking. The old cloister compound has been carefully renovated and currently houses seminar buildings, restaurants and a cloister shop in which you can purchase recordings of the cathedral's organ. The cathedral contains one of the largest organs in all of Germany, with 6,000 pipes, four manuals and 82 registers. Concerts take place here at various times throughout the year.

Zündorf, situated along the right side of the Rhine on Cologne's southernmost outskirts, has preserved its village character despite the fact it is actually a part of the city. The narrow streets and alleyways lined with half-timbered houses, the medieval market square and three old churches all contribute to give the visitor the impression that time has stood still here. The town has gained in attractiveness by the "Groov", a recreational area located directly along the banks of the Rhine encompassing meadows, bicycle paths, ponds where you can rent rowing boats, mini-golf and a combination indoor and outdoor swimming pool. Several different eating establishments within the old walls and having large terraces provide for hospitality.

The largest **brown coal mining area** in Europe and, consequently, the densest concentration of energy production generated at coal power plants is located to the west, between Cologne and Aachen. The coal-mining company Rheinbraun operates an information centre in Paffendorf Castle near Bergheim/Erft.

Other excursion destinations include:
Burg Castle on the Wupper. Hours: 9am–6pm daily and 1pm–6pm Monday 1 March–5 November, and between 10am–5pm daily except Monday 13 November–end February. For further information tel: (0212) 4 20 98 or 4 20 99.
Brauweil Church. Hours: all day during the weekend and on Thursday until 1pm. The abbey courtyards are open 10am–4pm. To book an appointment telephone Frau Kunz at (02234) 80 52 49.
Knechtsteden Monastery. Hours: open all day.
Zons. Sightseeing tours of this medieval fortified city are available upon request at the Heimat-und Verkehrsverein (the Local

and Tourist Information Agency). Tel: (02106) 37 72.

GARDENS & PARKS

Despite the fact that there are over one million people living in Cologne, the city is remarkably green; for every inhabitant there are about 75 sq. metres (800 sq. ft) of green area. Citizens have their long-standing mayor Konrad Adenauer (who later became the Chancellor of Germany) to thank for the **Äusseren Grüngürtel** (the Outer Green Belt) in the west part of the city. Within this 12-km (8-mile) stretch of forests and meadows there are a number of extensive footpaths, areas for playing or sunbathing, ponds where you can rent rowing boats and the Müngersdorf Stadium.

To the north of the city a recreational area encompassing 200 hectares (500 acres) of land has developed around **Fühlinger Lake**. Seven lakes (former gravel-pits) have been connected to one another. The 2,000-metre (6,670-ft) regatta course, an outdoor swimming pool surrounded by a large lawn for sunbathing and a lake for surfing provide the main attractions for thousands of people during summer.

Visitors will be delighted by the variety of flowers, trees and plants from all four corners of the earth to be found in the **Botanical Garden** in Cologne-Riehl. A population of rare trees has been cultivated here since 1864. Tropical and subtropical plants are on display in the greenhouses. In the immediate vicinity of the Flora is the **Zoological Garden**, spread out over spacious parkland. Visitors are drawn at all times of the year see more than 7,000 different kinds of animals from all over the world living here. The zoo includes an aquarium with an insectarium for reptiles, fish and insects. Hours: 9am–6pm during summer and 9am–5pm during the winter.

There are well over 4,000 different kinds of plants growing in the **Forst Botanical Garden**, located in Rodenkirchen (a suburb in the south of Cologne) at the intersection of Schillingsrotter Weg and Rondorfer Strasse. The variety of plants and trees here encompasses everything from the North American giant redwood tree to exotic specimens from Japan. Adjacent to the garden is the **Friedenswald** (the Peace Forest), where each country of the world is represented by examples of its indigenous trees.

The **Rhine Park** extends along the right side of the Rhine, directly opposite the city centre. This park has twice been the site of the German Garden Show. Large flower beds, and lawns provide enough room for more than 5,000 different kinds of plants to grow. A chairlift crosses the park, the separate seats spaced at intervals of a few metres. Playgrounds, cafés, fountains and sculptures punctuate the landscape and the panoramic view of the city centre from the Rhine's banks is unique. There's a funicular which goes from the north end of the Rhine Park up and over the Rhine itself, over the Zoobrücke to the left-hand river bank where it finally deposits its passengers directly in front of the entrance to the Zoological Garden.

The **Tanzbrunnen** (Dance Fountain), a unique open-air area used for a variety of entertainment events, is located at the southern end of the park by the exhibition grounds. During the summer season international show stars perform here. The spacious grounds offer room enough for approximately 2,500 visitors to find seats, some of which are under cover. The area is called "Tanzbrunnen" due to a dance floor and large fountain, both enclosed under a tented roof. Further information and a calendar of events are available from the beginning of May onwards at the Tourist Information Centre.

Indigenous wild animals can be seen in the **Stadtwald** (City Forest) near Cologne-Lindenthal, in the **Wildpark Brück** and in the **Wildpark Dünnwald**. The German Association for the Protection of Forests has also established a display of different kinds of trees here.

The **Leidenhausen Recreational Area** (Cologne-Porz Eil), located at the edge of the Königsforst in the east of Cologne, offers a variety of hiking trails, open spaces for sunning or recreational activities, a big playground for children, a bird of prey sanctuary and the forest museum "Haus des Waldes".

Groov, a "recreational island", is situated on the right-hand bank of the Rhine in Cologne-Porz Zündorf. There's a little lake (where you can rent a rowing boat), marina, mini-golf course and swimming pool, as well as a number of eateries where you can sit down and have a snack. When the weather is good, the island is particularly popular.

CULTURE PLUS

LIBRARIES & ARCHIVES

HBZ – Hochschulbibliothekszentrum (Rhineland-Westphalia University Library Centre): maintains a comprehensive catalogue of books available at all other university and college libraries. Classen-Kappelmann-Strasse 24. Tel: 40 10 05
Historisches Archiv (City of Cologne Historical Archives): Severinstrasse 222-228. Tel: 2 21-23 27
Dom-und Diözesan-Bibliothek (Cathedral and Diocesan Library): Kardinal-Frings-Strasse 1. Tel: 16 42-8 62 21
Evangelische Bibliothek (Protestant Library): Karthäusergasse 9. Tel: 33 82-318
Stadtbücherei - Zentralbibliothek (City Library – Central Library): Josef-Haubrich-Hof 1. Tel: 221-38 28

Other libraries and archives located in foreign cultural institutes include:
British Council, Hahnenstrasse 6
Amerika-Haus, Apostelnkloster 13
German-Finnish Association, Albertus-Magnus-Platz
Institut Français, Sachsenring 77
Institute for Italian Culture, Universitätsstrasse 81
Institute for Japanese Culture, Universitätsstrasse 98
Belgisches Haus, Cäcilienstrasse 46

MUSEUMS

With its eight municipal, numerous privately-run and ecclesiastical museums, Cologne is one of the most significant cities for art in all of Europe. This status has been re-emphasised by the construction of the new Wallraf-Richartz and Ludwig Museum between the cathedral and the Rhine in 1982.

The largest gallery devoted purely to painting in the entire Rhineland can be found at the **Wallraf-Richartz Museum**. The heart of this collection is composed of works by artists of the Cologne Painting School. On display at the **Ludwig Museum** are a selection of relatively recent works dating from the Expressionists through to the Moderns. The museum's focal points are provided by both the Haubrich and Ludwig Collections. The museum is located at Bischofsgarten 1. Hours: 10am–8pm Tuesday–Thursday, 10am–6pm Friday–Sunday. Closed: Monday. Guided tours take place Tuesdays at 6pm and Saturdays and Sundays at 11am.

Located right next to the aforementioned museums, the **Roman-Germanic Museum** is devoted to an account of culture and life beginning from the period following the death of Christ. The Roman settlement CCAA (Colonia Claudia Ara Agrippinsium) was established around the year AD 50 and the many exhibits include glassware, vessels, coins and jewellery, as well as the Dionysos Mosaic, the tomb of Lucius Poblicius, mural paintings, various other tombstones and holy stones date back to this period. Adjacent to the southern side of the museum at its original location, a Roman harbour road has been reconstructed. The address is Roncalliplatz 4. Hours: 10am–5pm Tuesday–Sunday, 10am–8pm Wednesday and Thursday. Closed: Monday. Guided tours are available upon request.

Just a few metres further on the **Diözesanmuseum** (Diocesan Museum) provides its visitors with an overview of sacred art. Here precious burial objects extracted from the tombs of Frankish princes are also on display. The address is Roncalliplatz 2. Hours: 10am–5pm Monday–Saturday, 10am–1pm Sunday. Closed: Thursday.

The **Stadtmuseum** (Municipal Museum) is housed in what was once the old municipal armoury which dates back to the 16th century. The museum contains exhibits depicting middle-class life as it was experienced from the Middle Ages until modern times. The address is Zeughausstrasse 1–3. Hours: 10am–5pm Tuesday–Sunday, 10am–8pm Thursday. Closed: Monday. Guided tours are available Saturdays at 3pm.

In 1952 the **Schnütgen Museum** was moved into the Romanesque basilica of St Cecilia. Christian art from the Middle Ages until the present day with an emphasis on the Romanesque and Gothic periods is displayed in surroundings truly worthy of such works. The museum is located at Cäcilienstrasse 29. Hours: 10am–5pm Tuesday–Sunday, 10am–8pm on the first Wednesday of every month. Closed: Monday. Guided tours offered on Sundays at 11am.

The most extensive collection of Chinese, Korean and Japanese art in Germany is on view at the **Museum für Ost-asiatische Kunst** (the Museum of East Asian Art). The museum is located at Universitätsstrasse 100. Hours: 10am–5pm Tuesday–Sunday, 10am–8pm on the first Friday in every month. Guided tours are offered on Sundays at 11am.

Around 60,000 different articles from a number of distant lands and continents can be numbered within the permanent holdings of the **Rautenstrauch-Joest Museum**, thus making it one of the largest ethnological collections of its kind to be found anywhere. In the special section "Spielzeugwelten" (World of Toys), there are several thousand examples of handmade toys from the Barbara Schu Collection. The museum is located at Ubierring 45. Hours: 10am–5pm Tuesday–Sunday, 10am–8pm on the first Wednesday in every month. Closed: Monday. Guided tours are offered on Sundays at 3pm.

The **Museum für Angewandte Kunst/Kunstgewerbemuseum** (The Museum of Applied Arts/Museum of Arts and Crafts) has now found a home in what was formerly the Wallraf-Richartz Museum. Examples of artistic trades from the Middle Ages as well as design, glass and porcelain are displayed here. The museum's address is An der Rechtschule. Hours: 10am–5pm Wednesday–Sunday, 10am–8pm Tuesday. Closed: Monday.

The **Josef-Haubrich-Kunsthalle** (Josef-Haubrich Art Gallery) on Neumarkt presents changing exhibits from all areas of art and art history. The Kölner Kunstverein (Cologne Art Association) is located right next to it and devotes its changing exhibitions to well-known artists of the 20th century. It's located at Josef-Haubrich-Hof, Kunsthalle. Hours: 10am–5pm daily and 10am–8pm Tuesday and Friday. Guided tours are held on Tuesdays and Fridays at 6pm. The Kunstverein is open 10am–5pm Tuesday–Sunday and is closed on Monday.

In the westernmost suburb of Cologne, **Weiden**, Roman excavations in a subterranean **burial chamber** are on public view.

The address is Aachener Strasse 1328. Ring for the attendant; groups should call to book an appointment in advance. Tel: (0 22 34) 7 33 99. Hours: 11am–1pm Tuesday–Thursday, 10am–5pm Friday and 1–5pm Saturday and Sunday. Closed: Monday and national holidays. There are also **Romanesque tombs** on view in the crypt of St Severinus's church. On every Monday and Friday at 4.30pm there is a guided tour conducted through both the excavations and the church. Those wishing to join a tour should call in advance Tel: 31 68 70.

The **Praetorium**, located underneath the Town Hall, is a Roman palace originally belonging to the governor and can be visited daily except Monday 10am–5pm. If you'd appreciate an extensive tour it is necessary to call and request one in advance. Tel: 221-34 68 or 221-41 98.

The city's automatic information service will provide you with a summary of all the exhibits currently on view in Cologne museums, tel: 221-43 43.

EXHIBITS/GALLERIES

There are more than 100 galleries and art dealers as well as auction houses in Cologne. Until the middle of the 1960s the city was most noted for its old art. This changed, however, with the advent of the first art market held in 1967. From this point onwards numerous galleries and artists established themselves in Cologne and, as a result of this, an international art scene emerged. Many of the galleries are located in the triangle created between Neumarkt, Rudolfplatz and Friesenplatz. The Kreishausgallerie (at the corner of Albertus-Strasse and Magnusstrase) is actually an arcade where several galleries specialising in modern art are grouped together.

The most important, internationally active galleries include:
Galerie Boissere, Drususgasse 7–11
Galerie Ricke, Volksgartenstrasse 10
Galerie Werner, Gertrudenstrasse 24–28
Galerie Zwirner, Albertus-Strasse 18
Galerie Max Hetzler, Venloer Strasse 21
Galerie Monika Spüth, Maria-Hilf-Strasse 17

Two other galleries also deserve special mention. The first of these is the **CCAA Glasgalerie Köln,** Auf dem Berlich 24, which deals in modern glass creations and replicas of Roman glassware. The second is the **Naive-Kunst-Galerie** in Dellbrück, Roteichenweg 5, where a permanent exhibit of works by internationally acclaimed naive artists is complemented by a variety of special exhibits. If you'd like to visit, it is necessary to call and make an appointment, tel: l: 68 83 38.

Every year in November the art market "Art Cologne" draws artists, gallery owners and visitors from all over the world.

CONCERTS

Advance Booking Office: Tickets for all important concerts and events which take place in Cologne can be purchased in advance at the following outlets:
The theatre box office at Neumarkt. Tel: 21 42 32
The theatre box office in Kaufhof (a large department store). Tel: 21 66 92
The Rudolphplatz Theatre Ticket Box Office. Tel: 23 83 57
Saturn Theatre Ticket Box Office. Tel: 12 19 12
KölnTicket, Roncalliplatz. Tel: 28 01

The quantity of musical events offered in Cologne has increased due to the construction of the **Philharmonie** (Philharmonic Hall), located in the Wallraff-Richartz and Ludwig Museum complex. The subterranean, ultra-modern concert hall can accommodate audiences of up to 2,200. At home here are the Gürzenich Orchestra, West German Radio Symphony Orchestra and the Köln-Musik. The repertoire encompasses everything from jazz to folk and chamber music, to symphony productions and contemporary music. Occasionally on Sundays at 11am Viktor Lukas presents the tremendous tonal richness of the Klais Organ.

The Rhineland Chamber Orchestra primarily performs baroque music and compositions from the classical period. Concerts take place in the Philharmonie or in the Schnütgen Museum.

The Gürzenich Choir, Kölner Kantorei, Männer-Gesang-Verein (Men's Choral Society), Philharmonic Choir, Kölner Kammerchor (Cologne Chamber Choir), Mülheimer Kantorei, Bach-Verein Köln (Cologne Bach Society) and the Kölner Kurende all put on vocal performances throughout the city.

Classical music venues:
Philharmonie, Bischofsgarten 1. Tel: 23 38 54
Gürzenich, Martinstrasse 29/37. Evening box office: Tel: 221 23 85
Musikhochschule Köln, Dagobertstrasse 38. Tel: 12 40 33
WDR Grosser Sendesaal, Wallrafplatz. Tel: 220-1

Rock, Pop and Jazz venues:
Luxor, Luxemburger Strasse 40. Tel: 21 95 06
Em Streckstrump, Buttermarkt 37. Tel: 21 79 50
Subway, Aachener Strasse 82-84. Tel: 51 76 69
Stadtgarten, Venloer Strasse 40. Tel: 51 60 39

OPERA & BALLET

The performance seasons of both the opera and ballet take the various school holidays into account and generally commence at the beginning of September and last until the middle of July. The Opera House repertoire includes both classical and modern works. The building, designed by Wilhelm Riphahn and constructed between 1957 and 1962, can accommodate 1,300 people. The municipal theatres support their own ballet ensemble, the Kölner Tanzforum. In July dancers from all over the world meet here to participate in the traditional "Sommerakademie des Tanzes" (Summer Academy of Dance). **Opernhaus**, Offenbachplatz, evening box office, tel: 221 82 52

THEATRES

Schauspielhaus, Offenbachplatz. Evening box office: Tel: 221 82 48
Schlosserei in the Schauspielhaus. Tel: 221 83 21
Kammerspiele, Ubierring 45. Evening box office: Tel: 32 79 90
Theater am Dom (light theatre), Glockengasse 11, Kölner Ladenstadt. Tel: 21 99 21
Senftöpfchen (cabaret), Grosse Neugasse 2-4. Tel: 23 79 80
Die Machtwächter (cabaret), Gertrudenstrasse 24. Tel: 24 21 01
Theater der Keller (contemporary theatre), Kleingedankstrasse 6. Tel: 31 80 59

Bauturm (contemporary theatre), Aachener Strasse 24. Tel: 52 42 42
Urania-Theater (contemporary theatre), Ehrenfeld, Venloer Strasse 265. Tel: 56 15 96
Comedia Colonia, Löwengasse 7-9. Tel: 26 76 70
Freies Werkstatt Theater, Zugweg 10. Tel: 32 78 17

The **Volkstheater Millowitsch**, Aachener Strasse 5. Tel: 25 17 47, is an institution which is particularly close to the hearts of many Cologne natives. At the present time the 6th generation of Millowitsch family members are performing theatre in Cologne; the company has performed here since 1936.

The **Puppenspiele der Stadt Köln** (Cologne's Puppet Theatre), Eisenmarkt. Tel: 21 20 95, is not a theatre just for kids. Both children and adults are sure to enjoy the performances. Typical Cologne characters like Hänneschen, Bärbelchen, Tünnes, Schäl and many other city originals are brought to life here as puppets.

In both theatres the local dialect is spoken: in the Millowitsch Theatre you'll hear the Rhineland dialect and in the Hänneschen Theatre the real Cologne dialect.

CINEMAS

The largest concentration of cinemas in Cologne is found along the Ring between Christophstrasse and Rudolphplatz. These are usually cinema centres, housing just a few large and small movie theatres under one roof.

The **Autokino** (Drive-in cinema) is in Porz, on Frankfurter Strasse. In Höhenberg (Im Weidenbruch 4) there is what's called "Filmdancing"; films are shown on a big screen while you're dancing. The **Lupe 2** on Mauritiussteinweg 102 and the **Cinemathek** in the new Wallraf-Richartz and Ludwig Museum both show avant-garde and old films.

In Hürth, situated east of Cologne and reached via Luxemburger Strasse, the new **Kinozentrum "UCI"** is in operation. This centre contains no fewer than 14 separate movie theatres and can accommodate a total of 2,800 people. Over 40 films are screened daily in these state-of-the-art cinemas. It's a good idea to reserve tickets in advance, tel: (0 22 33) 79 91 23.

SHOPPING

SHOPPING TIPS

The pedestrian zones in Cologne are perfect for undisturbed strolling and shopping. The covered arcades are ideal for shopping too, and not only when the weather leaves something to be desired. The **Bazaar de Cologne**, for instance, houses 63 shops and cafés, restaurants, ice-cream parlours, fountains and a glass elevator.

Olivandenhof is the name of the new shopping centre situated in the middle of the old business district between Neumarkt and Breite Strasse. Since 1988, 30 retail stores and a number of eating establishments have been conducting their business under a single glass roof. A number of oval galleries, connected to one another via glass escalators and a glass elevator, furnish a total of 4 x 160 metres (535 ft) of prime window space. All in all, this high-class shopping centre is designed for customers with good and expensive taste.

The art galleries and classy shops housed in the **Kreishausgalerie** also share a common roof. The **Kölner Ladenstadt** is the oldest shopping arcade in Cologne. In addition to stores which specialise in more sophisticated, luxurious items, there are also those which sell posters in general and film advertisement and art reproduction posters in particular. The Theater am Dom and the Pfeffermühle, (a restaurant serving crêpes to appeal to everyone's taste), are also located here. In the basement, "Colon" (a kind of a beer village) has spread out and a car park takes up the entire upper floor.

Without a doubt the most famous shopping street in the city is **Hohe Strasse**, the very first pedestrian zone in all Germany. Boutiques, trendy shops, department stores and speciality shops interspersed with restaurants suitable for either a quick bite or a leisurely meal are all strung out along the narrow North-South axis running through the city centre.

During the summer street painters and musicians take over the area where Hohe Strasse begins in the north, Wallrafplatz and the adjacent cathedral plaza. **Schildergasse** branches off from the southern end of Hohe Strasse towards Neumarkt. This broad street is lined with department stores like Kaufhof, Woolworth, Kaufhalle, Dyckhoff and Hertie, as well as with cinemas and cafés. **Breite Strasse** (Karstadt) runs parallel to this thoroughfare and offers a (nearly) car-free pedestrian paradise. Over the past few years **Ehrenstrasse** has developed into a modern shopping and entertainment street. A number of unusual boutiques have sprung up around the Sartory Theatre.

Eigelstein and **Weidengasse** (the latter branches off from the former), located in the northern part of the city centre, have fallen practically completely into Turkish hands. This is the place to buy excellent, top-quality Turkish culinary specialities like mutton, sheep's milk cheese, traditional round loaves of flat bread and exotic spices.

With a sales area encompassing 3,500 sq. yards, "Gonski" (Neumarkt 18), and its branch store located at Domkloster 2, is the largest **bookshop** in Cologne. Other big bookstores in the city centre include "Herder am Dom", Komödienstrasse 11, the "Bücherstube am Dom", which is located not at the cathedral, but rather at Neumarkt 2, "Sieger am Dom", Komödienstrasse 7, the railway bookshop "Ludwig", located in the main railway station and the "Buchhandlung am Barbarossaplatz", Barbarossaplatz. The bookstore "Gleumes", Hohenstaufenring 47–51, specialises in maps and travel literature.

Good antiques can be purchased in St Apernstrasse, near the Intercontinental Hotel. You can have works of art restored here as well as an expert's report drawn up. Mittelstrasse is distinguished by its exclusive **fashion boutiques**.

You can get nearly any **record** and **CD** that you can think of at "Saturn" on Hansaring. For those more interested in rock and pop, the place to go is WOM (World of Music), located in the basement of the Hertie department store at Neumarkt.

Unusual jewellery, for example Finnish designer pieces by Lapponia, can be found at Klaus Kaufhold (Quatermarkt 5 – near the intersection of Hohe Strasse and Schildergasse, or at Apostelnkloster 17, between Neumarkt and Mittelstrasse). In 1980 he established the first platinum workshop in his store at Quatermarkt and was thus instrumental in helping this relatively new material become popular in the world of jewellery production. Juwelier Hölscher (Hohe Strasse) carries a good selection of classic jewellery and Josef Becker (Hohe Strasse) specialises in silver articles.

Souvenirs of all shapes and sizes can be found in the small shops around the cathedral. An especially popular gift always was and still is, of course, Eau de Cologne 4711. This can be purchased in literally every perfume shop, but is also readily available in the speciality stores clustered around the cathedral and in the Glockengasse. (The latter address is where the firm had its original quarters.) If you're looking for a really special souvenir from Cologne, pay a visit to Brüggelmannhaus in the Mühlengasse. Here Lilli Balg-Baur sells her handmade puppets of original Cologne characters like Tünnes, Schäl, Hänneschen, Bärbelchen, etc. Each puppet is unique down to the tiniest detail. Lilli Balg-Baur received a first prize in the USA for her original Cologne waiter, the *Köbes*.

Balloons large and small, costing anywhere from 20 pfennigs for the smallest to a whopping 50,000 DM for the largest inflated decoration, can be found at Frau "Balloni" in Cologne Ehrenfeld, Gutenbergstrasse 10. Sybille Hartung makes dreams come true out of feather-light rubber. If you're looking for **magic tricks and equipment**, make sure you stop by the "Zauberkönig", Grosse Budengasse 3, near Hohe Strasse. In addition to magic articles they also carry a large selection of joke gimmicks. The "Postkarteladen" located at Breite Strasse 93 has the largest assortment of **postcards** around.

MARKETS

Although there is no main outdoor market in Cologne, there are about 37 different ones with over 80 events that take place on various days during the week in the Altstadt-Nord (the old part of the city in the north) and in a number of suburbs. Between 7am and 1pm you can stock up on fresh fruits, vegetables, meat, cheese, butter and eggs, as well as on spices, herbs and textiles. The Nippeser citizens have held their **Markt am Wilhelmplatz** ever since the turn of the century. Over the years it has become the oldest and biggest outdoor market in the city. It is held every day except Sunday. The **markets in Lindenthal and Klettenberg** each have more than 50 years of tradition behind them. Both are located in the "Belt"; the former on the third Cologne Ringstrasse and the latter in Buchforst on Waldecker Strasse.

Flea Markets take place every two months in the old part of Cologne, as does the **Antique Market**, in Cologne Ladenstadt. In spring and autumn there's a **Trödelmarkt** (a combination junk/flea market) held at Neumarkt. From the middle of April until the middle of May numerous visitors are drawn to the colourful, fragrant **Flower Market** at either Neumarkt or Rudolphplatz. Already from the middle of May until the beginning of June, just before the other wine festivals get rolling, the **Kölner Weinwoche** (Cologne Wine Week) is organised at Neumarkt. Growers from wine-producing areas all over Germany come together here to present their products and you can count on things getting at least a little wet and wild.

Neumarkt is also the site for **Bücherherbst** (Autumn Books), a book fair attended by some 60 different publishing houses and bookstores. It is held 10–18 September. The exhibits are complemented by a variety of interesting poetry readings, singing and cabaret performances. Things start taking on that Christmassy-feeling from around the end of November until the 23 December. The stands which make up the traditional **Weinachtsmarkt** (Christmas Market) are open for business on Alter Markt and on Neumarkt.

244

SPORTS

Cologne has acquired quite a good reputation as a "sports metropolis". Numerous athletes from the city have made it to the very top of their respective athletic fields. There are several arenas in Cologne suitable for staging large events. All are located conveniently and can be easily reached. The New Year is ushered in with the Cologne Six-day Cycle Race, held at the **Sporthalle in Deutz**, Deutz-Mülheimer-Strasse. Tel: 88 20 31.

The **Müngersdorf Stadium**, Aachenerstrasse 703. Tel: 49 83-224,. A generously laid-out athletic complex situated on the western perimeter of the city, this was erected in 1923, thus making it Cologne's very first stadium. It includes fields for soccer and track events, an area for horse shows, tennis courts, hockey fields, a large outdoor swimming pool, physical fitness course, gymnasiums and various open spaces. The German Sports College is also located here. The modern main athletic stadium offers covered seating to as many as 60,000 spectators and is the home ground of Cologne's first division side 1 FC Köln. Still in the second division, Fortuna Köln is based at the **Südstadion** (South Stadium) in Zollstock, Vorgebirgsstrasse. Tel: 36 20 43.

The Sport-und Bäderamt (municipal office for sports and swimming) has up-to-date information regarding events scheduled for both stadiums. Tel: 49 83 222.

The Cologne ice-hockey club "Die Haie" (The Sharks), several times over German Champions, fights out many of its battles in the **Eissporthalle** (Ice Sports Arena) of the Cologne Ice and Swimming Arena (Lentstrasse 30, on the road that leads over the Zoobrücke on the left side of the Rhine. Tel: 72 60 26).

Turf fans will find themselves irresistibly drawn to the **Horse Race Course** in Cologne-Weidenpesch, Rennbahnstrasse 152. Tel: 74 80 74. Horse racing began here on the 3 March 1898.

Nineteen indoor and 10 outdoor swimming pools, the Ice and Swimming Arena with its 61-metre (203-ft) long slide, two 30 x 60-metre ice-skating rinks (which are only in operation during the wintertime) and numerous private swimming pools provide a variety of opportunities to satisfy your urge to swim or participate in some type of athletic activity.

A few of Cologne's swimming pools are:
Martinsbad, located in the Altstadt, Lintgasse 10. Twelve 10 x 20 metre pools filled with water heated to 30°C. Hours: 10am–10pm Monday–Friday, noon–7pm Saturday, 11am–6pm Sunday.

Kurbad Marienburg, Marienburger Strasse 70. This 10 x 20 metre pool contains sea water heated to a pleasant 32°C. Hours: 10am–9pm Monday–Friday, 7am–8pm Saturday.

Familiensauna "El Paradiso", located in Rösrath-Hoffnungsthal, east of Cologne. Options offered here include Finnish, panoramic, organic and steam saunas, indoor and outdoor swimming pools, massage and physical fitness training equipment. Hours: 10am–10pm daily.

From the middle of 1991, **Aqua Land**, an extensive recreational water-world boasting ultra-modern facilities, is open for fun of the wet variety. It is located at the northernmost outskirts of Cologne, near Chorweiler, Merianstrasse 1 (at the corner of Merianstrasse and Neusser Landstrasse).

Bowling buffs should be sure to check out the modern alleys at **Alpha-Bowling** in Cologne-Klettenberg, Luxemburger Strasse 299. Open: 4pm–1am Monday–Friday, 2pm–1am Saturday and Sunday. A second option right in the city centre and maintaining four alleys is **City-Bowling**, Moselstrasse 44.

Tennis and squash aficionados can work up a sweat at any one of the four tennis and 16 squash courts at **City-Sport** in Cologne-Sülz, Rhöndorfer Strasse 8–10. A swimming pool and sauna on the premises round the options off nicely. Hours: 8am–midnight daily. There are 10 courts, a sauna and solarium at **Squash-Park** in Cologne-Weidenpesch, Neusser Strasse 718a. Hours: 10am–midnight Monday–Friday, 10am–8pm Saturday, Sunday and holidays.

If horseback riding is more your style, get into contact with the **Kölner Reit-und Fahrverein** in Cologne-Müngersdorf, Aachener Strasse 800. Tel: 49 14 32.

Golfers have a choice of two courses: **Marienburger Golf-Club e.V.**, Militärringstrasse. Tel: 38 40 53, or **Golf-und Landclub Köln e.V.**, Refrath. Tel: (02204) 6 31 14. Both clubs require that you have a valid membership card for another golf club.

Special Information

THE DISABLED

Most theatres, museums and public facilities in Cologne are equipped with special entrances and lavatories to accommodate disabled visitors. Additional help is also available upon request. Many subway stations can be reached by either escalator or elevator. Some of the pedestrian traffic lights also provide acoustic signals for the blind. The City of Cologne prints a brochure entitled "Freizeit – Bildung – Ferien" containing information regarding all the facilities in the city suitable for disabled people. The brochure is free and can be obtained at the Tourist Information Centre.

CHILDREN

Most children will enjoy a visit to the zoo or one of the wild animal parks in Brück or Dünnwald. In Gut Leidenhausen there are different birds of prey to see along with big game animals and wild boar. You can rent a rowing boat in Groov, in Zündorf, and on Decksteiner Pond in the western green-belt. A trip high over the river on the Rhine funicular or with the chairlift across Rhine Park is sure to please.

During summer well-known fairy tales are performed on the open-air stage in Zons, the fortified medieval city located to the north of Cologne. There are two **children's theatres** which are especially tuned into what might be entertaining to younger audiences. At Ömmes & Oimel the emphasis is on fairy tale-like performances that tend to stimulate a child's own fantasy. The theatre is located at Löwengasse 7–9. Tel: 24 76 70. The spectrum of children's and young people's theatre performed in Die Kugel in Rodenkirchen, Industriestrasse 170. Tel: 31 99 60, extends from adventure stories all the way to musicals.

Statt Reisen, a non-profit organisation, offers two different **tours**, each lasting about 1½ hours, for groups of 12 children or more. The emphasis here is on fairy tales, sagas and legends native to Cologne. For example at the Heinzelmännchen Fountain the story of the Wichtel (magical cleaning elves) is told. Games and a quick bout of painting on the cobblestones keep even the youngest members of the tour happy. Further information is available at: Statt Reisen, Herwarthstrasse 22. Tel: 52 64 64.

WOMEN

The Women's Historical Society organises **city sightseeing tours for women**. The tours lead primarily to those places where women played a special role in Cologne's history. Anyone wishing to participate should book in advance by writing to the: Frauengeschichtsverein, Marienplatz 4, 5000 Cologne 1. The Piccolo-Theatre, Zülpicher Strasse 28. Tel: 23 27 04, is a **theatre by women for women**. Most productions are plays which focus on women, for example *Antigone* by Anouilh, *Nora* by Ibsen, etc. Plays revolving around women-oriented topics such as *Die Töchter der Hexen* (The Witch's Daughters) or *Hören Sie mal* (Listen For Once), a female monologue, are also performed here.

George Sand, in Mauritiussteinweg, is a **café for women** which offers an extensive cultural programme oriented towards women's interests.

The **Frauenbuchladen** (Women's Bookshop), Moltkestrasse 66. Tel: 52 31 20, carries a selection of books dealing with specifically female themes, fiction and poetry works by women, as well as an assortment of biographies about particular women.

BUSINESS PEOPLE

Industrie-und Handelskammer (The Chamber of Industry and Commerce), Unter Sachsenhausen 10. Tel: 1 64 00
Köln-Messe (Cologne Trade Fairs), Messeplatz 1, Deutz. Tel: 82 11
Amt für Wirtschaftsförderung (Bureau for Economic Promotion), Richartzstrasse 2–4. Tel: 221 33 12

STUDENTS

University of Cologne, Albertus-Magnus-Platz. Tel: 470-1
University students in possession of a valid student identification card can eat relatively cheaply in the "mensa" (the student refectory) and are also permitted to use the student library, which stocks a selection of newspapers from all over the world (Universitätsstrasse 12, Cologne-Lindenthal).

The brochure "Studieren in Köln" (Study in Cologne) is available for free from the Kölner Studentenwerk (Student Administration Office), Universitätsstrasse 16, 5000 Cologne 4. Tel: 47 29 152 or 47 29 157. The Student Administration Office also has information regarding inexpensive student housing.

USEFUL ADDRESSES

TOURIST INFORMATION

Information of interest to tourists is available from the **Verkehrsamt** der Stadt Köln (The City of Cologne Tourist Information Office), Unter Fettenhennen 19, 5000 Cologne 1. Tel: 221 33 45.

CONSULATES

Belgian Consulate General
Cäcilienstrasse 46
5000 Cologne 1
Tel: 21 53 64

Costa Rican Consulate
Neumarkt 41
5000 Cologne 1
Tel: 23 00 08

Icelandic Consulate
Spitzweg 16
5000 Cologne 1
Tel: 48 78 78

Italian Consulate
Universitätsstrasse 81
5000 Cologne 41
Tel: 40 08 70

Dutch Consulate
Sechtemerstrasse 12
5000 Cologne 51
Tel: 37 14 23

Austrian Consulate
Glockengasse 1
5000 Cologne 1
Tel: 24 74 75

ART/PHOTO CREDITS

Photography by

Page 63, 84/85, 86/87, 16/17, 162/163	**Michael Bengal**
166, 168/169, 180, 184, 185, 188/189,	
190, 191, 194, 201, 203, 206, 218	
Cover, 12/13, 14/15, 27, 31, 32/33,	**Wolfgang Fritz**
35R, 39, 40/41, 42, 44L, 54, 56, 57, 58,	
76/77, 80, 98, 104, 106, 107, 105,	
110/111, 117, 112, 118, 127, 130, 132,	
133, 134, 141, 145, 146, 147, 151,	
155, 156, 158L, 172, 178/179, 182,	
192, 199, 207L, 207R, 209, 210, 216	
7, 26, 28, 30, 35L, 37, 38, 44R, 52/53,	**Günther and Margarete Ventur**
74/75, 81, 82, 88, 94, 95, 100, 101,	
102, 103, 109, 122, 123, 125, 126,	
128/129, 136, 139, 142, 143, 144, 148,	
149, 152, 153, 154, 158R, 159L,	
170/171, 173, 174, 176L, 176R, 177,	
181, 187, 200, 202	
1, 97, 159R, 160, 161, 175, 197, 214	**Heinz Mülow**
34, 36, 43, 50, 119	**Rheinisches Bilderarchiv**
78, 79, 164/165, 196	**Bodo Bondzio**
68	**Klaus Barisch**
51	**Bundersbildstelle Bonn**
71	**Electrola**
183	**Ford-Werke**
114, 115, 120, 121	**Rainer Gaertner DPGh, Bergisch Gladbach**
137, 212, 213, 215	**Karin Hackenbroich**
62L, 62R	**Dieter Klein**
66	**Klaus Lefebvre**
72	**Lindenstrasse/D. Krüger**
67	**Willy Millowitsch**
60	**Peter Peitsch**
70	**WDR**
45	**4711**
Maps	**Berndtson & Berndtson**
Illustrations	**Klaus Geisler**
Visual Consultant	**V. Barl**

INDEX

A
B

D
E
F
G
H
I
J
a
b

d
e
f
g
h
i
j
k
l